DOCTORS ON HORSEBACK

Pioneers of American Medicine

DOCTORS
ON HORSEBACK

Pioneers of American Medicine

by

JAMES THOMAS FLEXNER

FORDHAM UNIVERSITY PRESS
New York
1992

Copyright © 1937, 1992 by James Thomas Flexner
All rights reserved
LC 92–19615
ISBN 0–8232–1379–X
First published by Viking Press, 1937
Fordham University Press, 1992

Library of Congress Cataloging-in-Publication Data

Flexner, James Thomas, 1908–
   Doctors on horseback : pioneers of American medicine / by James
Thomas Flexner.—Fordham pbk. ed.
      p. cm.
   Originally published: New York : Viking Press, 1937.
   Includes bibliographical references and index.
   ISBN 0-8232-1379-X
   1. Physicians—United States. 2. Medicine—United States.
I. Title.
R153.F5   1992
610'.92'273—dc20
[B]   92-19615
                                                              CIP

Printed in the United States of America

To

Helen and Simon Flexner

ACKNOWLEDGMENTS

I am grateful to the following authors and publishers who have kindly permitted me to reprint source material from the books and articles named hereunder: Miss Ethel Armes for *Nancy Shippen, Her Journal Book*, published by the J. B. Lippincott Company; the *Atlantic Monthly* for "Dr. Rush and General Washington," by Paul Leicester Ford; Paul B. Hoeber, Inc., for *Crawford W. Long and the Discovery of Ether Anæsthesia*, by Frances Taylor Long; the J. B. Lippincott Company for *The Journal of Dr. John Morgan of Philadelphia from the City of Rome to the City of London, 1764*; the C. V. Mosby Company for *Life and Letters of Dr. William Beaumont*, by Jesse S. Myer; the *Pennsylvania Magazine of History and Biography* for "Historical Notes of Dr. Benjamin Rush," by Silas Weir Mitchell, and for "Extracts from the Journal of Miss Sarah Eve."

My debt to the authors of the books listed in the bibliographies at the end of this volume, and to many other authors whom lack of space has prevented me from listing, will be recognized by all students of the history of American medicine.

My especial thanks are due to the New York Academy of Medicine and to Miss Gertrude L. Annan, in charge of its department of history. The following libraries and institutions have permitted me to consult books and manuscripts in their collections: the New York Public Library, the New York Historical Society, the Pierpont Morgan Library, the Historical Society of Pennsylvania, the Ridgway Branch of the Library Company of Philadelphia, the University of Pennsylvania, the American Philosophical Society, the Army Medical Library, the Library of Congress, the Medical School of Washington University, and the Filson Club. Dr. Marshall McDowell placed at my disposal his collection of Ephraim McDowell manuscripts. I am grateful to the Frick Art Reference Library for assistance in securing illustrations.

I have modernized the spelling and punctuation of the letters and documents I have quoted.

FOREWORD

The early doctors of America fought on two frontiers: riding the wilderness of a new continent, they explored the mysteries of the human body.

During the eighteenth century they labored to cure the sick on a strip of sea-coast separated by months of ocean from the nearest medical professor and the source of drugs. Gradually, painfully, they groped towards medical institutions of their own, but the work was only started when shots rang out at Lexington. Then the doctors of America marched with an under-fed, ill-equipped army. Treating thousands of sick and wounded who were crowded into barns, often without drugs and instruments, they aided thirteen colonies to defeat an empire. No sooner had peace brought into being an independent nation than another call came: they climbed across mountain passes and drifted down unknown rivers; they struggled abreast of the pioneers. The settler in the most isolated log cabin could count on the ministrations of a doctor who had hanging from his saddle beside the bags of medicine a musket and an ax. When cities sprang up where forests had been, these men labored to make them healthy, fighting sometimes against new diseases the Old World had not known.

As they took part in every adventure that built a continent-spanning nation, America's pioneer physicians met a higher adventure than the darkest forests, the fiercest Indian wars, could offer. The world of medicine was also a wilderness only half explored whose mysteries challenged the mind. Laboratory technique was in its infancy. People had died of fevers for untold centuries, but no one knew why fevers came and there were a dozen theories of how to cure them. Foreseeing infections in every wound, surgeons limited themselves to simple operations on the extremities of the body, and never expected to cut without giving pain. Although the circulation of the blood had been discovered, no one understood the processes by which a wound healed, or the nature of digestion, or the cell structure of living matter.

Much of medical practice was a blind stumbling through darkness, yet the challenge of disease was always there, more insistent to the doctors on horseback than the challenge of the wilderness. Listening to the breathing of sick men, they did not hear the noises of the forest. And in the settlements of a new nation there appeared doctors of genius, explorers who, without laboratories or instruments of precision or even any formal training, made great discoveries that helped usher in the age of modern medical science. The modern physician, with all his varied resources, follows the trails these half-forgotten pioneers have blazed.

Contents

ILLUSTRATIONS

Seer and Continental Soldier

John Morgan

John Morgan
BEFORE THE REVOLUTION
FROM A PORTRAIT
BY ANGELICA KAUFFMANN

John Morgan
AFTER THE REVOLUTION
FROM A CONTEMPORARY PORTRAIT

1

T HE bright uniforms of the world's great generals dim
in the public eye when people realize that in the winning of wars battles are less important than bacilli. Dysentery
has been more deadly than all the cavalry charges of history.
Although vital statistics were lacking until recently, it is probable that the World War was the first major war in which more
soldiers died from wounds than from disease. Perhaps the historians of the future will write more of medical directors than
of generals; artillery bombardments and heroic stands will be
relegated to footnotes; while in the larger type we shall read
of drugs, epidemics, and the quarrels of doctors.

Ten thousand accounts of the American Revolution have
made everyone familiar with the Battle of White Plains, but
who ever heard of the hospital in Bethlehem? Yet during a
few months that hospital accounted for five times the deaths
suffered in that battle. During the entire war, roughly nine
American soldiers succumbed to disease for every one killed
by the British. It is significant that, for the two years while
Washington was in continual flight across New York and New
Jersey, the medical department was crippled by lack of supplies

and an internal feud. We know that the Continental Army melted away to almost nothing during the battleless encampment at Valley Forge, as much from disease as from desertion. Yet Washington was not the worst hit by epidemics. The most disastrous campaign medically was the attempt to capture Canada that ended militarily in utter rout. If the hospital department of the northern army had been decently supplied and decently efficient, almost all of the North American continent might today be one nation. Indeed, during the next year the same northern army enjoyed under a new medical organization the healthiest campaign of the Revolution, and immediately won the Battle of Saratoga, the greatest victory of purely American arms. Many facts show that disease and medical incompetence played a major part in the history of the Revolution.

The hospital department of the Colonial army got off to a bad start when its first director, Dr. Benjamin Church, was convicted of treason, but this opened the way for the appointment of Dr. John Morgan, who had a great European reputation and was considered the most brilliant physician in the Colonies. He had founded America's first medical school. No wonder a jubilant cavalcade of patriots rode out to meet him that gusty November day in 1775 when he appeared with his wife at Cambridge after the long ride from Philadelphia. In coaches and on horseback they escorted the new director general of hospitals to the house of Mrs. Mifflin.

Immediately there was a knocking on the door and four generals appeared to welcome Morgan. He respectfully greeted Washington, with whom he had served in the French and Indian War; he shook hands with Generals Gates, Charles Lee, and Putnam. No sooner were they all seated over cups of tea than a messenger rushed in carrying a dispatch box. Everyone waited tensely while Washington opened it, but his anxious look melted into a smile. The express stated that the British ordnance brig *Nancy*, loaded with a wealth of arms and ammunition, had been captured by an American frigate. "What delighted me excessively," Mrs. Morgan wrote home, "was seeing the pleasure which shone in every countenance, particularly General Gates's; he was in an ecstasy. And as General Washington was reading the invoice there was scarce an article he did not comment upon, and that with so much warmth as diverted everyone present."

Thus auspiciously did John Morgan take over his all-important command. As the four generals tramped back to their separate headquarters, they must have felt easy in their minds concerning the health of the army.

But back in Philadelphia there was at least one man who was not pleased, a tall, haughty man with the nose of a heroic steel engraving and a handsome, ruddy face that smiled easily but never betrayed what its owner was thinking. For years Dr. William Shippen, Jr., had had cause for enmity against the new director general of hospitals, and in his bitterness he had convinced himself that Dr. Morgan was an incompetent coxcomb. While Shippen circulated, gracefully as ever, in the Philadelphia society that was now swollen by members of Congress, whenever he remembered Morgan his brain churned angry thoughts. Morgan was the leading physician in the Colonies, indeed; he had founded the Medical College of Philadelphia, had he? Shippen knew that both these honors belonged to himself, that Morgan had stolen them from him by subterfuges.

When the passing months brought rumors about Morgan's incompetence and horrible cruelty in office, Shippen felt that what he had always known was being proved for the world to see. This was his triumph, but perhaps he could reach a greater triumph yet. Perhaps Morgan could be ignominiously dismissed as Shippen was sure he deserved to be, and Shippen given the post from which he was ousted. Fascinated by the vision of so perfect a revenge, Shippen whispered in anterooms with rebellious army doctors and with the members of Congress who had elected Morgan and could as easily bring about his disgrace.

Few of the farmer boys who dropped their plows to pick up muskets had ever heard of Dr. Morgan or Dr. Shippen, and probably not one knew of the old enmity that burned between the two leaders of American medicine. Yet many hundreds of these lads were to die horribly of disease, covered with typhus lice, literally melting away with dysentery, because once upon a time John Morgan had founded America's all-important medical school in a way that seemed treacherous to William Shippen.

2

ONE May afternoon ten years before the Revolution started, the citizens of Philadelphia had been amazed to see a young man walking along the street shading himself with a silk parasol. The mechanics in their aprons laughed uproariously, and even the gentlemen craned their necks to look. Rarely had convention been so flouted in this small provincial capital, where men considered themselves too virile to carry umbrellas even in a blizzard, and the ladies, afraid of being conspicuous, shielded themselves from the sun with huge fans. Newspaper editors hurried out of their print-shops to stare, and then hurried back again to compose articles excoriating such effeminacy. In the midst of all this bustle, the only person who seemed unconcerned was the young man under the sunshade. Although his small body was delicately formed, with graceful hands and little feet, he walked with the carriage of a soldier; the foppishness of his dress failed to obscure the energy of his stride. As the common herd laughed, his handsome face expressed disdain, and he smiled a little to himself to see that the better people straightened out their grins when they recognized who it was under the sunshade and bowed deferentially. The supercilious curve of his mouth seemed to say: "In a few days everyone will be carrying parasols; I will civilize this provincial city in time."

John Morgan found it easy to be nonchalant under many eyes, for he was used to attracting attention. Ever since his return from Europe a month before, he had been pointed out in the street as a genius. Philadelphia was still a painfully provincial city where any Englishman was certain of respect, but Morgan was better even than an Englishman; he was one of the colony's own sons who had gone abroad and made the impossibly erudite scientists of Europe admit he was a great man. The general attitude was expressed by Samuel Powel, a future mayor of Philadelphia, when he wrote from Europe concerning Morgan: "Pray use him as his merits deserve and don't force him from you. For the honor of our country make his residence with you agreeable. It is no small sacrifice he makes in returning, as fine prospects open upon him here if he would stay, but his *amor patriae* maintains the upper hand."

Morgan was born in 1735 of a wealthy family that traced its

lineage back to the days of King Alfred. The first Quaker meeting in America was held in his maternal great-grandfather's house. His father, Evan Morgan, a landowner and merchant and one of the first industrialists in the Colonies, was a friend of Benjamin Franklin and a disciple of the new science that, because of Quaker liberalism, had found its first American home in Philadelphia.

Morgan went to school at Nottingham, Pennsylvania, where he was joined a year later by another Philadelphian whose background was almost identical with his own. Billy Shippen also came from an influential family, and his father too was an associate of Franklin. We have no way of telling whether the youngsters liked each other in those days. Both learnt whatever their scientific families had failed to teach them about unquestioning obedience to authority, for the principal of the school was a Presbyterian divine who had taken so violent a part in religious controversy that his opponents had expelled him from Connecticut as a vagrant; he enforced rules for their own sake, entirely apart from their meaning. The curriculum stressed the classics and good manners; it was considered equally heinous to miss an ablative or to speak rudely to a classmate, and Morgan rarely sinned in either particular.

While Morgan was away at school, Franklin founded the College of Philadelphia. Harvard and Yale, like Oxford and Cambridge, were seminaries for the education of ministers; they specialized in Latin, Greek, and theological hairsplitting. However, the Quakers' lack of a paid ministry and scorn for dogma enabled Franklin to establish courses in mathematics, physics, chemistry, history, and modern languages. Morgan entered the first class of what the Beards term "the first liberal institution of higher learning in the western world."

A year before his graduation, Morgan apprenticed himself

to an experienced doctor; there was no other way of studying medicine on the North American continent. The apprentice system, which had prevailed exclusively for two hundred years, required for effectiveness learned practitioners, but there was not a single medical school, public medical library, or scientific journal to make them learned. Preceptors were limited to repeating what they had learnt from their own preceptors: dogmatic statements the theoretical bases of which had been lost in the retelling. To these they sometimes added remedies they had stumbled on and seen work with their own eyes, usually the last ineffectual thing they had tried before the patient got well of himself. Essential studies like chemistry and anatomy were unknown; the first recorded dissection for the purpose of teaching was done in New York the year Morgan took up medicine. Floundering in a morass of ignorance that made anything seem possible, some practitioners turned to the Indians for guidance and dried the juice of pokeberries in the sun to make a poultice "of great virtue for the cancer."

Since no colony had laws regulating the practice of medicine, any charlatan could hang out his shingle and compete on terms of seeming equality with all physicians. Truly the *New York Independent Reflector* understated the case when it reported that the city of 10,000 inhabitants boasted only forty doctors, "the greatest part of whom were mere pretenders to a profession of which they were entirely ignorant; and convincing proofs of their incapacity were exemplified by their iniquitous practices. The advertisements they published proved them ignorant of the very names of their drugs." Conditions in the backwoods were, of course, even worse.

Attempting to get as near the sources of medical knowledge as possible, Morgan apprenticed himself to John Redman, a young doctor who had just returned from extensive studies in

Europe. Morgan compounded medicines, read the few texts Redman owned, accompanied him on his rounds, and held the bowl into which patients were bled. After the first public hospital in America was founded by Franklin and Dr. Thomas Bond, Morgan, while yet Redman's student, became its apothecary, a position which enabled him to study the practice of all Philadelphia's leading doctors. When Redman graduated him after six years, Morgan was as well trained as a Colonial doctor could be.

At twenty-one, Morgan had a round, handsome face with blue eyes, a strong nose, and a large mouth curving scornfully above a small, pointed chin. Frequenting the best society, he dressed in the finest clothes he could square with his Quaker conscience. He enjoyed being seen with beautiful, faultlessly dressed women, and they enjoyed his company too, for he was scrupulously gallant; but they were always on their best behavior with him; they dared not tease or giggle. Morgan's letters suggest that he had a stilted sense of humor. "The officers in the town," he wrote at the beginning of the French and Indian War, "seem to do much more execution amongst the girls than ever they did among the Indians, and if they don't leave their hearts quite behind them, I hope they will give their pretty nymphs as good proofs of their courage next campaign in the field of Mars as they have done here of their feats under the banner of Venus."

Morgan was formal in everything: his courting, his humor, even his expressions of friendship. He was incapable of approaching people naturally, for fate had gifted him with little understanding of human nature. Entering a ballroom, he stepped into a strange country full of aborigines, whose actions he could neither foresee nor comprehend. Like a wise traveler, he consulted a guide book and followed punctiliously the ritual of eighteenth-century manners.

Morgan must have envied his old schoolmate, Shippen, who had made a brilliant reputation as an orator at the College of New Jersey, now called Princeton, and was studying medicine under his father, Dr. William Shippen, Sr. This young physician was so talkative and gay that, without working for popularity the way Morgan did, he won it as if by inadvertence. Often he would make the most awful breaches of etiquette which would draw Morgan up rigid, but the others laughed good-humoredly and liked the genial doctor the better for it. A suave man of distinguished bearing, Shippen was at home not only in drawing-rooms; in the tap-rooms of country inns Morgan watched with haughty embarrassment while Shippen joked with the farmer boys naturally, yet without forfeiting the respect due his station. Shippen's best friends could not remember ever having seen him out of humor. An implied slight, that would have made Morgan stalk off in outraged dignity, only made Shippen blander. His bantering manner was so perfect an armor that it ceased to seem like armor; his associates and perhaps he himself grew to believe it his true essence. Indeed, the ambiguities of his character were so well hidden that no contemporary account gives us insight into the passions that were to make him play his dubious role in the Revolution. Although Shippen's environment was almost identical with Morgan's, his character was the exact opposite.

Their apprenticeship over, Shippen went abroad for further study, but Morgan preferred to take advantage of new opportunities at home. The British army sent over to fight the French and Indian War had brought something rarely seen in America, a group of well-trained doctors; Morgan joined the Penn-

sylvania militia as a medical lieutenant so that he might watch
them at work. Probably he found military life much to his
liking, for here etiquette was elevated to law. He wished the
militia would imitate their betters, the English regulars, by
observing rigid discipline. "The officers," General Forbes wrote
of his Colonial allies, "except a few in the higher ranks, are
an extremely bad collection of broken inn-keepers, horse-
jockeys, and Indian traders." To this Morgan would certainly
have added: "Amen!" Although Washington was in the same
army, the two probably did no more than salute each other,
for Washington was a Virginia colonel and, like Morgan, a
believer in rank. During the famous march on Fort Duquesne
there was little fighting, but enough soldiers sickened in the
rain-drenched woods to keep Morgan busy. General Forbes
commended his skill in a dispatch.

When Morgan spent his leaves in Philadelphia, the gossips
noticed that a minx named Molly Hopkinson could break
through his otherwise impenetrable reserve. She was a tall girl
with features so well formed and delicate that men forgot her
face was too long and narrow. She swirled her dark hair boldly
back from her already over-high forehead, and wore low-cut
dresses that revealed a very long neck, "like a swan's," as well
as the startling yet graceful slope of her shoulders. Dangling
long earrings and trailing silken shawls, she could sweep into
a room on Morgan's arm with telling effect, but she had a gushing, girlish, sentimental side, too, that evoked a similar mood
from her companion. It would be an excellent match, the gossips decided; there were no better families in Philadelphia than
the Morgans and the Hopkinsons. Molly's father, Thomas
Hopkinson, was a member of the Governor's Council and an
amateur scientist who had impressed Franklin with his electri-
cal experiments. Her brother, Francis, was to earn fame as

poet, musician, member of the Continental Congress, and the designer of the American flag.

After three years Morgan had learnt all the army could teach him; he told Molly that he must study in Europe. When she asked how long he would be gone, he replied that he was determined to get the best medical education to be found in the world; it would take several years. Tearfully she gave him a miniature of herself which he clasped to his heart.

During 1761, Morgan started on the greatest adventure possible to a Colonial, a trip home. Whatever misgivings he may have felt about his success in the truly great world were soon dispelled, for Franklin, then agent for the Province of Pennsylvania, opened the best doors in London to him. A few trips to the tailor corrected the provincial details of his dress, and his manners, of course, needed no correcting. He remained in the city for a triumphant season, studying with the great anatomists, John and William Hunter.

Armed with letters from Franklin that spoke of his industry, application, natural genius, and sagacity, Morgan went on to Edinburgh to attend the leading medical school in the world. There he found Shippen already well established. His old friend was coming to the end of brilliant studies; in London he had lived with John Hunter and married Alice Lee, a Lee of Virginia. Sir Henry Pringle had used his influence to enable him to travel on the continent despite the war with France. It was impossible for the two Colonials not to compare the educational opportunities of Europe with conditions at home; they discussed it many an evening over the bitter Scottish ale. Shippen confided to his friend that he intended to expand the apprentice system by delivering lectures in anatomy as several other Americans had done before him. Perhaps when Morgan returned he would join him and lecture on physic. Morgan agreed, and that spring Shippen sailed back to put his part of the plan in operation.

Morgan proved to be one of the ablest students ever seen in Edinburgh, that capital of ability; the graduation thesis he presented after two years was an important scientific contribution. Since antiseptic methods had not been discovered, the pus that arises from infection was expected in every wound, but its nature was a subject of continual controversy. Morgan was the first to recognize that it arose not from the solid tissue but from the blood vessels. A hundred years later Cohnheim, by the aid of the microscope, proved this contention, showing that pus is made up of white blood corpuscles which have migrated through the vessel walls.

When Morgan went to Paris, he was already so learned that he became teacher as well as student. His demonstration before the Académie Royale de Chirurgie of anatomical methods learnt from the Hunters so impressed the members that they eleced him to their fellowship. In fact, the phenomenal success of Morgan's European tour proved how seriously lack of communication hampered the advance of knowledge. Every faculty, every city, was a self-contained unit whose discoveries rarely went beyond its walls; as he traveled over roads well-nigh impassable, Morgan was a bee spreading the pollen of knowledge, fertilizing minds up and down the continent. In Rome he visited Morgagni, one of the greatest scientists of all time, and was even able to teach that aged savant new tricks. The father of pathological anatomy gave the young medical student a copy of his epoch-making work inscribed to *"viro experimentissimo et humanissimo."*

An eighteenth-century gentleman, Morgan did not limit himself to science. With his fellow-Philadelphian, Samuel Powel, he made the grand tour in the manner of a British noble-

man; *"en cavaliers,"* as he himself said. Bouncing through
Europe in their private coach, complete with courier and lack-
eys, they demanded as their right "the countenance and notice"
of British officials everywhere. They were presented to the
King of Sardinia, joined the suite of the Duke of York in Italy,
and had a private audience with the Pope.

At Geneva Morgan and Powel called on Voltaire. The philosopher introduced them to his other guests with a histrionic
flourish: "I beg leave to present to you two English gentlemen.
O glorious nation, renowned conquerors of Canada! Though
they have fought against us, and well have they fought battles
by land and sea, we must now look upon them as our brave
friends, since we are now at peace." Having thus put his two
conventional-looking guests at ease, Voltaire promptly shook
them up again by asking: "What think you of that little dog;
has he a soul or not?" They avoided this *"mal apropos"* question—the adjective is Morgan's—as nimbly as they could and
soon, Morgan tells us, he became "quite familiar" with Voltaire, "asking him questions with as much assurance as if I
had been long acquainted with him." When they rose to go,
Voltaire again addressed the company: "Behold two amiable
young men, lovers of truth and inquirers into nature. They
are not satisfied with mere appearances, they love investigation
and truth, and despise superstition. I commend you, gentlemen. Go on; love truth and search diligently after it. Hate
hypocrisy, hate masses, above all hate priests."

Morgan's diary, which contains a lively account of this visit,
is with a few such exceptions made up of inscriptions copied
from tombs, notes on the dimensions of waterfalls, and essays
on local industries; obviously he could not relax even before
his own journal. Endless lists of pictures show that he visited
art galleries conscientiously. Certain of his taste, he praised and

blamed without hesitation, and could tell at a glance if a picture was ascribed to the wrong painter. Guido Reni was his favorite, and in a long discussion of Padua, he makes no reference to Giotto, Mantegna, or Donatello. He bought "old masters" as a gentleman should.

In Rome he cured an illness of Angelica Kauffmann, the beautiful young girl who was to become a famous artist. She was so taken with her handsome doctor that after he had left the city she painted his portrait from the image of him that floated in her memory, and sent it to him accompanied by a portrait of herself. Morgan, however, had left his heart in Philadelphia; it was the miniature of Molly Hopkinson, "which I valued above everything else," that he stared at during lonely hours. He commissioned Benjamin West to enlarge it to life-size.

One awful day he received a letter from Molly in which she exhorted him to be baptized. He, a Quaker, be baptized! In his dismay, he wrote an indiscreet letter to her brother-in-law, Parson Jacob Duché, in which he suggested that Molly was such a heathen she probably boycotted family prayers. When this letter fell into her hands, she replied with all the injured innocence of a virgin falsely accused. "I was much surprised to find you entertained the least doubt of my joining in family worship—had you been acquainted with the manner in which I have been brought up, you could not have imagined I would object to so necessary a duty." She then returned to the attack. "With respect to baptism, I think no more than you that a wicked man will enjoy the Kingdom of Heaven because he is baptized; neither do I think a good man will neglect so positive a command of his God." After quoting Scripture for a few paragraphs, she ended: "I once more, therefore, commend you to the direction of Heaven and your own conscience, and rest yours, Molly Hopkinson." Morgan continued to struggle, but it was a losing fight. In a little while he walked docilely to the font, bringing with him another former Quaker he had converted under his charmer's tutelage.

3

BEFORE Morgan completed his studies at Edinburgh, he came to realize that Shippen's scheme for reforming American medicine was not comprehensive enough. Colonial practice, he decided, needed to be completely made over, and this could not be done by two physicians lecturing on their own to whatever apprentices desired a little extra knowledge. In order to eradicate long-ingrained abuses, a university establishment would be necessary, capable of teaching all branches of medical science, of making rigid requirements for entrance and graduation, and of giving valuable degrees. As the dapper Colonial walked the Gothic streets of Edinburgh, his mind was busy formulating an ideal plan for rebuilding American medicine. After he had moved on to Paris, he wrote his revolutionary thoughts down in the form of an oration, and he argued them out with Powel point by point while their carriage rolled through Italy. Back in London, he showed the precious paper to Fothergill, Hunter, and Watson. When not a single phrase could be improved, he submitted it to Thomas Penn, the Proprietor of

Pennsylvania, and induced him to write the trustees of the College of Philadelphia, recommending that they authorize Morgan to form a medical school. Penn's seemingly innocent letter was to slaughter hundreds of soldiers in a revolution few people dreamed of, for it did not even mention Shippen's name.

That physician had already been teaching in Philadelphia for three years. He had returned from Europe with considerable *éclat*, bringing a valuable set of anatomical drawings which the famous Quaker physician, John Fothergill of London, had presented to the Pennsylvania Hospital. "I have recommended it," Fothergill wrote, "to Dr. Shippen to give a course of anatomical lectures to such as may attend. He is very well qualified for the subject and will soon be followed by an able assistant, Dr. Morgan, both of whom, I apprehend, will not only be useful to the province in their employments, but if suitably countenanced by the legislatures, will be able to erect a school of physic amongst you."

Shippen began his private lectures with obstetrics, eliciting not only jeers from those who thought "male midwives" comical, but determined opposition from the pious who believed he was undermining the modesty of American womanhood. However, when he began to teach anatomy, the real storm arose; he was rash enough to make his students dissect human bodies. This was felt to be a blasphemous prying into God's secrets, and, as he had no legal way of procuring cadavers, he was accused of stealing them from the graveyards. A contemporary rhymester wrote:

"The body-snatchers they have come
And made a snatch at me;

William Shippen, Jr.

FROM A PORTRAIT BY GILBERT STUART

It's very hard them kind of men
Won't let a body be!
Don't go to weep upon my grave
And think that there I be;
They haven't left an atom there
Of my anatomy."

Although Shippen published statements that the bodies dis-
sected were of suicides and executed criminals "with now and
then one from the potter's field," indignation mounted until his
life was threatened. Often his dissecting-room was stoned, and
once he escaped just in time down a back alley while his carriage was fired at. No coward, he continued his work and eventually won the people round.

Naturally Shippen was furious when Morgan returned from
Europe in an aureole of glory, bringing a plan that superseded
all his pioneering. He looked on sourly while Morgan, probably without consulting him at all, laid the scheme along with
Penn's letter before the trustees of the college, who accepted
it unanimously and elected him the first professor in the first
medical school on the American continent. But Shippen's anger
rose to its height when in an enthusiastically received oration
that lasted two days, his rival proclaimed himself the father of
a new era in Colonial medicine.

"It is with highest satisfaction," Morgan told his audience,
"I am informed from Dr. Shippen, Jr., that in an address
to the public as introductory to his first anatomical course he
proposed some hints of a plan for giving medical lectures
amongst us. But I do not learn that he recommended at all a
collegiate undertaking of this kind. . . . Private schemes for
propagating knowledge are unstable in their nature, and the

cultivation of useful learning can only be effectively promoted under those who are patrons of science, and under the authority and direction of men incorporated for the improvement of literature."

Morgan then proposed a plan which was perhaps most startling in its insistence on pre-medical studies. Although at that time any farmhand could make himself a doctor by hanging round a physician's office, Morgan demanded that candidates for his school must not only have served as apprentices long enough to have learned pharmacy and the rudiments of medicine, but must also be adept in Latin, mathematics, natural science, and preferably a modern language. Once admitted, students were required to attend lectures in anatomy, the nature and effect of drugs, botany, chemistry, theory and practice, and clinical medicine. After working in the Pennsylvania Hospital for one year, they would be ready for the degree of Bachelor of Medicine. In order to become Doctors of Medicine, they had to practice for three years before they returned and wrote acceptable theses.

When Morgan pointed out that the apprentice system, which offered no regular course in every distinct branch of medicine, must turn out ignorant doctors, he was insulting almost every physician on the continent. Conscious of this, he tried to reenforce his logic by an emotional description of the ill-trained practitioner. "Great is the havoc which his ignorance spreads on every side, robbing the affectionate husband of his darling spouse or rendering the tender wife a helpless widow; increasing the number of orphans, mercilessly depriving them of their parents' support; bereaving the afflicted parents of their only comfort and hope by the untimely death of their beloved infants; and laying whole families desolate. Remorseless foe to mankind! actuated by more than savage cruelty! hold, hold thy exterminating hand!" If, pausing for breath, he had caught Shippen's eye, he would not have been reassured.

Morgan next had the audacity to recommend specialization in a country where every doctor was physician, surgeon, dentist, and apothecary. No man, he insisted, could be skillful in all these pursuits. He told his startled audience that he would practice only physic and send all his surgical cases elsewhere. But, more amazing even than that, he announced that he had brought a well-trained apothecary from England, the first ever seen in America, to whom he advised all doctors to send the prescriptions that their apprentices now filled. Although his statement that a raw student could not be a good pharmacist was undoubtedly true, it struck a body blow at the financial basis of Colonial practice; most doctors made their livings more by dispensing their drugs than their services. This was unworthy, Morgan argued; a doctor should be paid as a scientist, not as a mere roller of pills. And, in order to afford the expensive education Morgan recommended, he should be paid more than was then the custom.

When Morgan stepped down from the rostrum after two days of oratory, he had torn American medicine to pieces and offered to rebuild it in a new pattern. His audience had listened to him with respect, but they regarded him as a visionary touched with the eccentricities of genius. Shippen joined other important practitioners in opposing specialization. Sitting in his office at Second and Spruce Streets, Morgan was probably the only doctor in the Colonies who refused surgical cases and did not dispense his own drugs.

Morgan, however, succeeded so well in organizing the medical school according to his own ideas that Shippen realized he would be unable to rival it with the kind of proprietary school he had in mind. After three months of angry hesitation, he wrote the trustees asking for the chair of anatomy and surgery and implying that Morgan had stolen his entire plan from him. "The instituting of medical schools in this country has been a favorite object of my attention for seven years past. . . . I should have long since sought the patronage of the trustees of this college, but waited to be joined by Dr. Morgan, to whom I communicated my plan in England, and who promised to unite with me in every scheme we might think necessary for the execution of so important a point." If Shippen had really intended to found a school under the university ægis, why did he wait so long to accuse Morgan of perfidy? Since his father was a trustee of the college, he must have known his rival's every move.

At Morgan's recommendation, Shippen was elected unanimously. They were the only professors during the first session of America's first medical school, but soon the faculty was increased to five, all graduates of Edinburgh and all but one under thirty-five. Although in a few years King's College founded another school in New York, Morgan's institution kept its leadership; in fact, it was to make Philadelphia the medical capital of the nation for well over half a century.

Insisting that he was the real father of American medical education and Morgan a mere imitator, Shippen claimed to be the senior professor. Morgan considered this preposterous. When the trustees decided in Morgan's favor, Shippen refused to accept their verdict. The pettiness to which this quarrel descended is shown by an exchange of letters between Morgan and Benjamin Rush, who hoped to be professor of chemistry, in which Morgan threatened to withdraw his promised support because Rush had put Shippen's name before his own in the dedication of an Edinburgh thesis. Only after Rush had reiterated that it was an error, not a comment on precedence, did Morgan continue his patronage toward his favorite pupil.

The enmity that was to have so disastrous an effect during the Revolution grew yearly. In 1768 Morgan organized the Philadelphia Medical Society and invited all the distinguished doctors to join except Shippen and his father. By this time, politics had come in to confuse the issue. The Shippens supported the Penns in their attempt to keep their vast lands untaxed, while Morgan followed Franklin into the other camp. Soon the two groups organized rival philosophical societies, both modeled on the British Royal Society; Shippen was a leader in one, and Morgan joined his medical society with the other. Since the Colonies lacked enough talent to support two such groups, they were eventually forced to combine into the American Philosophical Society, which has played so important a part in the cultural history of America.

Although in this case Morgan was on the liberal side, he disapproved of extreme Whigs; he was too much patrician to support any leveling tendency that would encourage a shopkeeper to treat him as an equal. During the dispute with England, he joined the moderates who sought a compromise, in 1766 winning a gold medal offered in London for the best essay on the advantages of perpetual union with Great Britain. Co-operation, he argued, was financially important to both sides, and necessary to the holy cause of Protestantism. However, he warned the British that lasting federation could be based only on mutual profit; if they continued to exploit the Colonies, the Colonies would rebel.

When rebel they did, Morgan was on the Colonial side, but we may be sure that like many other well-born patriots he regarded the revolt merely as a warning to King George and his

Tory parliament; independence entered his mind only as a dreadful and ultimate expedient. However, he was caught up in a whirlwind that broke from all control. On October 17, 1775, Congress elected him director general of hospitals for the revolutionary army.

4

DURING Morgan's months with the army in Cambridge, there was no fighting; the British remained in Boston while the Colonials prowled outside. Attended by an "obliging" maid, Mrs. Morgan did fine needlework, admired parades, and sang to the harpsichord while Colonel Kirkbridge played the violin. "You can have no conception of how agreeably we pass our time here," she wrote. "This is Sunday evening and we have never dined at home but once since last Friday week, and then we had company. We generally dine once or twice a week at headquarters. I find the ladies very agreeable." In fact, the siege was like a long house party; Mrs. Morgan was as happy as she had ever been in her life, and her husband must have been gay, for she boasts that he had made the reigning belle of the encampment into a family friend: "You know what an admirer of beauty he is."

Morgan was active in the field as well. The Colonial army was an amateur group that had sprung up according to no plan, and the medical organization was more haphazard than the rest, for it was thought unimportant. Each regiment had its own surgeon, often the family physician of one of its officers. Most of them, since the two Colonial medical schools had graduated only some fifty men, belonged to the old dispensation of apprentice-trained doctors; they knew infallible remedies for almost everything. Appointed by their own colonels, who were often appointed by Colonial legislatures, not Congress, many refused to admit the authority of the central hospital department, and Congress had not helped matters by drawing up its medical legislation so sketchily that differences of rank were not defined.

When Morgan arrived in Cambridge, he found the regimental surgeons in open revolt against his predecessor's scheme, based on British army practice, that they should treat only the slightly sick in their inadequate regimental hospitals, forwarding all serious cases to the general hospital created to receive them. The surgeons insisted on keeping their patients or sending them on as their whims dictated, and when the hospital doctors objected, they were defied; in the absence of regulations to the contrary, the regimental surgeons assumed they were the superior officers. To hold what sick they pleased, they needed drugs and instruments; so they demanded that the hospital department fill all their requisitions without question, but they refused to jeopardize their liberty by giving the slightest accounting. That alcohol was considered an important medicine did not make them less demanding. One of the regimental surgeons, Morgan complained, "drew on the hospital for above a hundred gallons of rum with wine and sugar in proportion in the space of six weeks, and from this regiment there was no return of sick made."

Not only was the resulting expense to the impoverished government reprehensible, but it was almost impossible to replace dissipated drugs and instruments since the Colonies had always relied on Europe for medical supplies. Yet when Morgan's predecessor had tried to conserve his little stock of medicines, the surgeons with their commanding officers behind them had raised such a fuss that Washington had been forced to appoint a committee of inquiry.

Morgan had no sympathy with half-hearted measures. Striding through the camp in his meticulous clothes, a great city practitioner supported by military rank, he curtly sent sufferers from sore throats back to their regiments, and raided the regimental hospitals, carrying away the really sick. When the ragged country practitioners objected in their backwoods accents, he lectured them on discipline. His lectures were not well received. Many militia companies elected and deposed their officers at will; they felt they had enlisted to fight tyranny, and that went for Colonial as well as British aristocrats. Perhaps as the country practitioners fidgeted angrily under his tirades, they remembered his public criticisms of apprentice-trained doctors and resolved they would show him which were the better men. When Morgan capped the climax by announcing that he was not a commissary department, that he intended to keep his irreplaceable supply of drugs for the rigors of the future, and that the regimental surgeons would have to send the patients they could not treat to the general hospital, many must have felt that he was a Tory who would be caught in treason as his predecessor had been.

Finding that his own hospital department needed reformation as well as the regimental surgeons, Morgan made all his doctors take an examination. Since in those days most physicians never had their competence to practice questioned, a few resigned rather than submit to such an indignity. Morgan did not bother with tact or worry about the enemies he was making, and for a time he triumphed as he always had; illness among soldiers did not get out of hand, nor were there battles to produce wounded. According to Thatcher's *Journal*, the sick were "destitute of nothing but the presence of their dearest friends to alleviate their sufferings."

The war was at a stalemate, for the British were not strong enough to march out of Boston and the Americans lacked ammunition to bombard the city. Finally Washington got some powder and threw up fortifications on Dorchester Heights one inky night. Awakening the next morning, Howe saw them there and realized that Boston was no longer tenable. He embarked his army and sailed to Nova Scotia, where he dawdled three months before moving towards New York. On July 2, 1776, the first of his ships anchored off Staten Island, throwing into panic the small city of 20,000 which occupied the lower end of Manhattan Island. But for weeks Howe did nothing while his transports straggled in and he made abortive peace offers to Congress.

When the British arrived, Washington's army, which had been waiting in New York several months, was immediately in a precarious position. Some 18,000 ill-trained and ill-armed miltiamen supported by no fighting ships were supposed to protect an island from 25,000 picked troops and a first-class fleet that could move almost at will over the intricate waters. But there was one good omen. The New England army which had besieged Boston had at last received important reinforcement from other Colonies; patriots in their letters described with joy the arrival of Virginia sharpshooters in their coonskin caps, of sword-waving gentlemen from the Carolinas. Now that the soft Southern drawl mingled around campfires with the Northern twang, visionaries saw a united and therefore invincible nation. But the newcomers were not altogether a blessing;

they brought with them a dread visitant that was to decimate the army. They brought disease.

Communication was so difficult in the Colonies that most people never traveled far from home; they built up immunity to the few diseases endemic in their areas, but had no specific resistance to other ills. Since the mingling of men from many States meant also a mingling of infections, sudden epidemics slaughtered the farmer boys, susceptible many of them even to measles. Typhus, typhoid, smallpox, and dysentery raced from brigade to brigade.

Although like all eighteenth-century doctors they did not know the real causes of disease, Morgan and his assistants had inherited thousands of years of pragmatic observation; they possessed many valuable drugs and could do much for their patients through diet and nursing. Harassed by a half-dozen epidemics raging at once, Morgan labored heroically; he collected medicines and fitted out whole streets of hospitals to which he commanded the regimental surgeons to send their sick. Once he found a regimental hospital in Chelsea where a hundred patients were crammed into one tiny dwelling, lying in shoals on the floor so that it was impossible to pass between them. In the heat of summer, the air was so foul that Morgan panted for breath as he stumbled over the dying. Furious, he ordered the surgeon to send half his sick to a general hospital and move most of the rest to a near-by barn. The surgeon, supported by his commanding officers, refused. He was soon infected by the bad conditions he had created and paid for his folly with his life, but there were always more backwoods physicians ready to flout Morgan's orders.

The regimental surgeons insisted so loudly that they lacked supplies for even their legitimate duties that Morgan asked Washington to command that they report what they had on

hand. The fifteen regiments that deigned to obey had altogether fifteen cases of pocket instruments, six sets for ampu-
tations, two for trepanning, seventy-five crooked and six straight
needles, four scalpels, three pairs of bullet forceps, half a paper
and seventy-five pins, a few bandages, ligatures, and tourni-
quets, and only two ounces of sponge. The regiments that did
not answer were probably even less well supplied. Both Morgan and the surgeons were horrified at this intelligence. To
Morgan's indignant demand how they dared enter the service
so badly equipped, they replied that the recruiting agents had
promised that the army would provide everything. When told
that the general hospital had only enough for its own use,
"they appeared," Morgan wrote the medical committee of
Congress, "quite confounded and expressed great uneasiness
at having no proper establishment." He begged the committee
to formulate some practical plan by which the surgeons could
be supplied.

Not that he could really have expected an answer. Congress,
jealous of its power and determined to control every detail
of the army, had divided its small membership into hundreds
of committees, of which the medical committee was considered
one of the less important. Its chairman, Samuel Adams, was
chairman of twenty-four other committees and a member of
ninety in all; he had no time to think of medical matters, but
his committee interfered with Morgan's every move. Although
the director general had been empowered to select his own
subordinates, the committee undermined his organization by
designating political favorites. They disapproved of Morgan's
acting on his own; yet when he wrote them for instructions,
they were usually too busy to read his letters. This was not the
first time he had asked them to do something about the regimental surgeons. He had even gone to Philadelphia to con-

sult them in person, but they had been too busy to give him any reply.

"I call for orders," he wrote Samuel Adams. "I shall shrink from no fatigue. Say what is my duty and to the best of my power I will obey. Every general, every colonel of a regiment, every surgeon in the army thinks I have full power and ample instructions, and know where to apply for the relief of their men, if sick or wounded and needing uncommon supplies, if I cannot afford them. It is a cruel situation."

Weeks passed, soldiers died from lack of drugs, and Adams did not reply to Morgan's letter. The director general made every possible effort. He organized the regimental surgeons for a concerted appeal to Congress. Whenever he could spare a few days from fitting out hospitals and attending the sick with his own hands, he galloped hundreds of miles in a vain search for medicines. He even had difficulty securing old sheets to be torn up into bandages. Dr. Binney, whom he had sent to Philadelphia for instruments, reported that there were none to be purchased and that the only workmen who could make them had been assigned by Congress to manufacturing arms. When brave surgeons close to tears complained that their patients died because they could get no knives suitable to amputate infected limbs, Morgan could only spread out his hands in despair. Finally a dispatch-rider brought him a letter addressed in Adams's familiar hand. "I have received several letters from you," he read, "which I should have acknowledged sooner if I could have found leisure." Adams added that he had laid them before Congress.

A few weeks before, Congress had enacted a topsy-turvy bill. Forbidding Morgan to issue articles of diet which the surgeons should have properly had for the slightly sick, it commanded him to give them "medicines and instruments." Reluctantly

Morgan depleted his hard-won supplies by issuing chests to forty or fifty regiments. Later Congress followed one of his suggestions by appointing a "Continental druggist," but that official's duties were never defined. The sad truth was, and Congress knew it as well as Morgan, that, whoever supplied the surgeons, they would be ill supplied since the breakdown of industry and commerce was complete.

The one good feature of the bill, strangely enough, did the most damage. Its provision that the regimental surgeons should be accountable to the hospital department made them so angry that they rose in open rebellion, securing the support of their officers by atrocity stories about Morgan's inhumanity. When the sick they refused to give up died in their unsuitable hospitals, they insisted Morgan was responsible because he capriciously denied them necessary medicines. General Greene heard that Morgan was "content so the sick did but die by rule." The surgeons whispered that conditions were so bad in the general hospital that to send sufferers there was the equivalent of murder. Fulminating against "inhuman neglect daily exhibited," General Smallwood withdrew all his sick from the general hospital and put them in charge of his regimental surgeons.

Washington supported Morgan whenever he could. In a letter to Congress, he called the surgeons "very great rascals" and said they were aiming to "break up the general hospital, and have in numberless instances drawn for medicines, stores, etc., in a most profuse and extravagant manner for private purposes." But Washington's influence with Congress was not great, and in the camp itself he was often powerless to enforce his own orders. The army that occupied New York was an ill-organized collection of militia companies which decamped the instant their short enlistments expired. Washington begged

Congress in vain to let him recruit a national, long-term force that would attract respectable officers and that could be trained and controlled; Congress felt such an organization would be undemocratic. The militia regiments, each accountable to its own State legislature, obeyed the commander-in-chief only when they were in the mood. There was "an entire disregard for that order and subordination necessary for the well-being of an army," Washington shouted at the deaf ears of his masters in Philadelphia.

Although a great diplomat, Washington was almost unhorsed in the troublous days that followed. Scorning diplomacy, Morgan made his contempt for the officers who supported the regimental surgeons very clear. The troops, he asserted later, elected to command them "men of the same mean, sordid, groveling disposition with themselves, void of the sentiments of brave soldiers, love of honor and liberty of principle; but ready to associate with them on a footing of equality; who would drink drams with them, allow them to plunder, or exempt them from duty when they did not feel themselves bold to fight; and who had no objection to fill the army with maligners, public extortioners and cowards."

Once Morgan came upon an officer shaving his soldiers, "whether for the pence he could collect or that he might stand a chance of interest and preferment . . . let casuists determine." Instead of looking the other way, he made his displeasure so plain that the whole militia company hated him. He insisted on obsequious respect from subordinates who did not even respect Washington. His battle for discipline was very important—the troops were wasting away with dysentery because it was impossible to make them dig privies—but Morgan helped his enemies represent his professional zeal as an attempt at self-aggrandizement. He was too busy to realize how strong these enemies were becoming, too much absorbed in Herculean tasks to feel the master hand which was beginning to direct the campaign against him.

Morgan heard the most frightening reports from Canada. The triumphant army, which had taken every British stronghold except Quebec, was suddenly stricken with disease on the Plains of Abraham. Soon it was in full flight, more from germs than from the enemy, the soldiers dropping in the wilderness as if raked by noiseless celestial guns. A pitiful remnant arrived at Fort George, bringing their microscopical murderers with them. Dr. Jonathan Potts wrote: "The distressing situation of the sick here is not to be described, without clothing, without bedding, or shelter sufficient to keep them from the weather. . . . We have at present upwards of a thousand sick, and crowded into sheds, and laboring under the various and cruel disorders of dysenteries, bilious putrid fevers, and the effects of confluent smallpox." There were only four surgeons and four assistants, and most of the medicines were completely exhausted.

Helplessly Morgan had watched this situation develop. When he had tried to reform the northern medical department by appointing competent physicians, its surgeon general, Dr. Samuel Stringer, had refused to accept them, insisting that because he had been appointed first, he was Morgan's superior. In a succession of letters to the medical committee, Morgan pointed out that "everything in the medical department in Canada displays one scene of confusion and anarchy"; he begged the committee to give him the power to act or to act themselves. Despairing at last of an answer, he wrote Charles Thompson, the secretary of Congress, to find out if Stringer's command really was independent. Thompson, without bothering to look the matter up, replied that Stringer undoubtedly had the right to appoint his own surgeons. "Your country will honor you," he added, "and posterity will do you justice even though Dr. S—— when you chance to meet should refuse to give you precedence." When Morgan secured a copy of the act appointing Stringer and found Thompson wrong, he wrote a furious letter saying that, had Thompson "been pleased to examine these resolves of Congress, his disobliging observations on rank and precedence might have been spared." Thompson replied with a rhapsody on commonwealths, and an attack on the etiquette of "courts or camps where rank stands for merit and that fantastical thing called honor supplies the place of virtue." Congress completed Morgan's chastisement by making Stringer autonomous. Had it not been for such foolishness—who knows?—Canada might today be a part of the United States.

When Howe finally became sated with inaction, he attacked the outpost of the American army that held the strategically important Brooklyn Heights. In the resulting Battle of Long Island his larger and better organized force crushed the patriots in an ignominious defeat that forced them to flee to Manhattan. Everything was confusion when the sick and wounded were ferried across the East River in a heavy rain; sufferers were landed at different wharves and carried without thought to the nearest houses. It took Morgan and his assistants all night to find and transport them to hospitals.

Under the weight of discouragement, the remnant of army discipline collapsed. Because of the new casualties, Morgan needed more laborers and waiters, but it took him days of petitioning to secure the assignment of fifty men, and an additional week to get action from the officers appointed to carry out the order. When the soldiers were marched to the hospital at last, they said they did not like the work and would not stay. A few months before, Morgan would have threatened them with court martial; now he pleaded with the abject urgency of despair. He promised to make their work as easy as possible and to allow them each a daily gill of rum. However, most of them deserted during the night and returned to their regiments.

Since it was clear the city would have to be abandoned, Morgan combed western New Jersey for another hospital site, while Washington asked the New York Convention to assign him four sloops to evacuate the sick. A few days later he complained they had not come. When it was certain that the New York Convention did not intend to supply them, Morgan was forced to agree to General Greene's plan of permitting all the sufferers who could walk to wander into the country under the command of their medical officers. Thus the sick escaped control and spread disease through the land.

Washington retired most of his army to Harlem Heights, leaving behind a few thousand men under General Putnam and about a hundred sick for whom he had been unable to secure transport. On September 15 British warships moved up the Hudson and East Rivers and fired at Putnam's force in between, while a landing party debarked at Kip's Bay, now East Thirty-Fourth Street. At the sound of firing, Morgan rushed from Harlem Heights with a few assistants, and rowed in a small boat down under the British guns. He saw whole brigades of militiamen on Powle's Hook and the Heights of Bergen "flee upon the firing of a broadside from a man-of-war . . . although not a man was hurt by the fire." The country boys had never heard such a din as the big guns made; those on the east fled west, those on the west fled east and, meeting in the center of the island, they all stampeded north in utter rout. Had the British moved quickly, the entire force would undoubtedly have been captured.

Morgan's party landed and proceeded to the hospital on foot. Finding that the militiamen in their anxiety to escape had appropriated the wagons in which he had hoped to evacuate the sick, Morgan put his charges on improvised stretchers and helped his assistants carry them to the boat. As the doctors hurried back and forth with their loads, weaving a perilous path among the fleeing troops, they heard the British muskets getting closer. When the redcoats came in view, Morgan was forced to cast off, leaving behind some of his assistants who were salvaging medicines.

Now that his wagons were gone, Morgan could not move his sick to the new general hospital at Newark; he was forced to crowd them into unsuitable houses, barns, and outbuildings at Kingsbridge and Harlem Heights. Often his heart bled to find the charges of regimental surgeons lying in fence-corners or under trees. Quartered in hastily constructed huts of straw, rails, and sod, the defeated soldiers were too discouraged to do anything but mope. "The shameful inattention," a general order read, "in some camps to decency and cleanliness in providing necessaries and picking up the offal and filth of the camp has been taken notice of before in general; after this time particular regiments will be pointed out by name." Naturally, the dysentery rate sky-rocketed. Since there were no ovens, raw flour was issued to the troops, who used hot stones or ashes to bake soggy bread that brought hundreds down with jaundice. Soon more than a third of the army was disabled by sickness. And Morgan was short-handed because many of the surgeons who had accompanied convalescents to the country had decided not to return.

Morgan was faced with a terrible lack of supplies. When he asked the Continental druggist for ten pounds of tartar emetic, he received four ounces. The representatives he sent to Hartford, Norwich, Providence, and Boston could find practically no medicines. He appealed to Governor Trumbull of Connecticut and went in person to the New York Assembly at Fishkill. Even the gift of an old knife or a linen sheet that could be made into bandages was welcome.

Often Morgan attended to the sick himself, not only amputating limbs and trepanning skulls, but undertaking the menial duties usually reserved for orderlies; when there was a wound to be healed, he forgot his rank.

Since the army was looking towards New Jersey, Morgan decided to open a hospital at Hackensack. The instant he arrived there, three hundred sick were brought to him although he was quite alone. In a few days there were over a thousand. The building was not ready and he had no bread, flour, or fresh provisions; however, he sent off dispatch-riders and labored heroically, spending day and night bent over the dying. It was a nightmare of torn limbs and wasting flesh and many anguished voices calling at once to one tired man. For a week Morgan never took off his torn clothes, which were so creased and dirty now it was impossible to believe they had been among the neatest in the army. Was this gaunt man with the tight face, lying on the ground for a half-hour's sleep, trying not to hear cries for help because he knew he must sleep or collapse himself; was this the same dandy who had amused himself by carrying Philadelphia's first parasol?

At last some more doctors arrived. Morgan did not take even a day's holiday; driven by that abnormal energy which pulls men through impossible crises, he galloped to Fort Lee to ask General Greene about supplies for the Hackensack Hospital. There he met Dr. Shippen, who he knew was in command of a small hospital in New Jersey. Shippen greeted Morgan with a cordial handshake; he seemed his old self; his clothes were meticulous as always and the same smile adorned his well-fed face.

Morgan was thin, he said; he hoped Morgan hadn't been ill. Then his smile vanished and his words became strange: "Why aren't you at your post on the other side of the river?" When Morgan's tired eyes looked at him in blank amazement, he explained that he was in command in New Jersey and Morgan belonged in New York.

Morgan's nerves were on edge. He laughed a little hysterically and then became furious. He was the medical director of all the armies, he shouted, and Shippen was his subordinate; Shippen should be careful how he talked to his superiors. But Shippen merely smiled blandly and advised him that a wise officer follows the acts of Congress.

Having little time to waste on such foolishness, Morgan rode on to his hospital at Newark, where he found Dr. Foster, the officer in charge, frowning with puzzlement. He asked if he might speak to Morgan alone. The director general walked out with him under the trees and listened with amazement while Foster said that Shippen had called on him and "with great art and address" proposed that Foster turn over to him the medical stores which Morgan had collected during months of hard riding and cached at Newark. Shippen had further stated that he was in command there, and that Foster should report to him, not Morgan.

Morgan's tired mind seems not to have grasped what was happening. He told Foster that it was ridiculous, that when Shippen had been appointed surgeon to the flying camp he had written Morgan admitting he was a novice in military medicine

and asking for advice; it was impossible that Shippen was trying to supersede him.

Probably Morgan intended to straighten matters out when
he returned to Washington's headquarters near White Plains,
but things happened too fast. On October 28 the British
attacked. At the sound of firing, Morgan rushed out of the
general hospital accompanied by all his surgeons, instructing several assistants to follow with instruments and dressings
in a wagon. The doctors established themselves right behind
the line of battle and did not move until the engagement was
over. Terribly short-handed because of desertions, they struggled to tend eighty or ninety wounded; despite their efforts,
some bled to death. The regimental surgeons who had refused
to give up their sick now dumped them in terror on the hospital
behind the lines. The resulting problem of organization was
tremendous. For days after the battle, Morgan struggled with
a completely broken-down quartermaster department, trying
to have beds and chimneys built to keep the wounded warm.
Watching his charges die of cold because he could get no action,
Morgan lacked the leisure to worry about his own problems.

5

WHILE Morgan was toiling on battlefields, building hospitals,
riding hundreds of miles to collect drugs, instructing insubordi-
nate assistants, and tending the sick with his own hands, Shippen

had been in Philadelphia talking to members of Congress. Later Morgan was to charge that all the criticisms of his regime were broadcast by a cabal with Shippen at the head; the medical department would have functioned smoothly, he insisted, had it not been for his old enemy. Of course, the situation was much more complicated than that, but it is true that Morgan's key trouble was the refusal of Congress to give him power to fight his other troubles. How far was this due to Congress's desire for authority that hampered Washington as well; how far to Shippen, who was always in the capital and whose father and two brothers-in-law were members? At this date it is impossible to be sure, for Shippen had no reason to write letters, and words vanish as soon as spoken. We may be certain, however, that he never tried to quiet the charges that flooded in from disgruntled regimental surgeons and misled officers; he hated Morgan too much.

An often overlooked angle is presented in a letter Washington wrote Shippen's brother-in-law, Richard Henry Lee, a few days after Congress had elected Morgan: "Tell Dr. W. Shippen that I was in hopes his business would have permitted him to come here as director of the hospital." Washington's wish may have been exclusively his own, based on his friendship with Shippen's father, for the physician's name was not before Congress at that time; yet it is interesting to speculate whether Shippen could have been director general instead of Morgan. Perhaps he did not find the cause of freedom worth disarranging his luxurious private life until he saw an opportunity to supplant his old enemy. We cannot take seriously the statement he later made in his own defense, that he used his political influence to get the appointment for Morgan; the single piece of evidence that might support this contention is too ambiguous to set up against the flood of evidence which proves the opposite.

In any case, when on July 15, 1776, Congress elected Shippen surgeon to a small flying camp in New Jersey and placed him under Morgan's orders, he accepted the post. Now that he was forced to write letters, the record of his scheming becomes clear. On the one hand he calmed any suspicion Morgan might have by meekly asking advice on military medicine; on the other, he greatly magnified his achievements to Congress. He boasted that "all the wounded from Long Island are now recovered," although, of course, he had never treated any of them. His statement that he had lost only ten or twelve men of twenty or thirty thousand passing through his camp was criminally inaccurate. Not half that number could have come under his charge, and concerning his wonderful record of cures we have Dr. James Tilton's unbiased statement that "the flying camp of 1776 melted like snow in the field, dropped like rotten sheep on their struggling route home where they communicated the camp infection to their friends and neighbors, many of whom died."

However, Congress believed Shippen's reports, which made him seem so much more able than his rival. On October 9, without consulting either Morgan or Washington, they gave Shippen autonomous command of all the hospitals on the New Jersey side of the Hudson. The Continental Army had already evacuated New York City. In order to get almost complete control of the medical department, Shippen merely had to wait for the British to drive Washington across the Hudson, as they immediately did.

Morgan's disgrace was still not complete, so Shippen soon wrote Congress: "I have not taken charge of nearly two hundred [sick] scattered up and down the country in cold barns and who suffer exceedingly for want of comfortable apartments because Dr. Morgan does not understand the meaning of the honorable Congress in their late resolve." A few weeks later he wrote Richard Henry Lee: "I saw on my first entering the army that many more brave Americans fell a sacrifice to neglect and iniquity in the medical department than fell by the sword of the enemy. I saw directors but no direction, physicians and surgeons, but too much about their business, and the care of the sick committed to young boys in the character of mates, quite ignorant and, as I am informed, hired at half-price. . . . How far my own department has been better filled does not become me to say." He enclosed a plan for a complete reorganization of the medical corps.

Lee replied that, since Washington had lately been invested with authority over the hospital department, Shippen should lay the plan before him. Shippen must have smiled. When he had written the commander-in-chief a month before asking him to forbid Morgan the west bank of the Hudson, Washington had upheld Morgan's right to establish hospitals for the Continental Army wherever it was most convenient. Not the least discouraged, Shippen had forwarded the letter to Congress with the suggestion that it make Washington's duty clear to him. The scheming physician was sure of his ground; did not Lee write him: "As for Morgan, the very air teems with complaints against him. If all charges against him be true, I would not have my conscience so burdened for mountains of gold."

The American army was being routed on all fronts and everyone, including Congress, felt the need of a scapegoat. Since defeat and disease were caused by the same lack of supplies and breakdown of discipline, they were always together; it was easy to blame one on the other. With sighs of relief, discouraged patriots took up the cry against Morgan, glad to hold someone responsible who could easily be removed. The misdeeds of the northern medical department, where he had been denied control, and of the regimental surgeons, who had refused to obey him, were all placed at Morgan's door. The men who lay dying by the roadsides cursed him with their last breaths. Many Congressmen felt that unless Morgan was removed it would be impossible to enlist a new army.

Riding the country in another of his arduous trips of organization, Morgan heard so many rumors of Shippen's activity that he became alarmed. When he reached Washington's headquarters near Trenton, he told his commander that he had been appointed to direct all the hospitals of the Continental Army, and that unless he was restored to his rank he would resign.

"I hope, sir," Morgan tells us that Washington replied, "you do not imagine it owing to me. I am here without any assistance from the hospital department. In case of need I know nobody here to take the direction. I think it very strange. I would have you lay the matter before Congress, that some steps may be taken to remedy this irregularity and inconvenience, and that I may know what I have to depend upon."

Accordingly, Morgan went to Philadelphia. Samuel Adams, he remembered, met him in the central passageway of Independence Hall under the fluted pillars, right before the swinging doors from which the voice of Congress issued in a monotonous drone. With the quick sentences of a busy man, Adams told Morgan he had been charged with such gross incompetence that he would be wise to resign. Morgan, who had been too active in the field to listen to attacks on his administration, was struck silent with amazement. Then the color rushed back into his face and he cried: "I do solemnly deny the charge, and

I entreat that I may this instant be introduced to Congress that I may have an opportunity of vindicating myself against every injurious aspersion." Smiling wearily, Adams said that Congress was engaged. "I ask an inquiry!" Morgan shouted. "I desire to know the particulars of the charge, and who are my accusers, to meet them face to face, and am willing—" His urgent voice went on while Adams, one ear cocked at the debate in the meeting-room behind him, edged the excited physician down the hall and out onto the steps, assuring him that in due time Congress would consider his demand for an investigation.

Morgan waited in Philadelphia, pacing the streets. He met his old friend Rush, who was a member of the medical committee, and tried to tell him of the situation. But like every Congressman Rush was too busy to listen; he said: "I am glad you have come; it will take a great burden off my shoulders," and hurried on. Then Morgan cornered Rush in his office and made him listen. The only reply he could get was: "I would not for ten times the consideration go through the toils and difficulties of your station." As we shall see, Rush soon had good reason to remember these words.

When Congress fled to Maryland for fear Philadelphia would be captured, it had not acted on Morgan's plea. Hearing that Washington had fought the Battle of Trenton without any assistance from the hospital department, Morgan rushed back to the commander-in-chief, only to be met by a new resolve of Congress that ordered him to the east side of the Hudson. He had to obey. From Fishkill he wrote a memorial in defense of his actions, but Washington received it on the same day he received a curt resolution of Congress that discharged both Morgan and Stringer from the army without giving any reason. Washington forwarded it to Morgan, adding: "What

occasioned the above resolve I cannot say. I only assure you
it has not been owing to any representations of mine." Shippen,
however, wrote Lee that he was delighted Congress had followed his advice by dismissing the two directors. "Would it
not," he asked, "answer a good purpose and save the Congress
much trouble if I were called inspector general of the whole?"

Morgan amplified his memorial into a book. Although all
his other writings had followed meticulously planned steps of
logic, this work is a wild scramble of documents, letters, statements, thoughts, and afterthoughts that sometimes discusses
the same incident in five or six different places. Following the
convolutions of a mind in anguish, it shouts, reiterates, rages,
weeps, and is above all stunned. "Who would believe in a future
day," he asks, "that so grave and illustrious a set of men as
compose the American Congress" would remove without trial,
and on the "misrepresentations of scheming men . . . one who
from his first stepping forth on the stage of action has always
met with public approbation and distinguished honors both at
home and abroad; who has served his country in posts of eminent trust and usefulness with applause?"

Morgan's attacks on Shippen indicate a persecution complex.
Under that villain's leadership, he shouts, the regimental
surgeons formed a cabal "to injure my character and misrepre-
sent my conduct with a view, if possible, to ruin me forever
in the public esteem." He believed that they purposely allowed
the sick to die so that he would be blamed.

The book contains a statement signed by most of the distinguished doctors in the army complimenting his efficiency,
intelligence, energy, and courage, and stating that "no person
whatever acting in the capacity of director general under the
same circumstances could possibly have given universal satisfaction." It was a remarkable tribute that these physicians, who

were still in the service, should have supported a discharged and disgraced officer against the man who was obviously to be his successor.

Morgan was quite alone; he did not know where to reach his wife, the only person with whom he could ever unbend. In fact, communication had broken down so completely that practically no letters circulated. Two months after his dismissal, Molly wrote him from Baltimore saying that she had not heard from him and that she did not know where to address her letter. "Did you, my dearest, ever receive a packet from Mr. Hancock discharging you from the service?"

In his book, Morgan demanded an official investigation. He sent copies to Congress which were submitted to the medical committee. Ten months to the day after he was cashiered, the committee reported: "Though no cause is assigned for his discharge, yet your committee on inquiry find that the general complaints of persons of all ranks in the army, and not any particular charges against him, together with the critical state of affairs at that time, rendered it necessary for the public good and the safety of the United States that he be displaced." They considered Morgan's memorial "a hasty and intemperate production," but agreed that a committee should be appointed to hear him.

Morgan at once published a notice in the newspapers asking all those who had charges against him to present them. He rode indefatigably over the war-torn countryside, allowing himself not a single day's rest as he collected evidence in his own defense and to Shippen's discredit. A letter to Washington elicited one of the temperate responses for which the commander-in-chief is famous. "The hospitals at Cambridge," he wrote, "being stationary and in a country full of every necessity, were well provided and I imagine well attended." No fault could be found with the economy of the department, but then "things in the first stage of the war were both plentiful and cheap." In New York City and Harlem Heights the troops "were exceedingly sickly and died fast," yet that might have been due to their inexperience, the want of necessities, to fatigue and extreme heat. Although a lack of transportation facilities hindered moving the sick to New Jersey during the retreat, "I do not recollect that you were charged with personal inattention or want of activity, but the clamors were loud against the department in general, and the miserable condition of the sick in all quarters a fact too well known and remembered.

"The resolves of Congress appointing Dr. Shippen and yourself directors in separate departments occasioned a disagreement between you, I think particularly as to the disposal of hospital stores. I remember that I was obliged for the good of the service to interpose in some manner, but without reference to my papers I will not undertake to say what orders I was under the necessity of giving. I have understood that this clashing between Dr. Shippen and yourself was no small cause of the calamities that befell the sick in 1776."

Armed with the letters, affidavits, and records his unceasing industry had collected, Morgan appeared before an investigating committee and won a complete vindication. The committee blamed his dismissal on the necessities of public policy, and Congress thereupon resolved that it was "satisfied with the conduct of Dr. John Morgan."

This decision served only as a cue for further activity; Morgan immediately agitated for revenge on Shippen, his successor as director general. Assisted by Rush, whom Shippen had also driven from the army, he had his old enemy court-martialed for "malpractice and misconduct in office." After Congress had passed a resolution by which evidence for the trial could be collected in the field if both accuser and accused were present, Morgan flooded Shippen with demands that he attend hearings all over the country. "Morgan," the defendant complained to Lee, "supposing himself the prosecutor as well as persecutor, cited me to attend through the deepest snow this winter, which he first broke for 200 miles, and was once dug out of a snow hill, and was once froze to his saddle. . . . He is so meanly industrious that there is hardly an action of two years I am not obliged to explain." Shippen, of course, did not appear; in fact, he used every subterfuge to impede the collection of evidence. Once he even had Morgan jailed for slander. "My adversary," he wrote General Greene, "is a malicious and insignificant animal, yet he is indefatigable and implacable."

When the court martial subsequently brought in its equivocal verdict, Morgan had made every possible move to vindicate his honor. There was nothing left now but to survey the past and prepare for the future.

6

"THE wounds that are given by the envenomed tongue of calumny," Morgan had written under the first shock of dismissal, "are deeper and more fatal than the sword. They destroy what is dearer than life itself, reputation and peace of mind. . . . He whose reputation is injured is ever suspected; his society is shunned; he is looked upon as dangerous, as a

walking pestilence." And again: "If the sacrifice of my life
would have saved my country, I could have cheerfully offered
it up. I cannot say so much for my honor."

Fighting against shame for three furious years, he had felt
that if he could win vindication and achieve revenge his life
would again be the glorious adventure it had been; again he
would be John Morgan, the father of American medical education, darling of the ladies and of the world's greatest savants.
Yet, when the abnormal activity that had blown him along
like a gale abated, he found beneath it still the unrelieved ach-
ing of his honor. Then he knew that the filthy blot which had
soiled his life could not be wiped out by all the explanations
in the world. Untouched by failure until he was more than
forty, he had never built up the resistance to misfortune that
is the boon of ordinary men. At one blow disgrace had annihi-
lated his self-esteem.

Sitting by the hour in his study, he failed to turn the pages
of the book before him. His wife tried vainly to entice him to
the receptions and balls he had once loved. How could he be
graceful now, kiss the young ladies' hands, and condescend
to the young men, when all the while he heard a whispering
behind him? Every time a lady tapped her escort on the arm
and smiled, he knew she was pointing him out in derision.
"Look," he imagined she was saying, "there's John Morgan
who was disgracefully dismissed from the army."

Perhaps he could have regained his self-confidence in the
Colonial drawing-rooms of his youth, but what was there in
republican society to make him want to live an active life
again? The fine manners that had been his joy were gone forever. Fighting for freedom, Morgan had with his own hand
helped to murder the graces that had made his life worth
living. Tradesmen discarded their aprons and walked the

streets like gentlemen; they considered him their equal. There was no dignity left in a land where mechanics voted and shop-keepers appeared at the best parties. People talked of freedom, not courtesy; the young were proud to be boors as long as they were not British gentlemen. It was best to lock oneself away from so mean a generation. Within one's own room, with the shades drawn, one could struggle to remember a world that had vanished.

The Revolution had taken everything from Morgan. Not only society and honor, but when the British had burned Bordertown, his fine library, his relics, the diplomas he had won in Europe, all his past, had gone up in flames. Was it possible, he must have asked himself as he sat in a dark room too lost to light a lamp, was it possible that the youth he longed for had ever been? Was he the British gentleman, secure in his social station, who had ridden in a private coach across Europe, winning praise from the wisest professors in the world?

Morgan's fortune, although halved by the Revolution, enabled him to live on his income, so he did not need to practice medicine; little by little his patients fell away and he was not sad to see them go. He no longer lectured at the medical school. During the war, the College of Philadelphia had been abolished for Tory sympathies and its property handed over to a new institution, the University of Pennsylvania. When all the old medical professors were re-elected, Rush and Morgan announced they would not serve unless Shippen's appointment was withdrawn. The trustees refused, and Shippen became the only professor in the new school. After a few years Rush capitulated, but Morgan could not make himself sit on the same faculty with his old enemy. Although his professorship was kept open for him until the year of his death, he never lectured again in the institution whose founding was his principal glory. For a while he kept his connection with the Pennsylvania Hospital, but he resigned from that body too because its board made a trivial decision without consulting him; his honor was as sensitive as a wounded hand.

Occasionally Morgan showed flashes of his old energy. He led a group of veterans of the French and Indian War in a campaign to secure lands on the Ohio granted them as a bonus by Governor Penn. He wrote a letter on the digging of canals. The meetings of the American Philosophical Society were among the rare occasions that brought him out into the world; he enjoyed reporting to them on natural wonders. One of the most picturesque was "a horse with a snake in its eye to be seen in Arch Street, between Sixth and Seventh Streets, not only possessed of mere life but endowed with a very brisk locomotive faculty. True philosophers will not treat this aberration as idle, fictitious, or romantic, but see and judge for themselves." At first Morgan thought it must be some condition of the eye that looked like a snake, but careful examination convinced him that it was a real reptile "which from the vivacity and briskness of its motion exceeds any worm and equals that of any kind of serpent I have ever seen." Was this phenomenon a proof of spontaneous generation? he asked; certainly the snake could not have got there by natural means.

Then there was Adelaide, the piebald Negro girl with splotches all over her body. "Upon the large black spots there are also many smaller and blacker which are very glaring. Many of these spots divide . . . resembling a star. . . . In several parts these spots, being of different shades, give an exact picture of lunar eclipses. . . . Monsieur Le Vallois [the girl's owner] relates that the mother of Adelaide whilst pregnant with her was delighted in lying out all night in the open air and contemplating the stars and planets. . . . Whether this strong impression made upon the mother of Adelaide by the nightly view of the stars and planetary system may be considered as the cause of the very extraordinary appearances in the girl everyone will determine for themselves." M. Le Vallois, who seems to have run a freak show which he carried from learned society to learned society, also possessed a mulatto boy with a white aigrette on his forehead. His grandmother on his father's side had been frightened by having some milk spilled on her.

Thus with speculations not behind the times but certainly not before them Morgan amused his darkening mind. As long as his wife lived he was never entirely solitary; the clink of teacups and the sound of feminine voices rose to the darkened study where he sat. Mrs. Morgan had not changed. She gushed and laughed; her eyes filled with sentimental tears or gleamed with childish sauciness as she told her husband all the gossip of the neighborhood. But on New Year's Day 1785, she died. She was buried four days later in St. Peter's church. "The morning," wrote Francis Hopkinson, "was snowy and severely cold, and the walking was dangerous and slippery. Nevertheless, a great number of the most respected citizens attended the funeral, and her pall was borne by the first ladies of the place."

After mankind had helped him bury the one person he had loved, Morgan turned his back on mankind. Childless, he lived alone, hunched up like an old man over the relics of the past. He was only fifty, but he awaited death like a long-desired friend. "Wearied with this world," he wrote his brother, "I have for some time past turned my mind more than ordinarily to the thoughts of a better where I wish to go." Disease weakened him more and more.

While he was in the South on an unenthusiastic search for health, the legislature restored its charter to the College of

Philadelphia. Shippen, disturbed by the competition of newer and less demanding schools, took the lead in a reorganization that abolished the degree of Bachelor of Medicine and gave the doctor's degree to men so ill trained Morgan would not have allowed them to be bachelors. The pre-medical requirements, which had been the most progressive part of Morgan's plan, were thrown onto the dump heap whence they were salvaged with great *éclat* by the founders of Johns Hopkins University; for more than a century any untrained lad was allowed to study medicine anywhere in America. Before the new regulations were finally adopted, Morgan returned to Philadelphia, but he was too ill and discouraged to fight. With dying eyes he saw his enemy wreck the fine structure of medical education his youthful genius and energy had built.

Under the date October 15, 1789, Rush's diary contains the following entry: "This afternoon I was called to visit Dr. Morgan, but found him dead in a small hovel, surrounded with books and papers, and on a light, dirty bed. He was attended only by a washerwoman, one of his tenants. His niece, Polly Gordon, came in time enough to see him draw his last breath. His disorder was influenza, but he had been previously debilitated by many other disorders. What a change from his former rank and prospects in life! The man who once filled half the world with his name, has now scarcely friends left enough to bury him."

Saint or Scourge

BENJAMIN RUSH

Benjamin Rush

FROM A PORTRAIT BY THOMAS SULLY

Saint or Scourge

Benjamin Rush

1

J OHN MORGAN was the greatest physician of the Colonial era; the Revolution swept him aside with other outworn things. Although only ten years younger, his friend and pupil Benjamin Rush lived in an entirely different world; from the beginning he rode the bandwagon of freedom, he signed the Declaration of Independence at the age of thirty-one, and he flourished in the new soil of democracy so mightily that he became the first great doctor of the United States and the most powerful physician our nation has ever known. Sir William Osler's influence on his colleagues did not compare with the influence of Rush, whose medical theories were accepted by succeeding generations of practitioners as direct from God. Until the middle of the nineteenth century most men who died on the North American continent had little Rushes standing by their bedsides with lancets in one hand and vials of calomel in the other. For their master taught heroic remedies. Nature was a devil to be kept out of the sickroom by a doctor who battled every symptom with a flaming sword.

Today Rush's reputation is engulfed in controversy. Some doctors call him the father of American practice, while others substitute the word "vampire" for "father," insisting that his disastrous methods bled countless thousands to death during fifty long years. The part he played in the Revolution is also equivocal; most historians believe he was active in a plot to oust General Washington, but his partisans call this a libel. Even his character is obscured by a fog of argument. A forceful pamphleteer, pioneer in temperance and prison reform, in the emancipation of slaves and humane treatment of the insane, Rush falls naturally into the pattern of a Protestant saint. Undoubtedly he himself was conscious of this, for he expurgated the papers he left behind him, and wrote an autobiography that seems to some readers an attempt at self-canonization. But was this powerful man who lacked none of the passions of power really meek and holy, or did he sometimes slip by inadvertence over to the side of darkness?

However we answer these questions, it is certain that Rush was one of the most important figures of his age. He was versatile and strong, ready to take up his cudgels in any battle, and bristling with ideas that were new and startling. His name is written large across the cultural history of the United States.

Unlike Morgan and Shippen, Rush belonged not to the Colonial aristocracy but to the solid bourgeoisie who were to capture the nation during the Revolution. He was born on Christmas Eve 1745, to a pious farmer and gunsmith near Philadelphia. When his father died six years later, his mother was forced to move to town and follow the conventional expedient of impoverished widows: she opened a grocery shop. A graduate of a female boarding school, she was a well-educated woman for those days. Little Benjamin's love for her was possessive, as is indicated by his meditations on looking at her corpse forty years later. "I thought of the misery it had felt

in an unfortunate early marriage which happily for her terminated in three or four years by the extravagance and intemper-
ance of her young husband." His father, whom she married
next, was, he insisted, "the husband of her warmest affections."
He then thought of the anguish she had felt "during the sixteen
years she had been connected with her last husband, who was
rough, unkind, and often abusive in his treatment of her."
Obviously he resented the fact that she had belonged to other
men than his father.

The principal of the Nottingham School was his uncle, so
he naturally went there. Too full of energy to study hard, he
ate the excellent food and occupied himself with hunting and
gunning. "From much reflection upon this subject," he wrote
as an old man, "I am satisfied that it would be wise for country
schoolmasters to forbid these amusements altogether. Rural
employments might easily be established in their room. These
establish early ideas of connection between industry and property."

In the College of New Jersey, which he entered at fourteen,
"I was an idle, playful, and I am sorry to add, mischievous
boy," yet he demonstrated such talents for composition and
public speaking that, when he was graduated after one year,
the president tried to persuade him to become a lawyer. However, he consulted his uncle at Nottingham, who said that the
law was "full of temptations," and that he should "set apart
a day for fasting and prayer and ask God to direct you in the
choice of a profession." God, Rush implied, told him to go into
medicine, which he immediately did, although once he was
deep in its studies he wondered why he had not entered the
ministry instead. "To have officiated at the sacred desk," he
wrote a friend, "would have been my most delightful employ-

ment. To spend and be spent for the good of mankind is what I chiefly aim at. Though now I pursue the study of physick, I am far from giving it any pre-eminence to divinity."

Rush apprenticed himself to Dr. Redman, who had been Morgan's preceptor, and attended Shippen's early lectures in anatomy. During five years, he was absent from work only eleven days and took only three evenings off. The memory of such regularity did not satisfy him as an old man, however; he considered that he had been frivolous until the final year of his apprenticeship when, he implies, a sin with a woman showed him the wickedness of his ways. "The early part of my life was spent in dissipation, folly, and the practice of some of the vices to which young men are prone. The weight of that folly and those vices has been felt in my mind ever since. They have often been deplored in tears and sighs before God. It was from a deep and affecting sense of one of them that I was first led to seek the favor of God in his Son in the twenty-first year of my age. It was thus the woman of Samaria was brought to a repentance of all her sins by the Son of God reminding her of but *one* of them, viz., her living criminally with a man who was not her husband."

Rush got on famously with his preceptor, whom he called "a sincere friend and tender father"; indeed, Redman often left him in complete charge of patients for days together before he had been an apprentice two years. When Morgan started his lectures, Rush matriculated under him and did so brilliantly that Morgan promised his twenty-one-year-old pupil the professorship of chemistry if he would study that subject in Edinburgh.

During August 1766 Rush sailed for Plymouth with Jonathan Potts, another young medical student. He was delighted that the ship's captain showed "a reverence for his Maker and a belief in His providence. Every part of his conduct was moral and his commands and conversation were always free from profanity and swearing. He had been educated, he once informed me, by a pious mother."

At Edinburgh, Rush worked hard and during the second term presented a thesis on digestion. By way of research, he ate three large meals, each of which he forced himself to regurgitate after three hours. The measures were heroic, but the conclusions were wrong. Since the contents of the stomach were always acid, he thought he had proved that digestion was acetous fermentation. When he mourned that the gastric juice was so far buried in the stomach it could not be extracted, he showed ignorance of the experiments Réaumur had published fourteen years before, in which the French scientist had isolated the gastric juice of a kite and demonstrated that far from causing fermentation, it resisted it.

Rush tells us that his years in Edinburgh were the most important of his life because he met there an English radical named John Bostock who had the courage to question the divine right of kings. Although as an apprentice Rush had denounced the Stamp Act, the idea that kings could be entirely dispensed with struck at the basis of his philosophy. "I had been taught to consider them as essential to the political order as the sun is to the order of our solar system." For days the young man forgot medicine while, almost frightened by his own thinking, he mulled over Bostock's insidious arguments. When at last he became convinced of "the absurdity of hereditary power," he resolved never again to believe any statement without question. Thus it was a political not a scientific issue that prepared his mind for his amazing medical career.

However, since he believed that the order of society was fixed and could not be changed, he thought it wiser to hide his radical opinions. A few months later we find him writing that distinctions of rank "are absolutely necessary to keep up the happiness and well-being of society."

Rush attended William Hunter's lectures in London. Benjamin West introduced him to Sir Joshua Reynolds, who invited him to dine with Dr. Johnson and Goldsmith. When Franklin found that Rush lacked the money to go to Paris, he lent him a letter of credit for three hundred guineas. The grave essay in which Rush described his trip is the work of a logical young man, lacking *joie de vivre* and incapable of introspection, but motivated by a tremendous intellectual curiosity concerning the manners and customs of other men. Remembering his Edinburgh conversion, he started his essay: "We are very apt to imagine everything we see in our country to be the standard of what is right in taste, politeness, customs, language, etc., and therefore we condemn everything that differs from [it]. This is a fruitful source of error in the opinion we form of different stations." However, he was soon pointing out the similarity between French civilization and that of savage tribes.

When the women of Paris fascinated him, he found it necessary to defend their virtue from the usual British slurs by pages of close argument. The fact that they received men in their bedchambers was no proof of lack of modesty, since ladies expose more of their bodies in ordinary dress than "under a pile of bedclothes." He employed learned ethnological parallels to demonstrate that the use of coarse language does not necessarily mean lack of chastity. And what if they did paint their faces? "No one will pretend to say that the works of nature are so perfect as to be incapable of receiving any improvement from the arts." In the salons of French aristocrats Rush was greatly impressed by the intellectual attainments of the ladies, and he had the audacity to suggest that Anglo-Saxon girls would be just as pure and more charming if they were permitted a little knowledge.

Watching the Dauphin dine in public confirmed Rush in his disapproval of kings; he saw the monarch take a piece of meat from his mouth with his hand, stare at it angrily, and throw it under the table. When Rush met John Wilkes, the famous radical shocked him to the core by saying that "he once dined with twelve gentlemen in Paris, eleven of whom declared they should think it their duty to surrender up their wives to the king if he desired it."

Not only worried about the state of the world, Rush was also terrified lest Morgan should not be able to hold the professorship of chemistry open for him. Since Redman did not seem as active in his behalf as he might be, Rush turned on his preceptor. "I cannot say I ever received a single idea from Dr. Redman. . . . He never conferred a favor upon me of any kind but such as he was obliged to do by the common rules of decency and good manners. . . . May he live to see the base ingratitude of his conduct towards me! That is all the punishment I wish him for it."

Rush's ambition mounted daily. When he stepped off the ship on his return from Europe, he told Dr. Ramsay of his resolve that "no circumstance of personal charms, fortune, or connections should tempt him to perpetrate matrimony till he had extended his studies so far that a family would be no impediment to his further progress." For the following years he worked from dawn till midnight, attending patients all day and studying at night. "When I began to feel languid or sleepy at late or early hours, I used to excite my mind by increasing the heat and blaze of my fire in winter, or by exposing myself a few minutes on the balcony." Only rarely could he spare the time to amuse himself with friends.

Although he secured his professorship of chemistry without difficulty, his family position was not good enough to attract a fashionable practice; he was forced to minister to the poor. There were few old huts in the city where he did not attend patients. "Often have I ascended the upper story of these huts by a ladder, and many hundred times have I been obliged to rest my weary limbs upon the bedside of the sick from want of chairs, where I was sure I risked not only taking their disease but being infected with vermin."

Rush alienated most of his colleagues by violently expounding a new medical theory. Eighteenth-century medicine, like the poetry and theology of the time, had little interest in nature; while Pope's disciples wrote end-stopped couplets about drawing-rooms, while divines tortured phrases in the Bible, doctors, forgetting to study their patients, devised theories in their own minds. American practice was dominated by the Dutch physician Boerhaave, who had never impeded his medical speculations with experiments. The "humors," those remains of ancient thought, were the basis of his therapy; he had different treatments for salt, putrid, and oily temperaments. He blamed all disease on "morbid acrimonies" in the blood which he tried to chase from the body through the urine, through the pores, and by mild bloodletting.

In Edinburgh, Rush had come under the influence of William Cullen, who had discarded Boerhaave's speculations for some of his own. Cullen contended that a physician should control his observations by his theory, for the mind was a more noble instrument than the eye. He demonstrated by metaphysical arguments that Boerhaave was wrong and that all diseases were due to disorders of the nerve force; even gout was a neurosis. Since Linnæus's botanical studies had made classifications fashionable, he divided diseases according to superficial symp-

toms into classes, genera, and species, 1387 in all. Opposing
bloodletting, he put his faith in an elaborate hierarchy of drugs.
His disciples merely had to fit their patient's symptoms into
his classification and then apply the remedies he detailed.

On returning to America a stripling of twenty-four, Rush
tried to convince his elders that they had been fools all their
lives because they had followed Boerhaave. Unable to admit a
doubt of Cullen's system, he excoriated the leading practitioners
with a condescension and a self-righteousness that brought a
flood of abuse down on his head. However, he was a brilliant
propagandist, and in a few years Cullen began to supersede
Boerhaave as the inspiration of Philadelphia's doctors.

Shippen seems especially to have resented Rush's arrogance.
In 1771 Jacob Rush wrote his brother Benjamin from London:
"I am sorry that Dr. Shippen has kept away students from attending your lectures. At the same time, I am not at all sorry
that you are at variance with him. Better, infinitely better is it
to be at eternal variance with a man of his cool malice and
treachery." Like Cassius, Jacob Rush warned, Shippen could
never be caught off his guard, yet his hatred was so deep that
he would murder Benjamin were he not afraid of the law.

Not content with making his colleagues change their methods, Rush attacked the public in pamphlets on many subjects.
The diatribe against slavery which made him unpopular with
the rich showed him a brilliant writer. His short, nervous
clauses are joined into sentences that, although complicated,
draw the eye down the page. Even his bravura passages of
eighteenth-century eloquence rarely go over the edge into
bombast; the description of a slave market is capable of misting
a modern reader's eye. In 1774 Rush helped organize the first
anti-slavery society in America, and many years later he succeeded Franklin as its president.

Rush's *Sermons to Gentlemen upon Temperance and Exercise* reveal some of the contradictions that made up his multiple nature. Although he argued against alcohol, we find some surprising breaks with the Puritanical attitude that usually dominated his writings. In support of dancing as "a most salutary exercise," he argued that cheerfulness "when well-founded and properly restrained is another name for religion." He loved to boast that his labors left him no time for society, yet he wrote: "We shall walk, run, dance, swim, fence, sail, and ride to little purpose unless we make choice of an agreeable friend to accompany us. Solitude is the bane of man."

In his twenty-eighth year Rush either decided his studies were far enough advanced to allow him to marry or else "a circumstance of personal charm" got the best of him. He fell in love with a fashionable, vivacious, and red-haired young lady named Sarah Eve. Perhaps he was motivated by passion, not prudence, for Sarah's diary hardly makes her out Rush's type. How, for instance, does she deal with the sacred calling of the ministry? "I never once thought of it before I heard Mrs. Clifford mention it, why such an exemplary man as Mr. Duché should sit every day and have his hair curled and powdered by a barber. Since, I have thought about it *greatly*, and I would like to hear *his* sentiments on the subject. But, my dear ma'am, what would a parson be without *powder*; it is as necessary to him as a *soldier*, for it gives a more significant shake to his head, and is as *priming* to his words and looks. As to having his hair curled . . . perhaps he may look upon it as more humiliating to wear his own hair than a wig, as then his head must serve as a *block* on which the barber must dress it."

What of her sense of duty? "In the afternoon Anna and I

went out to look for some calico for Mrs. Smith. We were to
return immediately, but instead of that we stayed and drank
tea with Betsy Guest. Sad girls, sad girls! But we really could
not help it; our cloaks and bonnets were taken off by force and
locked up—but that was from our desire. As we found they were
determined to keep us, we begged them to secure them which
they accordingly did. Worse and worse! Worse and worse!"

What must Rush have thought of her lack of conventional
hypocrisy towards sacred matters like funerals, when it was
usual for young ladies to walk sadly by the biers of their contemporaries? "In the evening B. Rush, P. Dunn, K. Vaughan,
and myself carried Mr. Ash's child to be buried. Foolish custom
for girls to prance it through the streets without hats or bonnets!"

In this love affair too Shippen appears as a villain, but Rush
would not have approved of Sarah's reason for disliking his
caresses. "In the morning Dr. Shippen came to see us. What a
pity it is that the doctor is so fond of kissing; he really would
be much more agreeable if he were less fond. One hates to be
always kissed, especially as it is attended with so many incon-
veniences; it decomposes the economy of one's *handkerchief*, it
disorders one's *high roll*, and it ruffles the serenity of one's
countenance; in short, the doctor's or a sociable kiss is many
times worse than a formal salute with bowing and curtsying, to
'This is Mister Such-a-one, and this is Miss What-do-you-call-
her.' 'Tis true, this confuses one no little, but one gets the better
of that sooner than to readjust one's dress."

Sarah Eve's journal is the gentle, high-spirited reflection of
a gentle high-spirited soul without a shade of pomposity or
put-on emotion. She made fun of pretentiousness, and used her
mind with pleasure, although limited to concocting quibbles

about the few situations that arose in her restricted life. "We are now," she wrote, "on Penn Park Bridge; you will say I am but a poor traveler when I tell you it is the best bridge I ever went over, although it has but three arches." She was thrilled by so noble a sight. Even when she moralizes, her sentiments do not fall into language that Rush would approve. "Will fortune never cease to persecute us? But why complain, for at worst, what is poverty? It is living more according to nature. . . . Poverty without pride is nothing, but with it, it is the very deuce."

We can easily understand how Rush, perhaps against his better self, was fascinated by this beautiful and clever girl of twenty-two, but what did she think of the rising young doctor? Although not handsome, he had a striking air of intelligence. His receding forehead, which repeated the curve of his strong nose, his high cheek-bones, tremendously long lower lip, and deep-set blue eyes gave him a sympathetic gravity that was never broken by a laugh. Yet his face, reflecting the movements of a nimble mind, had a vivacious rhythm of its own, and the words he spoke on a hundred different subjects were fresh and intelligent and often exciting. How did this combination of qualities, which inspired complete confidence in patients and gave Rush the most famous bedside manner of his age, affect the high-spirited young lady he courted?

We must look for an answer in the diary she kept during his wooing. That Sarah was not afraid of putting her emotions on paper is revealed by numerous passages about her father who was in the West Indies trying to recoup his vanished fortunes. "As soon as I got up this morning, I went out in the field to see them mow, and could not help thinking that I walked and kicked the grass just as my dear father used to do. The thought gave me so much pleasure I had liked to forget to eat my breakfast." When a letter from her father was due, she gave up an excursion so as to be sure not to miss its arrival, and after it had brought good news at last, she wrote: "Mama, the boys, and I came home ten o'clock without the least fear. Nothing could frighten me now; I could go anywhere."

Obviously she loved her father, but what about Rush? He is mentioned many times, always as Mr. Rush or B. Rush. A typical entry reads: "This day I spent at Mr. Rush's. In the evening Mama and my aunt walked to town for me." When he showed distress that she and her mother were ill, she made her only enthusiastic mention of him: "Are we not blessed with the best of friends!" Under March 27 we find: "In the afternoon Mr. and Mrs. Garriquise, Hannah Mitchell, Mr. Roberts, Mr. Rush (Bless me, what a girl! Mr. Rush should have been set down first, I am sure, but now it is too late), and J. Giles drank tea with us."

However, she soon became Rush's fiancée. Had her reticence about him been due to "female modesty," or was her lack of enthusiasm over-ridden by the eagerness of her recently impoverished family for so good a match? Rush was already well known and making nine hundred pounds a year. Perhaps Sarah was trying desperately to keep hold on the flood of life that had begun to ebb within her. Shortly before her engagement, she came down with a lingering illness, probably tuberculosis, and three weeks before her wedding date she died.

Rush, who needed to share all his emotions with the public, wrote a eulogy of her for the *Pennsylvania Packet*. Titled "A Female Character," it translated her into the kind of girl he undoubtedly wished she had been: "A person who had lived with her from a child declared that she had never once seen her angry or heard a nasty word from her lips." But eventually he seems to have realized that she had not been the proper type of fiancée for a Puritan worthy; in his autobiography he makes no mention of the beautiful and tragic Sarah Eve.

Rush had now set his mind on marrying, and the next time he did not allow his emotions to run away with him. In less than a year he visited his old friend Richard Stockton at Princeton and was gratified to find that a baby he had carried in his arms while he was an undergraduate was now a woman. "His eldest daughter," Rush wrote in his autobiography, "a young lady of between sixteen and seventeen years of age, soon attracted my attention. She was engaging in her manners and correct in her conversation. I had seen a letter of her writing to Mrs. Ferguson which gave me a favorable idea of her taste and understanding. It was much strengthened by an opinion I heard her give of Dr. Witherspoon's preaching the next day after I saw her. She said he was the best preacher she had ever heard. Such a declaration I was sure could only proceed from a soundness of judgment and a correctness of taste seldom met with in a person of her age, for there was nothing in Dr. Witherspoon's sermons to recommend them but their uncommon good sense and simplicity of style. From that moment, I determined to offer her my hand."

Dr. Witherspoon performed the marriage. Even in his letters telling friends of the match, Rush insisted that he was more influenced by Julia Stockton's prudence and understanding than by her beauty. She was a pretty, buxom girl who accentuated an oval face by piling dark hair up over a high forehead and allowing it to fall in ringlets down her neck. The marriage seems to have been happy, although in her letters Mrs. Rush was less expressive of affection to her husband than to her children. She had thirteen children, of whom nine reached maturity. Rush tells us: "She fulfilled every duty as wife, mother, and mistress with fidelity and integrity."

2

HATING kings, Rush was one of the most radical thinkers in the Colonies; that fire-brand Samuel Adams, for all his rashness, found it necessary to pretend that he quarreled with Parliament only because its attempts to tax America were an encroachment on the royal domain. Despite such precautions, the Boston representatives to the first Continental Congress were regarded with as much suspicion as Communists would be at a modern Democratic convention; rich Whigs suspected them of "leveling principles" and even an ignoble desire to let the common people vote. Rush, however, put both Samuel and John Adams up in his house. The physician's chambers rang with heady phrases about freedom and democracy and the resulting return of virtue.

Once, while Congress was still discussing conciliation, Rush accompanied the Adamses to Thomas Mifflin's. Although Washington and Charles Lee were present, John Adams had the temerity to argue that union with Great Britain was no longer possible. He sprang to his feet and with his glass upraised proposed the toast, "Cash and gunpowder for the Yankees!" With a beating heart, Rush clinked his glass against the others and raised it to his lips.

Rush was never a passive participant in any cause. Anxious to make the agricultural Colonies independent of England, he organized the company that brought the first spinning jenny to America and made the first cotton cloth. He used his position as a doctor to discover the conservative "errors and prejudices" of his middle-class patients, which he reported to the radical pamphleteers for refutation. Writing anonymous newspaper articles himself, he marshaled arguments for a conclusive pamphlet that would prove once and for all the necessity of complete independence. Although he felt he could persuade many patriots, he hesitated to commit himself in writing, for he knew such heresy would cost him his rich practice. Finally he asked a young Englishman with whom he had been associated in anti-slavery agitation to undertake the task. When Thomas Paine agreed, Rush gave him his notes, named the resulting essay *Common Sense*, and with much difficulty found a publisher brave enough to print what proved to be one of the most important documents in all American history; it converted thousands to views which a few weeks before they had regarded as high treason. Rush's part in the preparation of the pamphlet was recognized at the time. In a letter to him, Charles Lee calls it "your *Common Sense*."

Rush was outraged by the conservatism of the Pennsylvania Assembly, which, elected by the propertied classes alone, remained lukewarm to freedom. He was a leader among the Whig members who bolted to form an illegal revolutionary assembly. On June 24, 1776, as chairman of a committee, he submitted a resolution demanding complete freedom that foreshadowed many of the important points and some of the phraseology of the Declaration of Independence. During July, the radical Pennsylvania body elected him a member of Congress. Although he did not take his seat until after the Declaration had been passed, he became a signer.

Since he was incapable of compromise, Rush was not an influential member of Congress. He spoke his mind on every subject, even implying in open debate that General Lee had purposely allowed the British to take him prisoner. Like a loyal Pennsylvanian, he supported the large States against the small, wishing representation to be by population not provinces. His argument against trying to fix by law prices that were rising because of inflation was eminently sane, but he joined the other more radical members in demanding that Congress keep all power in its own hands. When it was proposed that the general staff of the army be allowed to appoint three major-generals, Rush sprang to his feet in a fury. Rome, he pointed out, "called her general officers from the plow and paid no regard to rank, service, or seniority. . . . If the motion is passed, I shall move immediately afterwards that all the civil power of the continent may be transferred from our hands into the hands of the army, and that they may be proclaimed the highest power of the people."

Like his friends the Adamses, Rush blamed all defeats not on the national breakdown for which Congress was partly responsible, but on the individuals in command. He wrote in his commonplace book that Washington would probably be dismissed because he was "unequal to the discipline and decision necessary to win a war," and dangerously popular with the people. As a member of the medical committee, Rush naturally thought the disorganization in the hospital department was the director general's fault; he joined the pack that hunted Morgan.

When Congress fled to Maryland during December, Rush did not go with them. In his zeal for freedom, he joined the Pennsylvania militia that marched out to make a last stand before Philadelphia. Washington consulted him concerning the march on Princeton and he carried the order which told General Cadwalader to bring up the militia. Though they did not arrive in time to take part in the main Battle of Princeton, they engaged in skirmishing, and Rush treated the wounded on the field of battle. As soon as the capital seemed safe, he hurried back to Congress.

Having long outraged his conservative constituents, he now angered the radicals by calling the unicameral Pennsylvania legislature they had set up "a mob government"; he wanted a system of checks and balances. He was not re-elected to Congress when his term expired in March 1777. Since it was impossible for him to be inactive, he immediately joined the army hospital department.

While Morgan was director general, Shippen had argued for decentralization of authority, but as soon as his enemy was removed, he pushed through Congress a new plan whose provisions concerning the inferior status of regimental surgeons were to bury their controversy with the general hospital forever. All the power in the department, over both the physicians and the handling of medical supplies, was to be exercised by one man. Probably Shippen was not amazed when that man turned out to be himself. Made director general, he established a hierarchy of sub-directors in an attempt to lure able doctors into the army. As surgeon and later physician general of the "middle department," Rush became one of these subordinate officials, but he did not remain a loyal subordinate for long.

In his pamphlet, *Directions for Preserving the Health of Soldiers*, Rush proved his ability as a military doctor. Although his statement that "the munificence of Congress" had made ample provision for the sick was hardly accurate, he was right when he blamed many deaths on the officers who failed to enforce hygienic regulations. His arguments for personal cleanliness and general sanitation would have saved many lives had they been listened to, even if some of his reasoning seems

comic today. "The hair," he wrote, "by being long and un-
combed is apt to accumulate perspiration of the head, which
by becoming putrid sometimes produces disease." Although
no one realized that insects spread maladies, Rush urged that
troops be not quartered near marshy ground.

Convinced that soldiers in encampments should never be
crowded together and should continually change the straw on
which they slept, Rush was horrified to find that Shippen's hospitals, which should have been centers of hygiene, violated
both these rules. In May he wrote his superior officer that the
hospitals were breeding disease, but Shippen paid no attention.
The huge Brethren House of the Moravian sect at Bethlehem,
Pennsylvania, which became the chief general hospital, soon
rivaled the British prison ships as the most dangerous place that
existed during the Revolution. It was safer to stroll under the
guns of the enemy than to be carried into this house of healing.

Over seven hundred sufferers were crowded into the barn-
like edifice, although, allowing four feet to each patient, there
was room for only three hundred and forty-six. Elementary
sanitation was disregarded. For weeks Shippen could procure
no brooms or cleaning instruments, and when they arrived at
last, the hospital was filthy beyond repair. Several sufferers
lay piled together on one pallet of straw. Dr. William Smith
reported that he had known "from four to five patients to die
on the same straw before it was changed, and that many of
them had been admitted only for slight disorders." Here was
a paradise for the typhus lice, which, when a dead body became
cold and unpleasant, only had to crawl a few inches to find a
new living man.

Two to three hundred sufferers, almost a third of the patients, died during the last three months of 1777; out of forty
members of a Virginia regiment only two emerged alive. Al-

though the subordinate surgeons who worked in this pest house struggled so valiantly that almost all of them contracted typhus and many succumbed, they could achieve nothing because of the filth, over-crowding, and lack of supplies. Morgan would have worked sleeplessly to alter this terrible situation, but when the doctors complained to Shippen, he replied with a genial smile that the sick had room and stores enough.

Soon some of his subordinates were in open revolt. Four of the surgeons swore out the following affidavit: "This is to certify that the wine allowed to the hospital at Bethlehem under the name of madeira was adulterated in such a degree as to have none of the qualities or effects of madeira; that it was common practice for the commissary general to deduct one third—sometimes more, sometimes less—from the orders for wine, sugar, and molasses, and other stores ordered for the sick by the surgeons; that none of the patients in the hospital under our care eat of venison, poultry, or wild fowl unless purchased by themselves, and that large quantities of these articles were bought by Mr. Hasse, the assistant commissary of hospitals, by order of the director general; that the director general never entered the hospital but once during about six weeks' residence in the village of Bethlehem although the utmost distress and mortality prevailed in the hospital at that time; that a putrid fever raged for three months in the hospital and was greatly increased by the sick being too much crowded and by their wanting blankets, sheets, straw, and other necessities for sick people."

Under pressure from Shippen, who as his superior officer controlled his future, one of the four signers of this statement wrote a recantation in which he tried rather unconvincingly to explain away the charges concerning adulterated wine and misappropriated venison, but even he did not have the face to deny that Shippen had visited the hospital only once or that over-crowding and lack of supplies had produced a terrible epidemic. Shippen procured several other witnesses to stand up for his conduct at Bethlehem, but they seemed equally half-hearted.

However we evaluate the testimony Shippen collected, in his own favor, there is no contravening the fact that on November 24, when the epidemic was at its height, he lied to Congress. "If we can be furnished with blankets and clothing our sick will soon be again fit for duty as no fatal disease rages," he wrote, and added doctored statistics on the number of sick and the percentages of deaths.

Of course, the nation was so disorganized and discouraged that even the most zealous hospital director would have had to face overwhelming odds that might have defeated him as they had defeated Morgan. Shippen, however, did not even try. An expert in the art of graceful living, he saw no reason why a war should make him change his habits. He resided comfortably in Bethlehem with his wife and never got within gunshot of a battlefield; later he was to continue his lectures and practice in Philadelphia although the medical department under his command was foundering. While many of his subordinates believed that the sick died for lack of the stimulus given by wine, he drank it in large quantities and, as he eventually admitted, speculated in madeira on the market. On October 18, 1777, Richard Henry Lee sent him seventy-five pounds in payment for "the wine I had of you." Shippen was to claim that the wine he sold was his own not the army's, but even if this were true the transaction was not to his credit. When thousands were giving their lives for freedom, he might well have given a little of his purse.

It is possible that Shippen did not feel freedom was of much importance. Since his family had reached greatness under

British rule, most of his close relations had Tory sympathies; his cousin Peggy is reputed to have influenced Benedict Arnold to commit treason. As Shippen sang convivial songs while his charges died, he may easily have excused his lack of zeal by reminding himself that the hospitals under his command were not much worse than the Hôtel Dieu in Paris, where four to six patients lay in one bed and twenty percent of those admitted expired. He may also have recalled that the type of graft of which he was accused was usual in the British army. During the eighteenth century the lives of common men were considered unimportant. The Landgrave of Hesse sold his Hessians to the British for thirty marks a head with the understanding that he would receive thirty more for each man killed, wounded, or captured. He scolded cautious officers who reduced his income through protecting their soldiers, and spent the money earned by the agony of hundreds on an Italian opera singer. Shippen's psychology may have been similar to the Landgrave's; he was also an aristocrat.

Although it is not fair to compare conditions in the north with those in Pennsylvania, where the national breakdown was much more complete, the record of Dr. Jonathan Potts, the commanding physician with Gates's army, forms an interesting contrast with Shippen's record. On the same terrain where disease had raged a year before, Potts lost only two hundred and five men out of an army of twenty thousand, although he treated five hundred who had been wounded in battle. When General Burgoyne surrendered at Saratoga, Potts, perhaps, could claim the victory as much as the American generals.

From his station at Princeton, Rush had watched the developments in the medical department of the Continental Army with horror. Powerless, he asserted, to help the sick even in his own hospital because Shippen would not listen to his sugges-

tions or send adequate supplies, he wrote three letters to his
friend, John Adams, accusing Shippen of ignorance and negli-
gence. "The present management of our army would depopu-
late America if men grew among us as speedily and spontaneously as blades of grass. The wealth of worlds could not support
the expense of the medical department above two or three
years." He begged that Shippen's power as commissary general
be checked by making him account for the supplies he purchased. "My heart is almost broken at seeing the distresses of
my countrymen without a power to remedy them." In a letter
to Congressman William Duer, Rush urged that the position
of purveyor be separated from that of medical director; he
pointed out that Shippen could, if he wished, steal supplies
"to the amount of a million a year," and proportion his reports of the sick "to his expenditures and to his fears of alarming Congress."

Rush agitated so successfully that Congress appointed a committee to hear his charges. Shippen immediately wrote to that
body that, while Rush was deserting his post to seek preferment, "I think it my duty rather to run the risk of suffering
in my reputation than that the sick soldiers should suffer by
my absence. Next week I shall do myself the honor of sending
or carrying a return of all the sick and wounded by which I
flatter myself it will appear that our sick are not crowded in
any hospital . . . that very few die, that no fatal disease pre-
vails, and that the hospitals are in good order. . . . I must
add, some amendments to our system may be made, but Dr.
Rush, from his ignorance of the state of our hospitals and not
knowing his duty, has not hit upon any of them."

Conscious that Congress was terrified of anything that might
reveal the desperate state of the army, Shippen insisted that
unless Rush were dismissed he would demand a public investi-

gation of the medical department. This bold stroke succeeded. Although its chairman was John Witherspoon, the divine whose sermons had been responsible for Rush's marriage, the Congressional committee announced that the troubles of the sick were due to a personal feud between Rush and Shippen. They forced Rush to resign, and then improved matters by taking the right to purvey supplies away from Shippen.

Rush immediately wrote his enemy that only his remembrance of their early association and his tenderness for Shippen's family prevented him from publishing facts that would ruin his rival's reputation forever. Despite the urging of his friends, Rush intended to restrain himself: "I have no revenge in me." However, in less than a month he sent Washington evidence against Shippen and demanded that he be court-martialed. But Washington was in no friendly mood.

While a member of Congress, Rush had grown to believe it was up to him to win the war. After he had been in the service only a month, he wrote the commander-in-chief, advising him to postpone the spring campaign. He confided to his commonplace book during October a note on "the state and disorders of the American army: 1. The commander-in-chief, at this time the idol of America, governed by General Greene, General Knox, and Colonel Hamilton, one of his aides, a young man of twenty-one years of age. 2. Four major-generals—Greene, Sullivan, Sterling, and Stevens. The first a sycophant to the general, speculative, without enterprise; the second weak, vain, without dignity, fond of scribbling, in the field a madman; the third a proud, vain, lazy, ignorant drunkard; the fourth a sordid, boasting, cowardly sot. The troops undisciplined and ragged, guns fired a hundred a day, pickets left five days and sentries twenty-four hours without relief, bad bread, no order, universal disgust."

The two Adamses, Rush's particular friends, and Richard Henry Lee had long been out for Washington's scalp; the defeat at Brandywine gave them great satisfaction, for it further lowered the commander's prestige. When the northern army under Gates won the victory of Saratoga, the more radical Congressmen, confident that they had found a savior, formed a conspiracy to displace Washington with Gates. It is easily proved that Rush joined with Generals Gates, Conway, Mifflin, and Charles Lee to become one of the principal supporters in the army of what is today known as the Conway Cabal.

Rush's letters to John Adams complaining of Shippen were full of attacks on Washington, who, he insisted, was so inefficient he did not know to within three thousand the number of men in his army. Criticizing the commander-in-chief for his inability to preserve discipline, Rush proposes a strange remedy: the general officers should be elected annually and all enlistments should be of short-term militia. "Good general officers would make an army of six months' men an army of heroes."

After Washington's defeat at Germantown, Rush wrote: "General Conway wept for joy when he saw the ardor with which our troops pushed the enemy from hill to hill, and pronounced our country free, from that auspicious sight. But when he saw an officer low in command give counter orders to the commander-in-chief, and the commander-in-chief passive under that circumstance, his distress and resentment exceeded all bounds. For God's sake do not suffer him [Conway] to resign. . . . Some people blame him for calling our generals fools, cowards, and drunkards in public company. But these things are proof of his integrity and should raise him in the opinion of every friend of America."

When the news of the Battle of Saratoga came, Rush was

beside himself with fury against Washington whose "imitation of an army" he compared to an "ill-organized mob." If Congress could overlook the contrast between Gates's victories and Washington's defeats, "then like the Israelites of old, we worship the work of our own hands."

As long as he confined himself to writing such sentiments to Adams, another supporter of the cabal, Rush was safe from criticism, but he was not furthering Washington's dismissal. His mind engaged in its usual conflict between zeal and caution. Journeying to Yorktown for the hearing of his charges against Shippen, he passed through the encampment at Valley Forge. He was shocked by the misery and disorganization he found there. General Sullivan, with whom he breakfasted, confirmed his impression. "Sir," he said, "this is not an army; it is a mob." In a burst of indignation, Rush sent Patrick Henry an attack on Washington, but he could not quite get up the courage to sign it. The author of the letter, he stated, "is one of your Philadelphia friends. A hint of his name, if found out by the handwriting, must not be mentioned to your most intimate friend. Even the letter must be thrown into the fire. But some of its contents ought to be made public in order to awaken, enlighten, and alarm the country."

Rush insisted that nothing was needed for victory but Washington's removal. "The northern army has shown what Americans are capable of doing with a general at their head. The spirit of the southern army is in no ways inferior to the spirit of the northern. A Gates, a Lee, or a Conway would in a few weeks render them an irresistible body of men."

Far from burning the letter, Henry sent it to Washington, who replied: "The anonymous letter with which you were pleased to favor me was written by Dr. Rush as far as I can judge from a similitude of hands. This man has been elaborate and studied in his professions of regard for me, and long since the letter to you. My caution to avoid anything which could injure the service prevented me from communicating but to a very few friends the intrigues of a faction which I know was formed against me, since it might serve to publish our internal dissensions." Washington then described the cabal at some length.

Washington naturally regarded Rush's attack on Shippen as part of the cabal's scheming; conscious that even the best medical organization might have broken down in those difficult days, he refused to court-martial Shippen. As a result, Rush's disapproval of Washington rose into a fury. The high point of the cabal, when Gates as president of the Board of War outranked the commander-in-chief, had already been reached; under the glare of publicity, the plot collapsed. The insurgent generals were demoted and the conspirators in Congress denied everything in an attempt to save their reputations from popular wrath. Rush, however, was too far aroused to retreat for some time. When General Charles Lee, whom a year before Rush had hinted to be a traitor, was court-martialed for disobeying Washington's orders at the Battle of Monmouth, Rush wrote John Adams: "General Conway who was the nerves, Mifflin who was the spirit, and Lee who was the soul of our army have all been banished from headquarters. The last has been most unjustly condemned by a court-martial for saving our army at the Battle of Monmouth on the 28 of June last. General Washington was his accuser." "Conway, Mifflin, and Lee," he told Dr. David Ramsay, "were sacrificed to the excessive influence of ONE MAN." More than a year after Rush's resignation, he hinted to Gates that, like Mifflin and Lee, he had been disgraced because of Washington's enmity, and warned that Gates himself would be next.

Although his descendants have tried to defend him from the accusation, Rush obviously regarded himself as a member of the cabal.

Discredited by his attacks on Washington, Rush got nowhere with his attempts to have Shippen court-martialed. When Morgan received his vindication a year later, he took over the role of prosecutor and soon succeeded where Rush had failed. In March 1780 Shippen was haled before a military court that presided during four months over one of the bitterest trials in history. Calumnious newspaper articles, charges and counter-charges, hysterical outbursts, and cries of treason followed each other so thickly that both the judges and the general public became disgusted. Since Morgan, Rush, and Shippen could not hide their hate for one another, the personal angle of their battle was all too plain. Shippen had not appeared when Morgan had summoned him to hear witnesses according to the act of Congress which allowed depositions to be taken if both accuser and accused were present; now he protested Morgan's evidence because he had not been there when it was procured. The court recessed while the enemies rode the old circuit together to ask the old questions once more. But two war-torn years had passed since the events on which Morgan's charges were based; many of the witnesses were dead or scattered, and those who remained had good reason to hide ancient scandals. The quarrels that had rocked the medical department since the very beginning of the war had so reduced confidence that Congress became less and less willing to vote money for doctors and supplies. Many surgeons, seeing the sick suffer from lack of appropriations, seeing the whole department being pulled down into general disgrace, were anxious to cover up all signs of inefficiency and graft even if it meant keeping an unworthy man in office. And the two years that had elapsed had given Shippen, who had remained in command the whole time, ample opportunity to recruit support with favors, to intimidate witnesses, and to send men he could not intimidate to distant posts. The wonder is that Morgan was able to collect any evidence at all.

Yet it was only by a majority of one vote that the court dismissed his charges for lack of proof, and the matter seemed so doubtful to Congress that it refused completely to uphold the verdict, substituting in its resolution for the phrase, "that said aquittal be confirmed," another: "that he be discharged from arrest." However, by some devious political maneuver, Shippen was re-elected director general of hospitals.

Rush thereupon published in the *Pennsylvania Packet* an open letter to his enemy. "Women," he screamed, "bedew the papers that contain the tales of your cruelties to the sick with their tears, and children who hear them read ask if you are made and look like other men. . . . Your reappointment to your present high and important office after the crimes you have committed is a new phenomenon in the history of mankind. It will serve like a high watermark to show posterity the degrees of corruption that marked the present stage of the American Revolution."

Perhaps because of a promise that was a condition of his re-election, perhaps because he could stand the criticism no longer, Shippen resigned a few months later. Morgan immediately published a broadside stating: "I am happy to inform my fellow-citizens that Dr. Shippen, at length unable to bear further investigation of his conduct, has been compelled to quit the station of director general of hospitals by a forced resignation." Washington, however, had never been convinced that the charges against Shippen were not part of the Conway Cabal; he gave the physician a certificate which blamed the troubles of the sick entirely upon the state of the nation.

Shippen returned home to an acute domestic crisis. His daughter Nancy was at eighteen the reigning belle of Philadelphia, surrounded with suitors. No one took seriously the clumsy attentions of Washington's favorite nephew Bushrod, but a keen rivalry existed between two outstanding men: the charming Louis-Guillaume Otto, a young and brilliant French diplomat, and the renowned soldier, Colonel Henry Beekman Livingston, heir to a vast New York fortune. A few weeks after his resignation, Shippen described the situation with cynical gayety to his son. "Nancy is much puzzled between Otto and Livingston. She loves the first and only esteems the last. On Monday she likes L—— and his fortune. On Tuesday evening when O—— comes, he is the angel. L—— will consummate immediately, O—— not these two years. L—— has solicited the father and mother; O—— is afraid of a denial. In short, we are all much puzzled. L—— has twelve or fifteen thousand hard. O—— has nothing now, but honorable expectations hereafter. A bird in the hand is worth two in the bush. They are both sensible, O—— handsome. What do you think of it?"

Nancy knew what she thought; she found Livingston a boor and loved Otto. When she engaged herself to the Frenchman, her mother was pleased, but her father flew into a fury; didn't Nancy realize that he had been impoverished by the war and that Livingston belonged to one of the richest families in the country? Shippen forbade Otto the house, and in less than a week after she had accepted the man she loved, dragged his terrified daughter down the aisle to an altar where the middle-aged rich man waited.

At her husband's home, Clermont, Nancy soon discovered he had many illegitimate children. Conscious that she had been forced to marry him against her will, he bullied her in eternal jealousy of Otto. The girl stood it for two years and then, taking her infant daughter with her, fled to her father's house. Shippen was not glad to see her, and when she sued for divorce, he took the husband's side; the Livingstons were an excellent connection. Discovering that she could win freedom only by giving her husband custody of the child, Nancy dropped her suit. She watched her adored Otto marry, lose his wife through death, and marry again. Finally the young man returned to France, where he became a famous diplomat and was named Count Mosby.

Nancy now lived only for her daughter, but Shippen was worried by the presence of the child; as long as she stayed in Philadelphia, she would be unlikely to inherit the Livingston fortune. He shipped the little girl back to her father. This culminating act of cruelty drove his wife into a nervous breakdown; retiring to the country, Mrs. Shippen collapsed into religious fanaticism. "Your beloved mother . . ." the doctor wrote his son, "begins to think it too great an indulgence for her to live with us any longer."

Nancy's high spirits shredded away; she also descended into deep religious melancholia. For days together she recognized no one. Her daughter, as soon as she was old enough, fled from the Livingstons to her side, but it was too late. The older woman merely infected the younger with her combination of torpor and religious mania. They lived together in an eternal twilight of silence, buried alive from the world. The daughter inherited the Livingston money but it made no difference; after her mother's demise, she became a rich, mad old spinster, living behind drawn blinds in a dusty, echoing house, growing older, more bent, more strange, until it seemed she had lived forever and that even death had forgotten to visit her. Not till 1864, when she was eighty-two, did this living relic of Shippen's greed find rest in the pitying dust.

When his wife and daughter sank into semi-madness, Shippen absorbed himself in ecstatic contemplation of his only son, whom he had always considered a paragon, like the younger Pitt suitable to be prime minister at twenty-four. But the young man developed tuberculosis; wasting away for six terrible years, he died. Then Shippen followed the rest of his family into pathological depression. He gave up his city house and retired to Germantown. His wife, who had somewhat re-covered, sat in one room mumbling and fingering the Bible; in another room sat the doctor, his handsome face now fallen in, staring motionless at a blank wall. For ten years he refused to lecture, to attend patients, to go to the convivial gatherings he had once loved.

At the age of seventy-two he contracted anthrax. It must have seemed fitting to him as he lay on his death bed that the hand that felt his pulse, the face that watched the anguished con-tortion of his limbs, were the hand and the face of Rush. Under the ministering eyes of his old enemy, Shippen died.

Rush promptly delivered an eloquent memorial oration. "The most ancient and most prominent pillar of our medical school is fallen, and the founder of anatomical instruction in the United States is no more. Hung be his theater in black! And let his numerous pupils in every part of our country unite with us in dropping the tribute of a grateful tear to his mem-ory." However, the entry in Rush's private diary was some-what different. "He had talents, but which from disuse became weak. He was too indolent to write, to read, and even to think, but with the stock of knowledge he acquired when young maintained some rank in his profession especially as a teacher of anatomy in which he was eloquent, luminous and pleasing. . . . His chief pleasures consisted in the enjoyments of the table."

3

RUSH had been unable to return to his practice when he was forced from the army, for the British still occupied Philadelphia, and in his father-in-law's house at Princeton he had nothing to do but write indignant letters. Since, like most active men, he could not bear idleness, his mind ran riot down descending slopes of depression. It gradually became clear to him that he must have misunderstood the answer to his prayers when he gave up law for medicine. Securing legal tomes from the library, he studied for the bar. However, the instant General Clinton evacuated Philadelphia, he hurried back. "From the filth left by the British army in all the streets," he reported, "the city became sickly and I was suddenly engaged in an extensive and profitable business." In the joy of purposeful activity, he forgot his discouragement.

He became ill himself with malignant bilious fever. "My physicians, Redman, Kuhn, and Morgan, shook their heads as they went out of my room. My friends could do little but weep at my bedside. I made my will and took leave of life." When he recovered, he played with the idea that his cure had been miraculous. A ragged crone, he tells us, appeared to him in a dream and begged him to attend her impoverished husband. At his reply that he was worn out attending the poor, she raised skinny arms to heaven. "Oh, sir!" she cried, "you don't know how much you owe to your *poor* patients. It was decreed that you should die by the fever which lately attacked you, but the prayers of your poor patients ascended to heaven in your behalf." This vision, he says, increased his interest in charity cases, and he was rewarded for his benevolence with a huge paying practice. His spacious three-story house in the middle of town was elegantly furnished and surrounded by a beautiful garden.

Rush soon quarreled with Dr. John Ewing, pastor of his church and provost of the University of Pennsylvania. He resigned from the church and organized a rival institution of learning near Harrisburg, Pennsylvania. All during his life, he kept Dickinson College alive; on his death, it closed for a time. It was eventually revived, and still exists today.

Believing that democracy cannot succeed without universal education, Rush wrote pamphlets urging that public schools be supported by taxes on all. Four colleges scattered through Pennsylvania should prepare their graduates for a university at Philadelphia. Rush's tendency to mix brilliant thinking with ill-considered idealism is exemplified by his desire to cap this structure of state education with a national university whose degrees in government would be a requisite for holding political office. How could Rush, who always sniffed the breeze for a trace of tyranny, recommend that every public official be forced to secure a diploma from an institution controlled by the party in power?

Rush's ideas concerning curriculum were amazingly modern. Supporting Franklin's opposition to Latin and Greek, he favored emphasis on modern languages and wanted grammar taught only by ear. He opposed all corporal punishment, and argued that practical manual pursuits like agriculture and carpentry should be mingled with more intellectual studies. Colleges should stress sciences and mathematics. On the other hand, he preferred denominational institutions. They prevented rather than caused intolerance, he insisted, "by removing young men from those opportunities for controversy which a variety of sects together are apt to cause and which are the certain fuel for bigotry." Convinced that religion was necessary to correct the effects of learning, he thought the University of Pennsylvania too secular.

Rush worked with untiring energy. "I obviated the usual effects of hot weather in producing an inability to read and thereby a waste of time by spending the hot months in writing for the press. The greater exertion necessary to compose than to read always obviated sleepiness." In his usual role of defender of the weak, he opposed continued discrimination against the Tories. He argued for the ratification of the Constitution with all his stupendous zeal, his letters to the newspapers over many *noms-de-plume* giving the impression he was a crowd of people. A prominent member of the Pennsylvania convention elected to consider federal union, he asserted that, since all vices and distresses were due to bad government, the Constitution would bring the millennium. The hand of God was as much employed in its provisions as in the division of the Red Sea to let the children of Israel pass. He wrote to his friends that once the instrument was ratified he would feel the nation was safe and he would follow "the first wish of my heart" by devoting the rest of his life "to the peaceable pursuits of science and the pleasures of social and domestic life."

However, Rush could not forget the drunkards; they must be reformed before he could retire. His *Inquiry into the Effects of Spirituous Liquors upon the Human Body* became one of the most influential temperance tracts of all time. His agents, descending on villages just before the harvest festival, in order to scare the poor farmers into drinking cider distributed thousands of copies of the physician's horrible descriptions of how the demon rum brought on dropsy, palsy, apoplexy, epilepsy, melancholy, and madness. Long after Rush was dead, the persuasively argued pages continued to strike such terror in the human heart that in 1885 the National Woman's Christian Temperance Union sent grateful delegates from forty States to his grave where they planted an oak tree "in token of their reverence for the memory of Dr. Benjamin Rush, instaurator of the American temperance reform one hundred years ago." In a prophetic moment Rush foresaw that by 1915 a drunkard would be "as infamous in society as a liar or a thief." But he did not foresee the repeal of the prohibition amendment.

Tobacco too was attacked by the crusading physician. Not only did it cause tuberculosis and madness, but the amount of time and money a man would save by shunning the noxious weed would "endow a charity school or nearly build a church." If only men who take snuff could be made to realize that, by opening the box and carrying the powder to their noses, they each wasted five whole days a year!

Rush helped organize the first free dispensary in America, but opposed a projected maternity hospital as contrary to "female delicacy." Usually, however, he was glad to flee medical issues for moral and political ones. Imbued by the Revolution with a tendency to test all authority, he had even questioned the infallibility of that idol of his youth, Dr. William Cullen. Once he considered the subject, he could not help noticing that

Cullen's remedies did not work as well as they should. He began to doubt, and doubt was the one thing most distasteful to his positive mind.

While Rush was still plagued with hesitation, Philadelphia was ravaged by one of the worst epidemics America has ever known. It was a rich city of 40,000 inhabitants whose red brick houses, two or two and a half stories high, stretched loosely between the two rivers. Dwellers on the Delaware looked across to the thick forests of New Jersey and watched the stately procession of sailing ships. The narrow streets and narrower alleys that led to where the fields began were rarely paved; in dry weather they were cloudy with dust and in wet sticky with mire. There was no sewage system and no water supply; housewives gossiped over street-corner pumps. Hogs rooted and chickens scratched everywhere, and dead animals were allowed to lie where they fell until the hogs and flies had eaten them.

Philadelphia was a jubilant city, alive with a post-war boom. Since there were too few houses to go round, rents mounted dizzily. Old Quakers foresaw the Lord's vengeance as their sons walked the streets brave in lace and ruffles, shoe-buckles agleam like twin moons. All day long clipper ships slipped into the harbor, and the waterfront rang with the chants of Negro stevedores. Heavy wagons, rolling down the narrow streets with merchandise for the back country, became entangled with a press of private coaches, coachees, and chairs; everyone was spending money because everyone knew the boom would go on forever. Evening brought no quiet, for the young ladies sat on their doorsteps in the dusk made by Benjamin Franklin's street-lamps and their laughter mingled with male voices until late in the night. Then the men hurried to taverns whose windows still gleamed palely in the dawn. As the dandies lurched home, disturbing sober folks with their shouting, farmers already whipped loaded carts down the street, anxious to change their produce for city luxuries. During twenty-four hours each day, riches showered on the greatest city of America.

No one noticed or cared when in an alley on the waterfront a poor varlet came down with a violent fever, turned a suspicious yellow, and died in a stupor. One by one the people sickened to the sound of prolonged revelry. On August 19, as Benjamin Rush left the death bed of Mrs. Peter LeMaigre, he was struck motionless in the street by realization. His announcement that yellow fever was abroad met with stubborn unbelief. Then suddenly the whole city seemed to be dying; hardly a street or alley lacked its corpse.

Revelry stopped over night, while the citizens pursued every wild expedient that promised escape from contagion. Since Rush and his colleagues blamed the disease on "noxious miasma," an evil air caused by rotting matter, stagnant swamps or the breath of infected patients, public-minded citizens lighted fires on every street corner to burn the miasma away. A committee of doctors headed by Rush announced that fires were dangerous and probably ineffectual. When they suggested burning gunpowder instead, the citizens got their muskets down from the wall and spent the evening firing at the miasma out of the window. So many people were wounded, that the mayor had to forbid this also.

People stayed in their houses behind locked doors. As tobacco smoke was supposed to counter-act miasma, women and children smoked cigars all day long. Many, putting their faith in garlic, chewed it continually or kept it in their shoes. Adults spent their entire time whitewashing their rooms, starting over again the instant they had finished, while their children followed them around, sprinkling vinegar, lighting gunpowder. No one had time to slap the mosquitoes that buzzed gayly through the smell of vinegar and powder, for no one knew that mosquitoes were the actual carriers of yellow fever.

When the richer citizens tried to flee, the neighboring cities passed laws barring all Philadelphians. Baltimore blocked the Philadelphia road with a militia company. Discovering that refugees landed at midnight in hidden coves from rowboats with muffled oars, the New York Council ordered that a watch of not less than ten men should patrol every ward after dark. If a Philadelphian on a stage coach showed the least sign of illness, the horses were reined in and he was made to alight wherever he might be. Since few farmhouses would admit such dangerous guests, some who were not even sick died of exposure in the woods; their corpses, which no one dared approach, rotted where they fell. At Milford, Delaware, a wagon of goods from Philadelphia was burned, and the woman who came with it tarred and feathered. Yet the refugees were made so agile by fear that a third of the population managed to find lodgings elsewhere.

In the terrorized city husbands abandoned sick wives, mothers their children. Ailing rich men, their wills forgotten, were deserted by their heirs, and could procure no attendants at the end of their luxurious lives except dissolute Negro laborers who drank up the wine in their cellars; Negroes were supposed to be immune. Many persons died alone in empty houses, their screams going on and on through the silent night while hundreds of anguished listeners stopped their ears. Sometimes a sufferer would use his last strength to stagger out into the deserted street, and pound unavailingly at the bolted doors of his neighbors. The next morning his corpse would be found lying face downward in the gutter.

In the midst of this panic, Rush attended innumerable patients every day. His gig and the many hearses alone kept the sound of wheels alive in the streets. The few frightened men who scurried past him kept handkerchiefs impregnated with vinegar to their noses, carried pieces of tarred rope, or hung bags of camphor round their necks. Walking in the middle of the street, they were furious if Rush's chair forced them to the curb, so afraid were they of contagion from the houses where people died. If he met a friend, Rush knew enough not to try to shake hands; many were affronted by the offer of a hand, while a doctor or a man wearing any appearance of mourning was shunned like a viper. Many persons prided themselves on their skill and address in getting to the windward of Rush as he hurried by. When the distant creaking announced the approach of a hearse, the few walkers fled lest a breeze blow over them from the cadaver. Driving on through complete emptiness, Rush would meet the body of one of Philadelphia's leading citizens lying in a clumsy coffin across the shafts of a chaise. There were no mourners, no sounds of weeping, only a solitary Negro whipping his horse so that he might quickly deposit his dangerous burden in the common pit; no one bothered to dig individual graves.

Stopping before the house of a patient, Rush poured vinegar on his handkerchief and pressed it against his nose as he walked up the unswept stairs to the room of death. Many were the horrible scenes of neglect and desertion he saw daily, but perhaps it was even worse when the sick man's relations had not fled. During the first weeks they begged him with hysterical tears—and later without tears, for the city was past weeping —to save a wife, a father, the surviving son of many sons who already stiffened in death. And Rush, although he made his rounds religiously, realized that he could not help. Certainty had deserted him when he needed it most; hesitating in his own mind, he noticed with agony that whatever he prescribed, the sufferers died.

Rush tried everything he could think of. First he gave gentle purges which were his closest approach to modern treatment; then he prescribed various barks, and applied blisters to the limbs, neck, and head. When this failed, he wrapped the body in blankets saturated with warm vinegar, and tried to stimulate the liver by rubbing mercurial ointment on the patient's flanks. Hearing that a West Indian physician who had often seen the disease was in town, he hurried to his lodgings to beg advice and returned jubilant with a new remedy. The next morning he ordered that buckets of cold water be poured over his patients. To his horror, three out of four who submitted to this remedy died.

Sitting in his study one midnight too tired to sleep, Rush took his head in his hands; he was entirely defeated. The creaking of hearses that rolled by in the street chimed in with his sepulchral mood, but the silence after they had passed was terrible; silence was inaction and defeat. He took up his pen to write his wife who was away in the country; there seemed nothing to say. He could not calm himself by composing helpful articles for the press, since he knew no advice to offer. Having his patients die by the hundreds while he could do nothing to aid them seemed the end of everything.

Suddenly, Rush tells us, he remembered that among his papers was the account of a yellow fever epidemic in Virginia which had been submitted to the American Philosophical Society some fifty years before by a local practitioner, Dr. John Mitchell. Perhaps he might find some wisdom there. Eagerly he rummaged through his closets. When the dog-eared sheets were before him at last, he found that Dr. Mitchell indeed had a new remedy to suggest. Physicians, the paper stated, should not be fooled by seeming weakness in a patient since yellow fever was caused by over-excitement of the body. Even if the pulse was so thin you could hardly find it, you should none the less prescribe the most violent purges.

In the silence of his room, these words struck Rush with the force of divine revelation; he understood everything now. Under all circumstances depletion was necessary. Away then with cowardice; he would purge and bleed to an extent never dared in Philadelphia before! Remembering that the strongest purges given in the army had been ten grains of calomel and ten grains of jalap, he added five more grains of jalap to this dose, and decided to give it three times a day. He would draw blood in proportion.

It was a different practitioner who emerged the next morning into the fever-ridden stillness of the streets; his patients were encouraged to see that his self-confident manner had returned. Somehow he managed to convince himself that his new remedy was an infallible cure. Soon he was stopping rival practitioners on the street to tell them about it. With a sense of renewed life, he sent an account to the College of Physicians, and began to campaign for his method in the press. When other doctors opposed it, he published a notice in the papers advising sufferers he could not treat to bleed and purge themselves, since his remedy, if used in the early stages of the disease, made yellow fever no more dangerous than measles or influenza. Anxious that the poor should not be deprived of so marvelous a discovery, he gave printed directions for depleting the system to two Negroes, Richard Allan and Absalom Jones, thus, he later asserted, saving two hundred additional lives. And yet his new method was the most fallacious of all that he had tried.

Under any circumstances Rush would have been frightfully busy—he soon was one of the three physicians well enough to leave his house while upwards of six thousand people were ill— but when he announced that he knew an infallible remedy, it seemed that the entire population swarmed to his door. Now that he was sure he could help, he found no labor too arduous or heroic. He visited more than half the homes in the city, attending one hundred and twenty-five patients a day while his pupils saw many more. Even during the brief intervals he allowed himself for meals, he prescribed to the poor who gathered round his table. "From my great intercourse with the sick," he wrote, "my body became highly impregnated with the contagion. My eyes were yellow and sometimes the yellowness was perceptible in my face. My pulse was preternaturally quick, and I had profuse sweats every night. These sweats were so offensive as to oblige me to draw the bedclothes close to my neck." Soon he was bleeding himself as well as his patients, and several times he fainted in sickrooms. However, he continued hurrying from house to house during twelve or fourteen hours a day. He discarded his vinegar-soaked handkerchief because he believed he already had the contagion and that his own home was as infected as any in the city; his assistants, when they treated the poor in his yard, could not find bowls enough to hold the vast amount of blood they drew. The blood putrefied on the ground. "Thus charged with the fuel of death, I was frequently disposed to say with Job, and almost without a figure, to 'corruption, thou are my father; to the worm, thou art my mother and my sister.' "

Three of his five apprentices died of the disease and the other two sickened. "At two o'clock my sister, who had complained for several days, yielded to the disorder and retired to bed. My mother followed her, much indisposed, early in the evening. My black servant man had been confined with the fever for several days, and had on that day for the first time quitted his bed. My little mulatto boy of eleven years old was the only person in my family who was able to afford me the least assistance. At eight o'clock in the evening, I finished the business of the day. A solemn stillness at that time pervaded the streets. In vain did I strive to forget my melancholy situation by answering letters and by putting up medicines to be distributed next day among my patients. My faithful black man crept to the door and at my request sat down by the fire, but he added by his silence and dullness to the gloom which suddenly overpowered every faculty of my mind.

"On the first day of October, at two o'clock in the afternoon, my sister died. I got into my carriage within an hour after she expired, and spent the afternoon visiting patients. According as a sense of duty or of grief has predominated in my mind, I have approved or disapproved of this act ever since. . . . From this time I declined in health and strength. All motion became painful to me. My appetite began to fail. My night sweats continued. My short and imperfect sleep was disturbed by distressing or frightful dreams. The scenes of them were derived altogether from sickrooms and graveyards. I concealed my sorrows as much as possible from my patients, but when alone, the retrospect of what was past, and the prospect of what was before me, the termination of which was invisible, often filled my soul with the most poignant anguish. I wept frequently when retired from the public eye, but I did not weep over the lost members of my family alone. . . . I saw the great and expanded mind of Dr. Pennington shattered by delirium just before he died. He was to me dear and beloved like a younger brother. . . . It was my affliction to see my friend Dr. John Morris breathe his last, and to hear the first effusions of the most pathetic grief from his mother, as she burst from the room in which he died. . . .

"The perception of the lapse of time was new to me. It was uncommonly slow. The ordinary business and pursuits of men appeared to me in a light that was equally new. The hearse and the grave mingled themselves with every view I took of human affairs. . . . I recollect further being struck with surprise about the first of October in seeing a man busily engaged in laying in wood for the approaching winter. I should as soon have thought of making provision for a dinner on the first day of the year 1800."

On October 9, Rush became so violently ill that he could not rise from his bed. The epidemic was then at its height, but in a few weeks a cold snap killed off the deadly mosquitoes, and suddenly the city was healthy again. Four thousand and forty-four had died, ten percent of the population but a much higher proportion of those who had remained in the city. Rush believed that, had he not discovered his method of bleeding and purging, another six thousand would have succumbed.

Like a true eighteenth-century theorist, Rush explained his new therapy logically, and believed his explanation would place him with the great scientists of all time. His ideas were a development of Cullen's speculations about "nerve force" and very similar to a theory devised by John Brown, one of Cullen's English pupils, from a misunderstanding of nervous irritability which Haller had just demonstrated. Brown asserted that all diseases were due to one of two causes: excess or lack of nervous stimulation. Combining these two causes into one, Rush insisted that every fever was due to excess excitability in the blood vessels brought on by a previous state of debility which had made the body liable to infection. The different symptoms which seemed to separate yellow fever from smallpox were superficial variations of little importance; all fevers were one and the same. They could all be cured by reducing the excessive action of the blood vessels through purges and salivation which weaken the body, but most effectively through bleeding. Once you had vanquished the excess excitement, you had won back to the previous debility, which it was now safe to counter-act with cordials and stimulating remedies.

Rush's theory encouraged him to carry purging and blood-letting, which were regarded as remedies by many of his contemporaries, further than any other influential doctor in modern history. "Bleeding," he instructed his disciples, "should be repeated while the symptoms which first indicated it continue, should it be until four-fifths of the blood contained in the body be drawn away." Although he fortunately underestimated the amount of blood contained in the body, he was known to draw more than nine pints of blood from one patient, about ten times as much as it is considered safe today for a blood donor to give.

Great doctors from Hippocrates to the most recent discoverer have realized that they can be most useful as a second line of defense, stepping in guardedly to help the body fight disease in its own way. Rush despised such cowards. "It is impossible," he wrote, "to calculate the mischief which Hippocrates has done by first marking Nature with his name and afterwards letting her loose on sick people." His system, he boasted, rejects "undue reliance upon the powers of Nature, and teaches instantly to wrest the cure of all violent and febrile diseases out of her hands."

Rush had been active in a revolution which he believed had brought Utopia within the reach of men. Having defeated the power of kings, like some mighty general he was going on to a greater conquest; he was defeating Nature herself. It was an expansive age, that period after the Revolution, when anything seemed possible to Americans; Rush wrote that there was twenty times more intellect and a hundred times more knowledge in the nation after the revolt than before. Why then should he merely serve as an ally while the body tried clumsily to fight disease? It was much more gallant to charge in with his lancet, and rout infection in a stream of blood.

The patriots slashed boldly through European red tape. Having reduced Cullen's hierarchy of fevers to one fever, Rush declared that he had cut materia medica to fifteen or twenty drugs, and made medicine "a science so simple that two years' study instead of four or more were sufficient." Although, of course, this was mistaken, the simplicity of his method brought one praiseworthy result. Unable to prescribe according to the names of diseases, his disciples were forced to vary their treatment by studying the conditions of the body. Rush, himself, could be an excellent observer; in his early days, he had written accounts that are considered classics of cholera infantum, dengue, and the thermal fever caused by drinking cold water when overheated.

However, Rush's observations often went amazingly awry. Although his therapy could have done little but harm, he firmly believed that he rarely failed to cure a case of yellow fever which was brought to him in its early stages. We may well wonder by what method he arrived at this conclusion. Looking down from the vantage point of years, the historian is often at a loss to explain why men were certain of beliefs which daily experience should have proved wrong. How could savages through numberless centuries have been sure that if you drove a stake through the footprint of a deer the animal would go lame? Can we explain the credence given to magic or to bleeding? Perhaps not, but sometimes we can hint at an explanation.

Under the stress of epidemic, Rush kept no statistics of his patients and did not even write down their names. The dead ones lay dumbly underground while the living came back to thank him. Innumerable well men must have been driven by terror to imagine they had the disease; bleeding could cure such. Postulating the unity of fevers, Rush believed that, while the cause of yellow fever was abroad, most people who showed any symptoms of illness had that disease; when sufferers from minor ailments recovered, he thought it a vindication of his methods. Indeed, it is possible that whenever he saw a real case of yellow fever he felt he had been called in too late.

To Dr. Adam Kuhn's assertion that the chief symptom of the disease was yellowness, Rush replied in a widely published letter that his therapy kept the skin from becoming yellow. "The yellowness of the skin occurs with few exceptions in such patients only as have been neglected in the beginning of the disorder, or who have recovered in spite of Dr. Kuhn's remedies. Dr. Kuhn will do a great kindness to the public by keeping his opinions to himself in this distressing juncture." The fact that so many members of his own household died did not shake Rush's conviction, for he believed that they had lived in a center of contagion.

Rush insisted that his colleagues instantly discard Cullen's theory, which he himself had made fashionable, to follow his own, and when they hesitated he attacked them with all the vehemence he had formerly reserved for those who refused to follow Cullen. Many physicians felt that his purging and bleeding did more harm than good; while the epidemic still raged, he fought a spirited encounter with them in the press. Unable to believe that their opposition could be on scientific grounds, he wrote: "The envy and hatred of my brethren has lately risen to a rage. They blush at their mistakes, they feel for their murders, and instead of asking forgiveness of the public for them, vent all their guilty shame and madness upon the man who convicted them of both."

Philadelphia was so infected that yellow fever came back yearly, though in a milder form. Rush blamed it on a "noxious miasma" generated by marshes and foul gutters that surrounded the city. Although he was ignorant of the part played by mosquitoes, the draining he recommended would have effectively outlawed the disease. Financial-minded doctors and real-estate operators, however, denounced him as a fool; afraid that the federal government would flee to a healthier place and end Philadelphia's leadership among American cities, they insisted the disease could not have originated at home; it was imported by boats from the West Indies. In 1794, many physicians asserted that cases of yellow fever were not yellow fever at all—perish so subversive a thought!—and when Rush announced their true nature he was regarded as a traitor. A group of chauvinistic citizens conspired to drive him from the city.

1797 brought another epidemic almost as severe as the one of 1793. Although the rich citizens again fled town, the panic was much less crippling; men can become acclimated even to death. Again Rush shed streams of blood and insisted that he could cure ninety-nine percent of the patients who came to him soon enough. A new factor, however, had entered the scene in the form of William Cobbett, a young Englishman who was later to become a member of Parliament and one of the most famous radical journalists of his time. He is a spiritual father of the "agrarian movement" preached today by some

American intellectuals, and his writings are still taught in colleges as examples of killing invective. Driven from home because of his attacks on corruption in the army, he had settled in Philadelphia, where in his disdain for the Colonials who had fought his beloved England he published a royalist newspaper called *Porcupine's Gazette*. He hated Rush because of his republicanism, and when yellow fever again appeared, he seized on bleeding as an issue with which to belabor his opponent.

> "The times are ominous indeed,
>   When quack to quack cries, 'Purge and bleed! . . .'

Blood, blood, still they cry, more blood!" he wrote. "In every sentence they menace our poor veins. Their language is as frightful to the ears of the alarmed multitude as the raven's croak to those of the sickly flock."

Cobbett made no secret of his intentions in regard to Rush: "He has long, very long, been sedulously employed in scuffling up his little hillock of fame. I will down with him just as the peasant with his foot undoes the labors of the pismire." Every morning Cobbett aimed new blows at the poor doctor. He insisted that Rush was up to the propagandist tricks "he learned from that crafty old hypocrite Franklin" of flooding the newspapers by prearrangement with letters praising his system, most of which appeared through "the channel, or rather the sink, of the quack-ridden *Philadelphia Gazette*." Rush's object was to make all other physicians seem "mere clyster-pipe Dicks under him." When Rush excused the death of one of his patients by saying the convalescent went riding too soon, Cobbett commented: "The Frenchman taught his horse to live without food, but just as his education was finished the poor thing died. So it is with the patients of the bleeders; by degrees they accustom themselves to live without blood, but the moment the process is completed they expire."

Rush tried to escape such abuse by fleeing to Princeton. "The unfortunate doctor who has so long been the object of public attention," Cobbett announced, "has lately had a return of those unhappy fits of insanity to which he has been liable ever since the memorable year 1793, and has been removed by advice of his friends to a purer air."

Rush felt that because of his zeal to aid mankind he was being made a by-word for cursing. Although he had his faction and his practice still was considerable, no new patients came to him. Perhaps he would be appreciated somewhere else than in Philadelphia. He wrote to New York, asking for an appointment to the medical faculty of Columbia. The professors were delighted to secure so famous a physician, but Alexander Hamilton blocked his appointment because he thought Rush's political beliefs too radical. For the third time, Rush decided to give up medicine. He resolved to become a farmer. However, before he picked up the plow, he must smash down his enemy; he sued Cobbett for libel. In the meantime, his old friend, President Adams, came to the rescue of his depleted income by making him treasurer of the mint.

The libel action did not come to trial until 1800. Rush's lawyer, Joseph Hopkinson, was John Morgan's nephew and the author of "Hail, Columbia!" Facing the jury, he intoned: "The injured father of an amiable family, the worthy citizen, the useful philosopher now sues before you. Professional science implores that countenance and protection without which she must wither and die. Virtue, bleeding at every pore, calls for justice on her despoiler, and the anxious heart of every honest man pants with impatience to meet in you the defenders of virtue and the scourgers of vice." The jury fined Cobbett $5000 and $3000 costs.

Fleeing the city, Cobbett allowed his printing plant to go under the hammer; Rush gave the money to charity. From New York, the Englishman continued his attacks in a new publication, *The Rushlight*, insisting that at the very moment he was convicted one of Rush's disciples had bled Washington to death. Concerning the sale of his effects, he wrote: "The sovereign citizens took printer's ink and drew the picture of the devil on the door of the house; they even bit the presses with their teeth by way of revenge for what the poor innocent things had done. Methinks I hear the reader say: 'It was well you were not there, Peter.' Not at all. I know the sovereign people of Philadelphia; I have wintered them and summered them as the man said by his hogs, and I know them to be at once the most malicious and the most cowardly race in existence."

Thus Cobbett fulminated for a few months, but it was hopeless; the suit had ruined him in America. On June first he sailed back to England and fame, leaving Rush in possession of Philadelphia.

4

THE remaining thirteen years of Rush's life were a gradual apotheosis. For the second time he remade the practice of the United States; little by little his colleagues discarded Cullen's system to follow his. Cobbett's hysterical attacks had helped him in the end, for they reduced what should have remained a medical dispute to terms of personal abuse and Federalist politics. After Jefferson's election in 1800, it was almost a patriotic duty to believe in the discoveries of a good Republican like Rush. Indeed, patriotism had much to do with the success of his system. The triumphant soldiers of the Revolution knew that the answers to all problems must grow up within their own shores, and who could be a better scientist than a signer of the Declaration of Independence? They were impressed with Rush's insistence that American practice must be different from the European, that American patients, being more virile, needed stronger purges and more heroic bleeding than effete foreigners.

Actually, Rush was not a progressive scientist for his time; in his whole life he never did an effective experiment. Evolving theoretical remedies by logic, he was typical of his age, it is true, but not of the best in his age. Scattered through the world there were a few men who had seen the vision of modern science, who realized that you can build a house only by putting one small brick on another, and who were content to spend their lives discovering seemingly unrelated facts about the body. Such careful technique was too slow for Rush, who solved all problems by an act of will.

It was the tragedy of medicine deep into the nineteenth century that too few facts were scientifically established to give a basis for practice. Intelligent treatment had to wait until much more was found out, but the patients could not wait; men sickened and cried for physicians to cure them. They wanted doctors who were sure of themselves, and the doctors needed for their own happiness to believe that their prescriptions helped. Thus self-confidence was a prime requisite for a great practitioner; woe to the man who used his eyes and saw that most of his remedies failed. A Svengali who could hypnotize himself, his patients, and above all his colleagues into believing he was right was certain to be regarded as a great scientist. Rush was such a man.

Standing on the lecture platform of the greatest medical school in the United States, he dominated his pupils with the personal magnetism of an orator. Never for a moment was there an intonation of doubt behind the words that found their way to his pupils' hearts. When he wished to emphasize a point, he rose from his chair with inexpressible dignity, elevating his hand as he rose and throwing back the glasses that covered the wise brilliance of his blue eyes. "I was enrapt," Dr. Charles D. Meigs wrote. "His voice, sweeter than any flute, fell on my ears like droppings from a sanctuary, and the spectacle of his beautiful, radiant countenance, with his earnest, most sincere, most persuasive accents, sunk so deep into my heart that neither time nor change could eradicate them."

The elegance of Rush's diction would have been less effective coming from a flashy man, but everything in his bearing bespoke simplicity. Years before he had discarded his wig, and long strings of gray hair softened his sharp features. He was not handsome, for the cheeks of his thin face had fallen in and many of his front teeth were gone, but his domed forehead, his hooked nose, his benign wrinkles, gave him the look of a savant grown old in the service of science. His clothes were neat and plain, generally of drab-colored cloth. Prophets do not smile or laugh; neither did Rush. He walked through the medical school with an erect, military step, and pupils were delirious with joy when, meeting them in the halls, he relaxed long enough to say firmly: "I hope you are well, sir."

Rush's obvious piety impressed his pupils. Whatever moderns may think of the way he used religious arguments to support scientific statements, it delighted his contemporaries. "From the affinity established by the Creator between evil and its antidotes in other parts of His works," Rush said, "I am disposed to believe no remedy will ever be effectual in any general disease that is not cheap and that cannot easily be made universal." Actually, Rush's religious career was stormy, for he could not subscribe to any authority not his own. He shuttled back and forth four times between the Episcopal, Presbyterian, and Unitarian faiths. However, he attended worship more frequently perhaps than any other doctor in Philadelphia, keeping pews in several churches at one time, so that he might visit the nearest during his rounds. As he told his pupils, it helped a doctor's practice to be often seen at prayer.

By far the biggest medical school in the country, the University of Pennsylvania graduated almost as many men as all the other schools put together. At one time more than half the members of the South Carolina Medical Society had been Rush's pupils; between 1779 and 1812 he lectured to 2872 prospective doctors. Many became professors themselves and taught his theories to young men in far corners of the land. Physicians everywhere wrote Rush for advice whenever faced with difficult cases and laymen wrote him too; he prescribed bleeding and purging by return mail.

His publications on innumerable subjects further enhanced his influence. An early advocate of prison reform, he opposed the death penalty and argued that felons should be kept employed at useful tasks. Public punishments were outrageous, he insisted, since the emphasis should be on rehabilitation not revenge. He wrote about slavery, drink, tobacco, the abolition of oaths, the customs of the Pennsylvania Dutch and the Indians, education, distinguished citizens, the diseases of old age and of Negroes, sugar culture, charity, the Bible, journalism, mineral waters, philosophy, paper money, chemistry, zoology, and a thousand medical subjects.

In order to turn out this vast mass of material, he recorded in notebooks every idea and observation that occurred to him. Temperamentally keyed to continual activity, he never gave himself leisure for quiet thought, but he did not feel the lack as the notations in his journals multiplied. Whenever he had enough entries on any particular subject, he compiled them helter-skelter into a pamphlet, without pausing to reconsider the judgments he had hastily written down. The result was a curious mingling of truth and error, brilliance and absurdity. A partisan commentator on his works could select extracts that would show him one of the most brilliant men of his time or one of the most foolish. Rush was among the first to observe focal infections, the relation of decayed teeth to chronic diseases; on the other hand, he argued that Negroes were black because they had a kind of leprosy, and insisted that he could cure hydrophobia with mercury and bloodletting!

The same self-confidence that made Rush the most influential physician of his day kept him from using his undoubted powers to their best advantage. Had he been willing to question his inspirations, to separate the wheat in his mind from the chaff, he might have contributed greatly to the advance of science. It is intriguing to speculate whether his career would have been different had Sarah Eve lived to marry him. Could he have suppressed her mocking intelligence into the proper attitude of worship for the head of the house and a great man, or would the barbs she always leveled at pomposity have passed through his armor in the end and taught him self-criticism?

Be that as it may, he was idolized by the doctors of his own period, who called him the Fothergill, the Sydenham, the Hippocrates, of American medicine. A great medical college in Chicago was named after him. So deeply did he root in the minds of American doctors his theory of the unity of fevers and their cure by depletion, that long after his death it was the dominant American practice; truly, he shed more blood than any general in history. Indirectly he was the father of homeopathy, that reaction to overdrugging which in time undermined his dangerous therapy by showing that patients recover more quickly if reliance is put on the healing power of nature. However, Rush's influence persisted in the back country almost into the twentieth century; Sir William Osler gave it the *coup de grâce*.

Rush himself was conscious of his present fame and anxious to preserve it for the future. The autobiography he wrote in 1800 is so self-righteous, that we are led to wonder whether it is sincere. Certainly his omission of Sarah Eve is suspicious, but we must remember that Rush was the least introspective of men; perhaps he believed he was the Puritan saint he described. All his writings about himself reveal a startling disingenuousness. He boasts, for instance, that during his six years as an apprentice he spent only three evenings away from his preceptor's shop, but in the next breath he follows the conventional pattern for saints by saying that during this period he was so wicked that he had to be saved by an emotional conversion. He complains that his virtuous crusades ruined his practice, and tells us how nobly he bore this martyrdom, but he cannot resist adding that during his twenty-one years in

Philadelphia he did more business than any other doctor. A thousand times we see him detail his grievances against his enemies with great bitterness, but only, he assures us, that he may say he heartily forgives them.

Rush's defense against the accusation that he was egotistic in believing he could cure all diseases is sophistical, to say the least; he points out that God often chooses the most imperfect instruments to carry out His will. Almost against his desire, God appointed him to drive the scourge of sickness from the world. "It is not to him that willeth or to him that runneth, but to the over-ruling hand of Heaven that we are to look for the successful issue of events."

Rush realized that his anonymous attack on Washington was a blot on his career. When he learnt that his letter to Patrick Henry, together with the general's reply, was to be included in John Marshall's *Life of Washington*, he inundated Bushrod Washington with requests that both letters be expunged. "In suppressing the letter or passages alluded to, you will prevent a great deal of pain to a large family of children," he wrote, insisting he would be forced to justify his actions by mentioning some "military anecdotes" to Washington's discredit. "It has been my constant wish and intention that those anecdotes should descend to the grave with me." When young Washington asked angrily if that was a threat, Rush backed water. "You have misapprehended me in supposing I intend to publicly defend myself against the charges contained in General Washington's letter to Governor Henry. Far, far from it. I had determined to submit to them in silence. To my family and friends only I had intended to justify myself." Although he was engaged in lecturing and publishing on innumerable subjects, Rush added: "To a man disgusted as I have long been with public pursuits and anxious for retirement, and wishing to pass the small remnant of my days unnoticed by the world, the favor will be remembered with the most grateful emotions." Marshall insisted on retaining Rush's letter to Henry, but deleted from Washington's reply the words: "This man has been elaborate and studied in his professions of regard for me, and long since his letter to you."

Rush's conscience continued to torment him. In 1812 he wrote John Adams, defending his attacks on Washington by citing a long list of other revolutionary figures who had also slandered the commander-in-chief. He himself, Rush pointed out, had supported Washington for president because he believed the councils of Steuben, Greene, and Hamilton had qualified him for the station. "I thank God that my destiny in the world of spirits to which I am hastening is not to be determined by slaveholders, old Tories, Latin and Greek schoolmasters, judges who defend capital punishment, Philadelphia physicians, persecuting clergymen, nor yet General Washington, all of whom I have offended only by attempting to lessen the misery and ignorance of my fellow-men." Nobly he wrote: "I do not even wish to make it known that General Washington was deficient in that mark of true greatness that characterized Cæsar, Henry the Eighth, and Frederick the Second, the ability to forgive."

Anxious to bury the record of his revolutionary heresy, Rush destroyed the hundred pages of his notebook which dealt with the men and events of the war. He did this, he insisted, out of patriotism; he did not want the Americans of the future to know that the founding fathers he attacked had not been altogether perfect.

Rush's private life was, like his public, a combination of benevolence and self-will. He loved his children in order to improve them, and in return for this love demanded unhesitating obedience. When he failed to receive letters, he wrote: "The distress I have felt in being thus disappointed, neglected, and ungratefully treated by two children upon whom I have lavished acts of parental kindness has been to me very great. It has prevented my sleeping and impaired my health. Lord, lay not this conduct to their charge!" His son, Richard Rush, was later to become one of the most important political figures of his day, but Benjamin used every emotional appeal to keep the young man from accepting his first federal appointment because it would remove him from Philadelphia. "Oh, my son, my son Richard, may you never be made to feel in the unkindness of a son the misery you have inflicted on me!"

A year before his death, Rush published what was probably his most important scientific contribution, one of the first systematic works on the diseases of the mind written in the western world. Since his early days, he had crusaded for more humane treatment of the insane, who were still believed by many to be suffering from their own sins or obsessed by the devil. As a result of his campaigning, decent quarters had been built for them in the Pennsylvania Hospital. In his book and in pamphlets, he made the brilliant suggestion that madmen be treated by occupational therapy. Not only did he want the hospital to supply workshops and spinning wheels, but also intelligent companions for the insane "to direct and share in their amusements and to divert their minds by conversation, reading, and obliging them to read and write about subjects suggested from time to time by their physicians." When he urged that patients be encouraged to talk out their troubles, he foreshadowed the technique of modern psychoanalysis.

He believed, of course, that much madness was caused by overstimulation of the blood vessels of the brain, and could be cured by his universal technique, bleeding, purging, and salivation, but even this was a step forward; he had realized that conditions of the body often caused disorders of the mind. Although he recommended a particularly cruel kind of straitjacket called a "tranquilizer," in which a heavy hinged block was clamped over the head of a patient tied to a chair, his book, which remained standard in American medical schools for over half a century, was a major influence towards a saner treatment of the insane.

On April 14, 1813, Rush complained of chilliness and took to his bed. Fever accompanied with heavy pain in his limbs and side kept him tossing all night; anxiously he awaited the dawn so he might send out for a bleeder. After ten ounces of blood were taken from his arm, he felt better. As soon as his symptoms returned, he wanted to be bled again. His physician, Dr. John Syng Dorsey, thought him too weak and, when the great doctor insisted, called in the most venerable of his disciples, Dr. Philip Syng Physick, who agreed that another bleeding would be dangerous. Rush, however, pleaded so insistently that they were forced to let him lose three ounces from his side by cupping. He maintained that he felt much relieved, but in less than two days he was dead.

Though it was thought even by admirers as enthusiastic as Dr. John Coakely Lettsom that Rush had hastened his end through bleeding when stimulation was required, it would be rash to judge now what was the true cause of his death. His doctors disagreed concerning the nature of his illness, and Rush was an old man. In any case, his demanding for himself when he was desperately ill the treatment he gave his patients was a final proof that America's most influential physician believed in his own methods with complete sincerity.

A Backwoods Galahad

Ephraim McDowell

Ephraim McDowell

FROM A CONTEMPORARY PORTRAIT

A Backwoods Galahad

Ephraim McDowell

1

AT the sound of hoofs the door flew open, disgorging a flood of people. A huddled crowd in a forest clearing, they stared over the hill. Behind them a cabin smoked, its black walls varied by white stripes where the logs were chinked with lime. The crowd waited silently while the hoofbeats grew louder on the frozen earth, and then a rider appeared over the crest of the slope. He was so tall that his legs almost touched the ground. As he approached, the knot of people moved forward to meet him, and a dozen hands reached out to hold his mount.

"You're Dr. McDowell?"

The newcomer nodded. In the gap between his coonskin cap and his fur collar nothing was visible but tiny, brilliant eyes and a huge nose blue with cold. After he had dismounted with the slow movements of fatigue, he painstakingly distinguished the people before him. Then he stepped aside with the two local doctors.

They treated him deferentially, for this man of thirty-eight had during the ten years since 1799 been the leading surgeon of the Kentucky frontier. Ephraim McDowell's name was known in every forest settlement where the language spoken was English, not the guttural accents of Algonquin tribes. Whenever a pioneer required an operation that was beyond the skill of the rural doctors, word was sent to Danville by pony express, by courier, or by some traveler going that way, and McDowell hastily crammed his instruments and drugs into worn saddle bags. The sixty-mile trip he had taken through the wilderness to treat Mrs. Thomas Crawford was a routine matter; often he rode a hundred.

Reconstructing what occurred after McDowell reached her cabin is like the task of an archæologist who must piece together scattered fragments into the statue they once formed. McDowell left three separate brief accounts of the events that were to make him immortal. By combining them with facts we know about the frontier and statements by McDowell's contemporaries, we can rebuild an image which, even if occasionally inexact, will resemble the truth more closely than the uncombined fragments could ever do.

The two local doctors told McDowell that Mrs. Crawford was pregnant; she knew the symptoms well for she was already the mother of five children. Although the ninth and tenth months brought the most terrible labor pains, there were no signs of a birth. By the time the doctors were consulted, she was so big they were convinced she would have twins. When all their skill failed to bring on a delivery, they had called McDowell.

He preceded his colleagues into the cabin. A short, tremendous woman who lay in a box bed filled with willow boughs attempted a smile of greeting, but a spasm of pain pulled her mouth tight. McDowell sat down beside her, asked a few questions, and then launched forth, as was his custom, into a discussion of politics, repeating the news so precious in isolated settlements. While he talked, he began his examination, his hands moving with extreme gentleness over her tortured frame. Suddenly the words died on his lips. He walked to one side with his colleagues and, after a hurried exposition, asked to be left alone with Mrs. Crawford. When all had filed out, he told her that he brought her bad news. She was not with child; she had a tumor of the ovaries. But perhaps there was some hope.

As dusk faded into night beyond the window of oiled paper, the surgeon and his pain-racked patient held a dialogue that will be famous as long as medical history is written. The little room that housed a whole family was lighted by one candle and an open fire over which heavy iron kettles simmered. The flames became brighter in the growing dimness, the flickering more distinct, while the tall doctor, overflowing a home-made chair, told Mrs. Crawford the truth and gave her a heroic choice.

McDowell has left a short account of their conversation. He explained that he had studied in Edinburgh with some of the world's greatest surgeons, who had taught him that women with ovarian tumors must invariably die; they could promise a patient nothing but two years of gradually increasing misery unless God worked a miracle. However, beneath the pessimism of the professors, there was an undertone of self-communion; they wondered whether ovarian tumors might not be cured by cutting out the diseased part. The operation would be similar to spaying, and animals recovered from being spayed. But no sooner was this suggestion made in the halls of the medical great than it was taken back again, McDowell told Mrs. Crawford. Surgery, as he supposed she knew, was practically limited to dressing wounds and amputating limbs; operators did not dare invade the great cavities of the body. He explained that

"John Bell, Hunter, Hey, A. Wood, four of the first and most eminent surgeons in England and Scotland, had uniformly declared in their lectures that such was the danger of peritoneal inflammation that opening the abdomen to extract the tumor was inevitable death." They believed that once the inner wall of the abdomen was exposed to the atmosphere, nothing could protect it from infection.

During the hundred years in which excising tumors had been discussed, no surgeon had ever dared hazard an operation. And so the patients had always died in long-drawn-out agony. McDowell could not understand, he said, why no one had ever made the test. He believed that a patient would be likely to recover even as animals did, but supposing it was a fifty-to-one chance—was not even that desperate gamble better than no chance at all? Perhaps the doctors were thinking more of themselves than of their patients, of how their reputations would be destroyed by a failure.

McDowell knew that if he operated and if Mrs. Crawford died, as all medical authority said she must, no doctor would disagree with a coroner's jury that found him guilty of murder. And even should he escape criminal prosecution, the practice he had built up over many years would be wiped out at one blow; who would dare trust again to a surgeon so reckless and mad?

"If you think you are prepared to die," he none the less told his patient, "I will take the lump from you if you will come to Danville."

A woman like Mrs. Crawford could never look heroic. Short, her naturally heavy body distorted by a tremendous tumor, her face marred by features too large and a long mouth too firmly set, she was a figure for pity, not romance. Yet there must have been a strange look in her gray eyes as she spoke quietly.

"I will go with you."

It seemed a mad scheme to make Mrs. Crawford ride sixty miles through the wilderness in mid-winter, but McDowell's examination had shown that she was strong enough, and there was nothing else to do. Only in his own home, where his drugs, instruments, and trained assistants were at hand, could he give her the care that would be essential to the success of an operation so hazardous that no one had ever tried it before.

The next day Mrs. Crawford was helped from bed and onto the quietest horse that could be borrowed; her huge tumor pressed against the pommel of the saddle, but that was unavoidable. Mrs. Baker, a neighboring housewife, accompanied her, since her husband had to care for the farm. He stood in the doorway of his log cabin surrounded by his sniveling children and watched the little cavalcade move slowly away. It took them minutes to arrive at the crest of the rise, and then they were gone. He gathered the children together and returned to the cabin, certain he would never see his wife again.

When the three riders passed through the near-by village, the faces of the settlers who crowded to the doors showed pity for Mrs. Crawford, but only hostility for the tall doctor who was sacrificing her to his foolishness and pride. The instant the houses were left behind, the forest locked over their heads, a braided canopy of glass, for every branch was sheathed with ice. They rode through gleaming vistas of silence, and although they moved continually, they did not seem to advance, so unchanging was the wilderness. Only the increasing agony of the tumor, which, as McDowell tells us, chafed against the pommel, testified to miles traversed. At night they sought lodgings in some cluster of log cabins that appeared beside the trail. Always the settlers received Mrs. Crawford with sympathy and her doctor with suppressed indignation. Long before he reached Danville, McDowell must have begun to expect trouble from the mob.

At last the sixty miles were behind them. They rode down the main street of a hamlet boasting less than a hundred houses and stopped before one of the finest. Standing at the doorway under the fanlight was the doctor's wife, a tall, graceful woman who received Mrs. Crawford with the expert kindness of long usage, and put her to bed.

When the surgeon's nephew and partner, Dr. James McDowell, heard what his uncle intended to do, he was horrified. Well educated in Philadelphia, he knew that Mrs. Crawford would certainly die, dragging their reputations and their practice to oblivion with her. He argued with his uncle. He washed his hands of such madness several times a day, only to return to the attack a few hours later.

The proposed operation soon became the only topic of conversation in the tiny community of Danville, which had for a long time known no such excitement. Naturally, McDowell's less successful medical rivals did not fail to point out that the butchery he planned was contrary to all medical canons and certain to end fatally. At first the popular murmur ran on the note of gossip, but soon the pitch heightened, the voices became emotional, and men began to say that McDowell must be stopped, either by the law or by the people if need be.

He had decided to operate on Christmas Day, when the prayers of all the world, rising up to God, would create a propitious atmosphere. In the meantime, he engaged in intensive preparation. Anxious to have Mrs. Crawford as strong as possible, he saw to her every comfort and fed her on a planned diet. He studied the plates of the abdomen in his medical books and tried to re-enact in his mind every dissection he had ever made. Since James McDowell had refused to take part in the experiment, he was forced to rely for assistance entirely on his apprentice, Charles McKinny. Each day he rehearsed the youngster, going over and over the operation in pantomime to be sure there would be no slip.

Christmas Day dawned with a ringing of bells. No sooner had Dr. McDowell arisen than his nephew came to him, his face tight with determination. He had struggled with himself all night, he said, and decided at last that, since a life was at stake, it was his duty to help if he could. McDowell must have gone about his preparations with a lighter heart; such trained assistance might make a vast difference.

As Mrs. Crawford walked into the operating-room, the streets were quiet, for everyone was at church. One of the ministers, an exhorter famous for snatching brands from the mouth of hell, chose the operation as the subject of his sermon. He told his congregation of pioneers, who were used to being a law unto themselves, that, although only God had a right to deal out life and death, Dr. McDowell was preparing to destroy one of God's creatures.

The chamber where Mrs. Crawford found herself had no resemblance to the operating-theater of a modern hospital. It was a room like any other in the house, bare except for a plain wooden table onto which Mrs. Crawford was strapped. Since ether had not yet been discovered, she could be given no stronger anæsthetic than a few opium pills; naturally she had to be fastened down. Devoid of white uniforms and gauze masks, the surgeons waited in their ordinary clothes, their coats off and their sleeves rolled up to avoid the blood. The instruments did not repose in steam sterilizers, for antiseptic methods lay far in the future. The knives and forceps had been washed like table silver and laid on an ordinary linen cover.

McDowell tells us that he bared the patient's swollen abdomen, marked with a pen the course of the incision, and handed the knife to his nephew; if James were to share the possible danger, he must share the possible credit too. Seeing the gleaming blade poised over her body, Mrs. Crawford closed her eyes and started to sing a hymn. When the knife bit deep, her voice quavered but the tune continued to fill the little room.

After his nephew had completed the incision, McDowell started on the serious part of the operation. His hand never shook, but his face burned red and he sweated at every pore in the icy chamber. Whenever Mrs. Crawford's voice, attempting hymn after hymn, shook with unusual agony, he whispered tender and soothing words, as he might to a frightened child.

Suddenly the silence of the street gave way to a confused murmur; church was out. More than a hundred people gathered in front of the house, some curious, some sympathetic, but the most vocal screaming with righteous indignation. In the room where Mrs. Crawford lay, her anguished hymns were drowned out by loud shouts of male voices calling for the operation to stop. James McDowell's inwards must have rocked queasily to think what might happen if Mrs. Crawford died. He searched her prostrate body for some symptoms of approaching death, but the suffering woman, her knuckles white where they clenched the table, sang bravely on.

According to McDowell's daughter, the mob swung a rope over a tree so that they might not lose any time in hanging the surgeon when Mrs. Crawford died. As the long minutes passed with no news from the silent house at which all eyes stared, the ringleaders could control their excitement no longer; they dashed for the door and tried to smash it in. But the sheriff, assisted by the more sober citizens, intervened; for a moment there was a struggle outside the surgeon's house. If McDowell heard the uproar, he gave no sign as he proceeded with the operation he later described as follows:

"I made an incision about three inches from the musculus rectus abdominis, on the left side, continuing the same nine inches in length, parallel with the fibers of the above-named muscle, extending into the cavity of the abdomen, the parietes [walls] of which were a good deal contused, which we ascribed to the resting of the tumor on the horn of the saddle during her journey. The tumor then appeared in full view, but was so large that we could not take it away entire. We put a strong ligature around the Fallopian tube near the uterus, and then cut open the tumor, which was the ovarium and fimbrious part of the Fallopian tube very much enlarged. We took out fifteen pounds of dirty, gelatinous-looking substance, after which we cut through the Fallopian tube and extracted the sac, which weighed seven pounds and one-half. As soon as the external opening was made the intestines rushed out upon the table, and so completely was the abdomen filled by the tumor that they could not be replaced during the operation, which was terminated in about twenty-five minutes. We then turned her upon her left side, so as to permit the blood to escape, after which we closed the external opening with the interrupted suture [a series of stitches placed a short distance apart], leaving out, at the lower end of the incision, the ligature which surrounded the Fallopian tube. Between every two stitches we put a strip of adhesive plaster, which, by keeping the parts in contact, hastened the healing of the incision. We then applied the usual dressings. . . ."

The sound of hymns, which had been getting weaker and weaker, stopped at last. Ephraim and his assistants carried the half-unconscious patient to her bed. When the mob learnt that the operation was over and that Mrs. Crawford lived, there was silence for a moment, and then the air was riven by a cheer. Actually the real danger was yet to come; would Mrs. Crawford develop peritonitis, that deadly infection of the abdominal wall? Dr. McDowell put her on the depleting diet then thought essential for combating fevers, and waited. When he came into her room five days later, he was horrified to see her standing up and making her bed. At his grave reproof, she laughingly replied that she had never been able to lie still. By means of persuasions, dire warnings, and threats he induced her to remain an invalid for twenty-five days, but at the end of that time she insisted on riding back to the neglected household tasks that had been worrying her more and more. With renewed energy she threw herself into the active life of a pioneer, moving on a short time later to a frontier outpost in Indiana, where there was new land to conquer from the forest. She remained in excellent health until her death at the age of seventy-nine.

McDowell's operation was one of the most important in the history of surgery. Although ovarian tumors are so common a malady that some specialists now treat more than a hundred a year, his cure for this otherwise fatal condition was only the lesser part of his discovery. More significant still was his demonstration that the abdominal cavity could be cut into with impunity. Indeed, his operation was a forerunner of a major part of modern surgery; its success combined with the revival of Cæsarian sections to destroy a false taboo and blaze the way for other surgeons who invaded the uterus, the spleen, the kidneys, the gall-bladder, and the liver. Every operation for appendicitis or gall-stones is a lineal descendant of one daring experiment made in the wilderness of Kentucky.

McDowell was not the first physician who, when confronted

with a woman dying of an ovarian tumor, considered the possibility of cutting it out. As early as 1685, Théodore Schorkopoff wrote that the extirpation of the infected ovary might bring a permanent cure were it not so dangerous. Twenty-seven years later Eherenfried Schlenker made a similar observation, and from then on the suggestion was made again and again. In 1787 the great English surgeon John Hunter asked: "Why should not a woman suffer spaying without danger as other animals do?" but he saved his reputation for sanity by adding in another lecture that an ovarian tumor was incurable "and that a patient will have the best chance of living longest who does the least to get rid of it." It is hard to understand why, since women were almost certain to die anyhow, someone did not take the risk of operating during the one hundred and twenty-four years that separated Schorkopoff from McDowell; but such was the case. When a surgeon was confronted with a fatally stricken patient, he would call in a committee of distinguished colleagues and, after a long and learned discussion, decide not to commit murder by using the only possible means to save the sufferer.

It was no accident that the all-important step which broke this deadlock was taken in the wilderness. Since McDowell did not add any new theoretical conception to surgery, he did not need the inspiration of distinguished colleagues; indeed, they would have got in his way by insisting, with all the prestige of fame behind them, that he was mad. McDowell's greatness lay in his skill as an operator, and in the courage and self-reliance that prompted him to dare what no physician had ever dared before. Courage and self-reliance were the necessary virtues of the frontier. That he came by them naturally, the story of his early life will show.

2

MORE than any other American doctor, Ephraim McDowell has become a legend. Strange myths cluster about his memory, and his attributes have been warped and heightened in the telling until he has come down to us in several manifestations that contradict each other. Indeed, McDowell's story falls naturally into the world of romance. It is a simple story of heroism, easy to comprehend, and its hero is a simple man untainted by the complicated psychology of a Rush or a Morgan. There is no place in legend for neuroses. Like Beowulf or Lancelot, McDowell attacked his ogre without heroics, or introspection, or even hesitation once he had made up his mind.

But more essential to the McDowell myth than its substance is its lack of substance. The inarticulate surgeon, skillful with his knife, was bewildered by his pencil; he wrote few letters, no memoirs, no records of what he thought and felt. And so unassuming was this backwoods hero that he never impressed his contemporaries into preserving the few scrawled pages that at one time or another necessity forced him to write. "Ephraim certainly writes a bad letter," you can hear his friends say. "There is nothing here worth keeping." And so the sheet that would today be a great find was torn up and dropped into the fire. Thus McDowell left few footprints for the historian to follow. Like Nature, the mind of man abhors a vacuum; where facts are not, there legends grow.

However, it is not impossible to separate the true McDowell from his mythological counterpart, and even to discover new data in dull tomes where the legend-maker fails to look. Since McDowell's childhood was lived among great events in the history of Kentucky, we may find many clues from which to reconstruct the early influences that molded him into a great man.

His father, Samuel McDowell, was born in Pennsylvania of a Scotch-Irish family that had been in America several generations. When Samuel was two, he was carried to Rockbridge County, Virginia, then the frontier of the Colonies, for it bordered on the Alleghenies over whose sheer woods the savages still ruled. On Christmas Day, 1742, Samuel's father was mortally wounded by an arrow as he fought to defend his home. However, the family prospered and became people of importance. When he was eighteen, Samuel married Mary McClung, a Scotch-Irish girl who had just reached America. Within a year he left his bride to fight in the French and Indian War, earning such distinction as a soldier that he was continually in demand for the border strife which continually flamed up anew. Between battles he practiced law. Elected to represent the frontier in the Virginia House of Burgesses, he was an active patriot who helped put his State in the forefront of the Revolution.

His wife in the meantime was kept busy bearing children. Born on November 11, 1771, Ephraim had five older brothers and three older sisters. His earliest memories must have concerned the revolutionary war in which his father and three of his brothers fought. There was, for instance, the exciting week when his brother James hurried home to get married with much military festivity, with the clanking of spurs and the firing of muskets. After James had ridden back to the front, there was a new woman in the house who brooded silently over her spinning and paled whenever a straggler brought news from the front. One night Samuel, Jr., the fourth brother, who was seventeen, ran away to join Lafayette at Yorktown.

The war over, the house was filled with silent heroes who, following the custom of their breed, treated their exploits as commonplace and were annoyed when asked about them. Having by this time a younger brother and sister, Ephraim belonged to the underprivileged middle group typical of all large families; he was neither petted nor praised. He had his tasks to do about the house and farm—many of them, since by the time he was ten he was considered old enough for a man's work—and woe to him if he neglected any particular; then he would receive the attention from his father he otherwise lacked. Samuel McDowell's square and prominent forehead rising to a great height above his ears, his narrow nose, firm mouth, and determined chin seemed made to express grave disapproval. However heinous Ephraim's crime, the old warrior never lost his temper; his displeasure was revealed in a few low-spoken words that had the energy of blows. Nor were blows lacking if the youngster showed the slightest disobedience or disrespect. The McDowells worshiped a Presbyterian God, slow to anger but terrible when His children transgressed His laws, and their household was organized on the inflexible principles of the universe. Ephraim's father was remote and clothed in awe, as a deity should be. If he had forgiven the child his misdeeds, the child would have despised him, for in the McDowells' universe the sinner demanded his punishment even as the righteous demanded his reward; to deny either would have been unjust, and above all the McDowells hated injustice.

When the boy behaved, he was privileged to eat three meals a day with the rest of the family, and to amuse himself as he pleased during the few hours he could rescue from his chores. A healthy youngster, large and gangling for his age, he hunted, vied with his companions in feats of strength, and fought with them periodically just to keep his hand in. Practical jokes were his particular joy, and when he made a friend look ridiculous he indulged in Gargantuan laughter that was immediately stilled if his father should happen by, frowning as always in deep thought about the future of the Union.

Although Nature was his most constant companion, Ephraim was not the kind to charm his idle hours with a sentimental worship of the works of God. Birds were targets for sling-shots, trees existed to be climbed or cut down if they got in the way, and apple blossoms were good because fruit was sure to follow. The study of Nature for her own sake could never have appealed to his practical mind. Although he might have spent hours collecting edible mushrooms, he would have been overcome with mirth at the idea of collecting butterflies.

When Ephraim raised his eyes to the west, he saw the green flanks of the Alleghenies lifting in light and shadow to the sky. He found these mountains romantic, for they were a challenge to human endeavor. His father and his brothers had penned the Indians on the far side of the barrier, but a new empire existed over there from which the Indians must in turn be driven. Perhaps it was in these wars that he would hunt more dangerous quarry than the raccoons and partridges that now fell before his rifle.

Only eleven years before Ephraim was born, Daniel Boone had climbed the mountains for the first time and, looking down from the other side, seen a forest stretching with its glades and watercourses as far as his eyes could reach. He had carved into a tree Kentucky's earliest written record, "D. Boon Cilled A. BAR in THE yEAR 1760," and returned with tales of country rich as the Promised Land. Then followed the days of moccasined explorers who paddled up the rivers and walked in Indian file through a hostile wilderness. The few settlers who found their way into Kentucky before the Revolution were driven back by the Indian wars that followed when British governors offered the tribes bounty for American scalps. The Alleghenies became again the natural border of the Union, and along it Colonel Samuel McDowell prowled for months with his Virginia militia, the rough troops lying between the rocks in eternal vigilance for Indian raids.

The return of peace in 1781 brought a sudden migratory excitement such as birds must feel at the first cool winds of autumn. Tories driven from their estates, revolutionary soldiers disbanded after years of fighting, the new poor of the inflated continental dollar, small farmers ruined by the competition of slaves, all these surged across the Alleghenies like the flood waters of a freshet when the dam goes down at last. By 1783 there were 13,000 settlers in Kentucky; within a year the number had doubled. A colonization fever, rivaled in American history only by the gold rush to California, had swept over the land.

Since the water route down the Ohio was still too dangerous because of Indian attacks, most of the immigration was from Virginia through the Wilderness Trail. Ephraim must have felt like the one bird who stays behind in autumn. Every day farmhouses were emptied. How often he helped the neighbors tie their possessions on the back of plow horses, for no wheel had yet entered the promised land. How often he watched little cavalcades start down the valley, the men in front carrying their muskets, the women driving the laden horses and perhaps a few cows or goats, while the dogs ranged back and forth, and the children taunted Ephraim as a sissy who stayed behind in the dull, safe fields of Virginia.

By 1783 it was no longer possible to govern every detail of Kentucky life from the capital of Virginia. A law court was set up and Samuel McDowell appointed one of the first three judges ever to sit in the Mississippi Valley. Thus at the age of twelve Ephraim achieved his ambition of riding the Wilderness Trail. For days the cavalcade moved warily on a worn track between ridges whose rocks and trees might always hide an ambush; for days they passed no settler's cabin, for a white man could not live with safety in this turbulent land. Indeed, the Alleghenies were a natural barrier more difficult and dangerous to cross than the channel which separates England and France. Long after Kentucky had become a State, it did not touch the older settlements anywhere; an expanse of uninhabited mountains, a hundred miles wide, stretched in between.

Since the Wilderness Trail was too rough for wagons, the Mississippi and its tributaries gave Kentucky its only practical means of transport. When the McDowells came out of the mountains on the other side at last, they were effectively cut off from the Atlantic seaboard; the geography of the Mississippi basin turned their eyes to the south, where the remains of the Spanish empire still flourished. Indeed, it was not a foregone conclusion that the western settlements would join up with the thirteen colonies which were struggling towards a precarious union. As late as 1804 Thomas Jefferson wrote: "Whether we remain in one confederacy or form into Atlantic and Mississippi confederations, I do not believe very important to the happiness of either part." Was Samuel McDowell then to become a ruler in a new nation? As we shall see, he had the chance.

The court began its functions by creating a town in which to hold its sessions. Selecting a favorable spot at the end of the Wilderness Trail, they laid out Danville, for many years to be the capital of Kentucky. Although a handful of log cabins sprang up around them, by 1790 Danville had only 150 permanent inhabitants. Here Ephraim spent his adolescence. If he wandered a few yards from town, he stepped into a forest so thick it made a permanent barrier between the sun and the earth; he could walk interminably in a glimmering midday twilight through which rose tree trunks thicker than a dozen men. Tiny gaps in the foliage sometimes showed him stars dim in the noonday heavens. When he came to a clearing, the southern sun would strike with the force of a thunderbolt, and he would stand on the rim of the forest dazzled by brilliance. It was a land of contrast: light and shade, Indian warfare flaming continually to the west and at home the arts of peace.

The McDowells lived in a two-room cabin built of logs. What furniture they possessed was home-made, since only a madman would try to haul a chair over the Wilderness Trail. Judge's son and village vagrant went round in clumsy homespun woven of wool they themselves had sheared from the sheep's backs. Shoes were rare and for state occasions only. Although they lacked space in their packs for all comforts and many necessities, the strange settlers of this forest carried books over the mountains. Ephraim could have studied had he wanted to; he went to a "classical seminary" at Bardstown, Kentucky; but in his later years he showed few signs of grammar and none of classical knowledge. In the simple economy of the frontier the daily tasks of life fell on everyone; Ephraim worked as hard in the fields as the son of the poorest farmer, and in his spare hours he had better things to do than to study what other people had thought and observed. Outside the

window an exciting world, fresh from the hand of God, waited
to show him its wonders, and there were companions too, tough
muscular fellows like himself, anxious to explore and hunt
with him or fight when the mood came on them.

The coins his elders clinked in their pockets taught Ephraim
geography. Since what American money the settlers had
brought with them soon returned east in payment for necessities, barter became the local means of exchange. It was sup-
plemented, however, by gold and silver coins from the corners
of the earth, coming to Kentucky God knows how and staying
there because no other region would honor them. With excited
eyes, Ephraim fingered strange disks from Spain, France, Hol-
land, Austria, Prussia, and Italy, as well as Arabian sequins
and Indian rupees.

The coins were symbolic. Danville, although lost in the
wilderness, became the center of an international intrigue which
might have changed the history of the world. Kentucky at this
time had two overwhelming needs. It needed to become a
State, for only by controlling its own militia could it protect
itself from the Indians who were massacring its inhabitants,
and it needed permission from the King of Spain to navigate
the Mississippi down to the Gulf, for its commercial prosperity
depended solely on its ability to get its farm products to the
sea. When Kentucky petitioned the Continental Congress for
statehood, the national government was framing the Constitution; unwilling to give the South another vote in its councils,
it put Kentucky off. At the same time, the Secretary of Foreign
Affairs negotiated a treaty with Spain giving up all claims to
navigate the Mississippi in return for concessions of value to
the North. Although the treaty failed of ratification by Congress, that it had been proposed showed a dangerous callousness
towards the needs of the frontier.

The King of Spain saw his chance. Anxious to destroy the power of the United States, he let it be known that, while Spain would never allow a part of that nation to trade down the Mississippi, it would be glad to extend every courtesy to an independent Kentucky. He bribed John Wilkinson, a famous revolutionary soldier, to agitate secretly for secession. Since Wilkinson could with truth argue that the United States had rejected both of Kentucky's prime needs, he gathered a powerful faction behind him. One simple act of self-assertion, he pointed out, no more treasonous than the Declaration of Independence had been, would enable Kentucky to fight its own battles unhindered by red tape and to navigate the Mississippi in peace. Indeed, had the settlers behind their shield of mountains declared independence, the thirteen States, embroiled among themselves over establishing a federal government, could have done little but submit.

Since it would have been to Kentucky's immediate advantage to set up a separate nation, the patriotic party, with Samuel McDowell as one of its leaders, could only procrastinate and hope the situation would change. The question was discussed in nine successive territorial conventions held at Danville between 1784 and 1792. McDowell presided over them all, and saw to it that nothing was done beyond rephrasing the demand for admission to the Union. On the face of it, this would seem an impossible policy to pursue. While the conventions were kept wallowing in parliamentary detail, the Indians, unchecked by an effective militia, killed or captured fifteen hundred settlers. As the survivors sank into poverty, Wilkinson, who had a private trading treaty with Spain, swaggered before them in the new-found wealth which they by seceding could share. That McDowell and his friends were able to hold a population of Indian fighters in check for almost a decade shows the power of these leaders and the stuff of which their constituents were made. The society where Ephraim reached manhood was no conglomeration of adventurers seeking sudden wealth. Kentucky was settled by farmers hungry for land; although unafraid of the wilderness and quick to reach for their rifles when the Indians attacked, they were as deliberate in thought and as slow to anger as Samuel McDowell himself.

All the issues of these difficult years passed under Ephraim's eyes in his own house. The Danville Political Club, which his father had organized among the patriotic statesmen, met there frequently and acted as an unofficial steering committee for the conventions. Ephraim came in daily contact with the towering figures of the frontier, quiet men in leather coats and coonskin caps who controlled the future of an empire and knew it. During dinner Ephraim sat silent at the table while Isaac Shelby, the hero of King Mountain, or Colonel Benjamin Logan spoke with slow unemotion of exploits so romantic that the poets of the future would fall over themselves seeking hyperbole with which to describe them. Ephraim saw the traitor too, saw the mercurial Wilkinson orating with a Spanish gesticulation of hand, and perhaps he then made up his mind about such plausible talkers.

Although the men he admired were grave and deliberate in action, they were in their ideas the wildest radicals of those days, almost Jacobins. The Danville Political Club was opposed to slavery and wanted to limit capital punishment to murder and treason. Despite the fact that Indian outrages were a daily occurrence, they insisted that the Indians could not be legally deprived of their hunting grounds without their consent. In discussing the federal Constitution, the club anticipated Jefferson by desiring a Bill of Rights. The Kentucky constitution that was largely their handiwork incorporated universal manhood suffrage, leading the rest of the world by twenty-five years in a measure considered as wicked then as communism would be today.

Influenced by men both high-minded and ambitious, Ephraim decided to study a profession. Surgery was a natural choice, since it would enable him to use his practical, manual skill for the benefit of humanity. In 1790, two years before Kentucky was admitted to the Union, he journeyed back across the mountains and became an apprentice to Dr. Alexander Humphreys of Staunton, Virginia. A short time previously, an Englishman had disappeared from Staunton and a sack of bones was found in a cave; Humphreys's enemies whispered that he had murdered the Englishman so that his students might dissect the body. Humphreys admitted the bones were his leavings, but said they belonged to a Negro he had lifted from a graveyard. When the coroner insisted that the dismembered body was that of a white man, Humphreys took the stand and swore that "after a Negro lays some time in his grave the odds cannot be known between him and a white person as to color." All during McDowell's apprenticeship the unsavory squabble went on with suits and counter-suits for slander, malicious persecution, and false imprisonment. A few years after he had finished educating McDowell, Humphreys gave up the battle and immigrated to Kentucky.

This story shows that Humphreys was unusually progressive in a period when most preceptors taught anatomy with a pile of bones thrown in a closet. Humphreys had studied in Edinburgh. Anxious to follow in his master's footsteps, Ephraim asked his father to finance a trip abroad. Before the dour judge agreed, he wrote Andrew Reid, his son-in-law, to say: "If you have any doubt of his [Ephraim's] economy or prudence, pray let me know, for I would not be for his going to Scotland, if he was of an imprudent behavior in any respect whatever."

Reid's answer must have been satisfactory, since in 1793 Ephraim crossed the ocean with Samuel Brown, another of Dr. Humphreys's apprentices who was also to become famous. Ephraim wrote no letters home and eventually received the following from his father: "I would be glad to hear how you like your situation there and how long you think it will be necessary for you to stay, for I assure you it will be very hard for me to send you a supply of money. But I will endeavor to support you if in my power, and to enable you to bring with you some books, and a quantity of medicine to serve you for some time, and to set up a decent shop. But I fear I will not be able to send you money sufficient." Samuel McDowell, whose salary was only two hundred pounds a year, managed to send his son three hundred, but even this was not enough to enable Ephraim to get his degree.

Perhaps the young man was not as parsimonious as he might have been; far from home, he could not resist a little gayety and display. When he and two other Kentuckians toured the highlands that summer, they walked, it is true, but if they had a letter of introduction to present they hired a carriage and drove up in state. Trying to appear like English gentlemen on a grand tour, they marched with much formality into the drawing-rooms of their new friends, but the instant they admitted they were from Kentucky, all formality was thrown aside and the delighted Scots haled them out on horseback or in a coach and exhibited them to the whole neighborhood as gentlemen from the extreme backwoods of America.

When Ephraim finally wrote home about his adventures, the account was not enthusiastically received. "The opportunity you have had of seeing so much of that old and well-cultivated country," Reid replied, "must have been very agreeable. I hope it has and will ease your mind on that score." And again, in a later letter: "I hope that you are laboring away at your studies, and should you be pretty well accomplished in the branch you are studying, have hopes you will be excused by your friends should you not return to them altogether a master of *Politeness.*"

During his later years McDowell loved to boast of his contest with an Irish footracer who appeared in Edinburgh and annoyed the scholars by insisting that he could out-run, out-hop, and out-jump any student in their dandified university. The students replied by electing the long backwoodsman their champion. A course of sixty yards was laid off and the stake set at ten guineas. Disappointed that the bets had not gone higher, McDowell allowed himself to be beaten. When he challenged the Irishman for a return race over a greater distance, his partisans were able to get a hundred guineas at odds. With all this money on his nose, McDowell could not lose; his heavy body charged down the course with such speed that it became a legend in Edinburgh.

However, his elders had no cause to fear that Ephraim would neglect his studies. He worked hard, although he showed little interest in the elaborate reasoning on which internal medicine was based. He did not sit at the feet of the theorists as Rush had done, but concentrated rather on practical sciences: chemistry at the beginning, anatomy and surgery at the close. Dissatisfied with the courses at the university, he matriculated outside with John Bell, the father of surgery of the blood vessels, who won his confidence by denouncing "the fascinations of doctrine and hypotheses." Sentimental writers like to dwell on the picture of the young man, whipped to emotional frenzy by Bell's description of the hopelessness of ovarian tumors, dedicating himself in the Scotch lecture-room to rescuing the human race from this scourge. It is more likely that he wondered why the operation had never been tried, and went on with the business of the day. Indeed, he so rarely spoke up in class or showed enthusiasm, that his fellow-pupils thought him a bit stupid. Samuel Brown remarked that McDowell went to Edinburgh a gosling and came back a goose.

Although McDowell's money ran out before he had secured a degree, when he returned to Danville, he was the best-trained surgeon beyond the mountains. Since his family position was impressive as well, he was immediately called upon to do all the difficult surgery in the Mississippi Valley. One of the most dangerous operations current in those days was lithotomy, tapping the bladder for a stone, and in this he proved himself especially proficient; had he never seen an ovarian tumor, he would have passed into medical history, like his younger contemporary, Dr. Benjamin Dudley, as "a great lithotomist." During the autumn of 1812, James K. Polk, a grievously ailing youngster of seventeen, came to him all the way from west Tennessee, and returned home joyously with the stone not in his bladder but in his pocket. When he was elected to the House of Representatives, Polk wrote McDowell to thank him for making his career possible: "'I have been enabled to obtain an education, study the profession of law, and embark successfully in the practice; have married a wife, and permanently settled in Tennessee; and now occupy the station in which the good wishes of my fellow-citizens have placed me. When I reflect, the contrast is great between the boy, the meager boy with pallid cheeks, oppressed and worn down with disease, when he first presented himself to your kind notice in Danville nearly fourteen years ago, and the man at this day in the full enjoyment of perfect health."

Before he was thirty, McDowell became a person of importance and property. He sponsored a library at Danville in 1800 and a few years later was one of the founders of Center College. During his thirty-second year he made an excellent marriage. His eighteen-year-old bride was the daughter of Isaac Shelby, the famous revolutionary general who had been the first governor of Kentucky. She was an Episcopalian, but in most other respects her background was identical with her husband's: their fathers had fought together in many a campaign and schemed together against the Spanish plot. General Shelby was famous for "glorified common sense," for "headlong bravery balanced by unwearying self-control." The words might have been written about Samuel McDowell.

Sarah Shelby was tall and dark. Her high-arched brows under a high forehead, her light-colored eyes, and her small firm mouth gave her a beauty untouched by frivolity. Although she had a considerable local reputation as a poetess, she was so shy she could hardly be induced to show her work to her friends and never to publish it. How this sensitive girl whose soul found peace in verses must have impressed her matter-of-fact husband! Indeed, the couple were well matched. Coming from similar backgrounds, they faced an identical philosophy from compensating viewpoints: practical strength contrasted with sympathetic weakness, the mind of action with the mind of dream.

His wife gradually led Ephraim from the McDowells' rocky universe into somewhat greener pastures. Under her influence, he renounced the Presbyterian for her gentler faith; later he donated land for a church. She it must have been who persuaded the practical-minded surgeon to build the slightly arty house where he received Mrs. Crawford. When Samuel Mc-

Dowell came to call, he certainly scowled at the paneling decorated with pillars which held up nothing but the empty air. In the McDowells' universe, things were good only if they served some utilitarian purpose; had not God made the apple round so it would fit into the hand?

As the leading consultant of the wilderness, McDowell was always on horseback, riding forest trails beyond the ends of civilization. One spring when the brooks were swollen to rivers and the rivers to floods, he was called, his granddaughter tells us, a hundred miles for an emergency operation. Mrs. McDowell begged him not to go, but in vain. After he had ridden forty uneventful miles, he came to a canyon that roared to the brim with water. Saplings as thick as his arm were bent horizontal by the force of the torrent, and the white-eddied surface was black with driftwood.

McDowell forced his mount into the stream. While the animal struggled against the current, he stood in his stirrups trying to fend off the timber that swept down upon them. When a huge log appeared, its ten-foot length wallowing like a crocodile, he struggled with it but found it too heavy. It struck the horse's chest; the sound was audible above the roar of water, and the stunned beast went under. For a moment the torrent flooded over them both, dragging them down; then somehow the horse got his head up again. After they had reached the further bank at last, drenched, half-drowned, McDowell turned in his saddle and looked back over the flood he had crossed. Perhaps the exultation that rushed through his veins was the same emotion his father had felt when he saw the shattered Indian tribes flee in terror from the Battle of Point Pleasant.

3

WHEN McDowell sent Mrs. Crawford home cured, he was aware that the fight against ovarian tumors had only begun. A doctor with no reputation in the centers of civilization had operated successfully on one patient, but perhaps his success was the result of chance, and even if it were not, who would believe a single voice crying from the wilderness against the accepted teaching of centuries? In doubt himself and conscious of the opposition he would have to face, McDowell waited seven years before announcing his discovery. "Although the termination of the case was most flattering," he wrote, "I was more ready to attribute it to accident than to any skill or judgment of my own, but it emboldened me to undertake similar cases; and not until I had operated three times, all of which were successful, did I publish anything on the subject."

In 1813 he cured one Negro woman, in 1816 another. Then he undertook a more difficult task. For days a blank sheet of paper lay before him while a goose-quill wilted in his hand. Undoubtedly his literary-minded wife was called in to help, but her talent ran to flowers, not tumors. Although they struggled interminably to get the unadorned facts down, the result was neither elegant nor detailed. The completed paper gave no history of the origin of Mrs. Crawford's condition, on the all-important questions of diagnosis and after-treatment it was hazy to say the least, and the description of the actual operation, which we have already quoted, was not voluminous. He was even more sketchy concerning the other two cases.

McDowell sent one copy of his paper to his old master, John Bell, in Edinburgh, and another to Dr. Philip Syng Physick. "The father of American surgery" was too knowing to be taken in by a nonentity's crude description of the impossible; after glancing through it scornfully, Physick refused to have the paper published. McDowell then sent it to Dr. Thomas C. James, the professor of midwifery at the University of Pennsylvania, who took the trouble to read it carefully and published it in 1817 in his journal, *The Eclectic Repertory*.

Most surgeons paid no attention whatsoever to McDowell's "nonsense," and the two who did, wrote articles for the same journal blaming the inadequacy of McDowell's account for the deaths of patients on whom they had not dared operate. It was unfortunate, Dr. Ezra Michener of the Philadelphia Dispensatory commented, that cases as interesting as McDowell's "should come before the public in such a manner as to frustrate their intention of being useful. . . . Few persons will be likely to venture their reputations on such uncertain data."

We can imagine the scorn of Dr. McDowell, who had ventured his reputation on no data at all, for these city practitioners who demanded to be spoon-fed. During September 1819 he answered his critics in a letter to Dr. James: "I thought my statement sufficiently explicit to warrant any surgeon's performing the operation when necessary, without hazarding the odium of making an experiment; and I think my description of the mode of operating, and of the anatomy of the parts concerned, clear enough to enable any good anatomist, possessing the judgment requisite for a surgeon, to operate with safety. I hope no operator of any other description may ever attempt it. It is my most ardent wish that this operation may remain, to the mechanical surgeon, forever incomprehensible. Such have been the *bane* of the science; intruding themselves into the ranks of the profession, with no other qualification but boldness in undertaking, ignorance of their responsibility, and indifference to the lives of their patients; proceeding according to the special dictates of some author, as mechanical as themselves, they cut and tear with fearless indifference, utterly incapable of exercising any judgment of their own in cases of emergency; and sometimes, without even possessing the slightest knowledge of the parts concerned. The preposterous and impious attempts of such pretenders, can seldom fail to prove destructive to the patient, and disgraceful to the science. It is by such this noble science has been degraded in the minds of many to the rank of an art."

McDowell then went on to report two more ovariotomies he had performed since his previous article. One patient had recovered and the other had died of peritonitis, his only fatality in five operations. Although his letter was published in *The Eclectic Repertory* for October 1819, it did not embolden any other surgeon to follow him. Women who might have been cured continued to die in agony.

The second surgeon in the world to perform ovariotomy was also an American, but communication was so faulty that he had never heard of McDowell; Nathan Smith's operation was entirely independent. Born in Massachusetts in 1762, Smith was carried while yet an infant into the northern wilderness of Vermont, a region as wild as was Kentucky in McDowell's childhood. There he labored in the fields, received a meager education in the district schools, and served in the militia at the end of the Revolution. Having studied medicine at Harvard, Edinburgh, and elsewhere, he founded the Dartmouth Medical School; for years he was the entire faculty. His impressiveness may be judged from the evening prayer the president of the university offered up after attending one of his lectures: "O Lord, we thank Thee for the oxygen gas; we thank Thee for the hydrogen gas and for all the gases. We thank Thee for the cerebrum; we thank Thee for the cerebellum and the medulla oblongata."

Smith helped start the medical department at Yale, where he held three professorships simultaneously. In his spare time he founded several other schools, often lecturing at two or three a year, and carried on a vast consulting practice. One of the towering figures of American medicine, he was equally distinguished as a physician and a surgeon; his paper on typhoid fever was the best in the world up to that time. During July 1821, twelve years after McDowell had operated on Mrs. Crawford, Smith successfully excised the ovarian tumor of a Mrs. Strobridge at Norwich, Vermont. Ignorant of McDowell's work, he was encouraged to operate by an autopsy he had previously made which showed that such tumors "adhered to no part except the proper ligament, which was no larger than the finger of a man." An account of his operation, published in the *American Medical Recorder* a year later, went unnoticed and never came to McDowell's attention.

The Kentucky surgeon would certainly have rejoiced over this confirmation of his work. He had heard nothing about the paper he had sent to John Bell in Edinburgh, and his practice was falling off at home. Whenever he rode down the street, the Negroes dived into their houses and threw the bolts behind them. One evening, his granddaughter tells us, he met a huge colored man on a solitary part of the road. The man fled, but at McDowell's command to halt fell on his knees and, rolling white eyeballs to heaven, burst into shrill prayer. As the surgeon reined up beside him, he crossed himself without stopping, his hand flying like the shuttle of a loom. McDowell dismounted and shook him until he stopped screaming. "Why are you afraid of me?" he asked. "My master," the Negro answered, "he say Dr. McDowell am next to the devil; Dr. McDowell goes around cutting people open and killing them."

McDowell's daring operations had injured his reputation. His enemies denounced him as a cruel man who enjoyed slicing into the bellies of women, and they had little difficulty persuading the simple pioneers who had long wondered how so ordinary-seeming a man could be great. The surgeon scorned the pompous tricks by which his contemporaries impressed their patients. On entering a house he did not issue commands to set everyone running; when he felt a pulse he did not frown portentously or finger a gold watch the size of a cart-wheel; he failed to wear fine clothes and condescend to the humble. Dressed always in black broadcloth, he walked into even the meanest dwelling as a friend of the family might; he spoke pleasantly to the children and, while he examined the patient, gossiped about local matters. "He is exactly like one of us," the people thought. "Obviously he can't be a great doctor."

The word went about that McDowell "was not much in fevers." A patient who was deprived of a quart of blood according to the prevalent method of Rush, and then dosed with calomel and jalap until he was about to explode, knew that heroic efforts were being made to cure him. But McDowell, far ahead of his time, did not believe in Rush's violent therapy. First swearing them to secrecy lest the damaging heresy be spread abroad, he told his private pupils that a sick man left to Nature's healing care would do better than one so dosed and harried. When McDowell, having quietly examined his patient, prescribed nothing but rest, the sufferer naturally felt he was being neglected and called in another doctor. Why, McDowell even went so far as to let fever patients drink cold water and breathe fresh air, two things known to be terribly dangerous!

The great surgeon, not particularly proud of his method of treating fevers, left them whenever he could to his partners. Internal medicine, based as it was on guesses and theories and almost no real knowledge, did not appeal to his practical mind. Surgery, however, was another matter. Surgery was a science not an art; how he despised arts! If you knew your anatomy well enough, you could be sure of exactly what you were doing, and McDowell always knew his anatomy. In those days when most doctors had never made an autopsy, he fitted up a dissecting-room in an abandoned jail. He continued all his life to examine cadavers and forced his students to do the same. Naturally this impious practice, revealing a curiosity inspired by the devil, did not help his popularity.

It would, however, be wrong to think of McDowell sinking into insignificance and poverty; many frontiersmen stuck by him to the end. In 1822 he was called several hundred miles to Hermitage, Tennessee, where he removed an ovarian tumor from the wife of John Overton, Andrew Jackson's wealthy backer. His aide in this operation was Old Hickory himself, who handed him the instruments and put him up in his house; the two men of action got on famously. McDowell asked five hundred dollars, but Overton sent him a check for fifteen hundred. When the doctor returned it, pointing out the error, Overton replied the operation was worth at least that. According to Samuel David Gross, the great surgeon and medical biographer of the next generation, this fee was the largest paid in America until that time.

About then, McDowell accepted as a private pupil a second nephew, Joseph Nashe McDowell. This preternaturally cadaverous young man looked as if he had pared his own flesh down so that he might study his bones; he was an enthusiastic anatomist. In fact, enthusiasm was his principal attribute; he was never happy unless his tiny, sunken eyes gleamed with baleful fire and his high-pitched voice was screaming in bombast. He loved to boast of his manly prowess, tell how he had beaten up a bully or nailed a squirrel at five hundred yards. People could not help laughing to see this scarecrow carry on, swaggering as if he were a complete man, and when the inevitable laughter came, Joseph would throw his bony head back and yell in a shrill, feminine tantrum. His fellow-pupils called him "saw-bones," a satisfactory nickname which never failed to drive him into a fury; but McDowell backed his nephew, for Joseph loved every bone and muscle in the body with a personal passion. While he pored over a cadaver, all the bombast vanished from his thin face which became both sensitive and intellectual.

McDowell's daughter, Mary, had grown into a plump and rosy young lady. Whenever the emaciated Joseph saw her eyes resting on him, he leapt into a paroxysm of boasting: not only would he be the greatest doctor in the United States, he would be the greatest general as well and drive the dirty Spaniards from the continent. Although Mary laughed, he was not discouraged. Following her everywhere, he wooed her so violently that she appealed to her father. McDowell's gentle remonstrances, however, merely drove Joseph into a heroic fury. Mary loved him, he insisted; McDowell was trying to come between them. The surgeon lost his temper too, and the scene ended with Joseph stamping out of the house, shouting that he would show McDowell who was the better man.

Joseph went to Lexington, Kentucky, to study medicine at Transylvania University, then the medical center of the west. Soon it became common gossip there that McDowell had stolen the credit for discovering ovariotomy from his dead nephew and partner, Dr. James McDowell, who had done the operation against his advice. Joseph even went so far as to consult Mrs. Crawford and magnify her story that James had made the first incision into a statement that he had carried out the entire operation while his uncle assisted. The scandal mounted until McDowell was forced to issue a defensive statement accompanied by affidavits from Mrs. Crawford and others who had been present. However, the rumor continued to circulate. Joseph, as we shall see, became an important medical figure, and all his life he never ceased his efforts to take the credit from his uncle. When he became bored repeating the same story over and over, he embellished it with one John King, a retired Indian hunter who, he said, had made his living spaying animals and had anticipated even James by using his veterinary technique on a lady whom McDowell had cruelly refused to treat. There is no telling how much these lies hurt the surgeon's reputation.

Not until McDowell's fortunes had reached a low ebb did the copy of his first paper which he had sent to John Bell make its appearance in England. On its arrival at Edinburgh seven years before, Bell had been dying in Italy; the paper fell into the hands of his successor, John Lizars, who kept it hidden away until he was able to publish it as an incidental part of the history leading up to an operation of his own. He did not even bother to spell McDowell's name correctly, and he entitled the article in which the American's epoch-making discovery was included "Observations on the Extirpation of Ovaria, with Cases, by John Lizars."

Lizars recounted his one case at three times the length Mc-Dowell had used for three, and he summoned all his literary skill to make the narrative as moving as possible. He introduces us to a young binder of shoes whose husband beat her so cruelly that she was forced to leave him. When a year later a swelling developed in her abdomen, she ascribed it to the beatings, but the hospital to which she went accused her of bearing an illegitimate child. From time to time other doctors "cruelly taunted her with being pregnant." Then Lizars describes how he came to the rescue: he told her she had an ovarian tumor and that he would save her by cutting it out. Although he dwells at great length on his courage in over-riding the advice of distinguished colleagues, he gives Mc-Dowell's successful cases only passing credit for influencing him to operate.

The amphitheater was filled with students, three venerable surgeons were in attendance, when Lizars prepared to introduce ovariotomy to the civilized world. Conscious that history recorded his every gesture, he made the incision under a hundred admiring eyes, but when he had laid the abdomen open, bewilderment took the place of self-confidence on his features. With growing dismay he examined the patient, and then he called over the other three surgeons. After each in turn had peered gravely into the wound, the four looked at each other blankly, for, alas, there was no tumor whatsoever to be seen; the swelling was caused by a pathological fatness of the intestines. Sadly Lizars sewed his patient up again. However, as she regained strength after the operation, his self-esteem returned; was he not the first reputable doctor to demonstrate that the abdomen could be cut into with impunity?

Proudly he wrote the case up and published it in the *Edinburgh Medical Journal* for October 1824.

McDowell's paper, thus backhandedly brought before the cultured British medical profession, excited nothing but guffaws of incredulous mirth. Dr. James Johnson, editor of the *London Medical and Chirurgical Review*, laid down a veritable barrage of scorn, impugning McDowell's veracity and his grammar. Although forced to admit at last that the backwoods surgeon had done what he said he did, Johnson still had arguments. "When we come to reflect," he wrote, "that all the women operated on in Kentucky, except one, were Negresses, and that these people will bear cutting with nearly, if not quite, as much impunity as dogs and rabbits, our wonder is lessened." Auguste Nélaton, the famous French surgeon, followed this lead by insisting that McDowell did the operation only on Negresses and not from humanitarian motives, but in order to save the property of slaveholders.

The Europeans, and the English in particular, were outraged by the idea of crediting so important a discovery to an American. As late as 1883 Sir Thomas Spencer Wells, whose success at ovariotomy earned him a baronetcy, wrote that, although McDowell did the first operation, still greater merit was due to the series of British surgeons who pointed out the physiological possibility of excision. In fact, the British were to be praised for not having made the experiment. "In this country, such is the sacredness of human life, even when threatened by fatal diseases . . . that men, even of the stamp of the Hunters and the Bells, naturally shrank from the responsibility."

Lawson Tait, another famous English surgeon, adopted a different line of attack. McDowell, he said, was not an American but a Scotchman. Probably he was born in Scotland, and even if he was not, his parents certainly were, and anyway in 1771, the year of his birth, there was no United States.

Obviously, Lizars's object in phrasing his report the way he did was to have McDowell's work regarded merely as a fore-runner to his noble experiment. Who can doubt that he would have succeeded as far as the British medical profession was concerned had his subsequent attempts at ovariotomy been successful? He operated on three women really suffering from tumors; one recovered, one died, and in the third case he did not dare finish the excision. He never tried again, and ovari-otomy was outlawed in Scotland for another twenty years.

Lizars, the professor of surgery at Edinburgh, was con-sidered one of the most skillful operators of his time, and yet, with all the expert assistance a great medical school could offer, he was unable to approach the record of a country doctor who often had no trained assistants at all. In a letter written during the last year of his life, McDowell reported that he had done eleven ovariotomies with but a single death. Although one patient was so debilitated when she came to him that there seemed little possibility of her surviving the ordeal, Mc-Dowell, knowing there was no other hope, went ahead, un-afraid of marring his record with another fatality. The lady recovered and engaged herself to be married the next year. "This case proves that appearances in surgery are often de-ceitful," McDowell commented, "and that while the taper of life continues to burn, although it be faint, there is yet hope. . . . How it is that I have been so peculiarly fortunate with patients of this description, I know not; for from all the information I can obtain there has not one individual sur-vived who had been operated on elsewhere for diseased ovaria. I can only say that the blessing of God has rested on my efforts."

There was more to it than that. Although McDowell was helped by the sturdy constitutions which all pioneers were forced to develop, he must have been a brilliant surgeon. The abdominal cavity is particularly sensitive to the type of handling it receives. If the normal flow of fluid is not disturbed, it is almost immune to infection, but once this delicate balance is upset by an inexpert hand, nothing but antisepsis, which had not then been discovered, can save the patient from peritonitis.

Ovariotomy remained so dangerous in hands other than McDowell's that it was frowned upon by medical faculties all over the world until long after his death. Of course, even under the worst circumstances it was no more dangerous than not operating, but the mechanical surgeons McDowell so despised had their reputations to look after. If they operated and killed a patient, it would hurt their practices, and if they permitted others to operate successfully, their lack of skill would be made plain. So they argued that a doctor who takes terrible risks for his patient, even if the patient is otherwise certain to die, is blasphemously encroaching on God's right to mete out life and death.

Forty years after McDowell had cured Mrs. Crawford, Dr. Washington Atlee was denounced by the entire profession for proposing to do an ovariotomy in Philadelphia, still the medical capital of America. One professor called from the rostrum for the police to intervene, and an eminent surgeon visited the patient to tell her she would be dead in twenty-four hours. She recovered. Professor Meigs thereupon wrote that the operation was not justified by any amount of success. "Dr. Atlee's coolness in cutting open a woman's belly does not, I should think, entitle him to judge more clearly than I as to the morals of such surgery." Meigs wanted the operation forbidden by statute.

During the winter of 1856–7, the Academy of Medicine in Paris engaged in a five months' battle to determine whether ovariotomy should be permitted in France. Only one distinguished surgeon supported it, and the eventual conclusion was that so frightful an operation should be proscribed even if the cures announced were real. Indeed, although daring surgeons continued to save their patients, ovariotomy did not become a regular part of practice until the discovery of anæsthesia and antisepsis made it safe for mechanical surgeons.

While the controversy that was to outlive him raged, McDowell quietly attended his patients in Danville, excising ovarian tumors whenever they appeared in his practice. Although in 1825 he was given an honorary degree by the University of Maryland, the only degree he ever received, he was accorded less praise than censure for carrying out an operation most doctors felt should not be attempted. He remained successful as a lithotomist—Dr. Gross says he cut thirty-two times for bladder stones without a death—but his popularity continued to decline, and the calumny of which he was the object reached amazing proportions.

Once when he was away attending a distant case, his wife came down with an acute illness. Of necessity McDowell's rival, Dr. Anthony Hunn, was called in. Hunn took one look at the ailing lady, threw the prescription McDowell had left her out of the window, and announced that she had been poisoned. Immediately it was whispered that her husband had tried to murder her and, but for Dr. Hunn's timely intervention, would have succeeded. As the story passed from mouth to mouth, accompanied by the click of a spindle or the creak of rockers, it grew until gossip authoritatively stated that the bright-eyed young apprentice who accompanied McDowell everywhere was a girl in man's clothing. The surgeon had tried to kill his wife so that he might marry this paramour. From then on, a contemporary account tells us, he was "the object of the utmost contempt in the neighborhood."

But McDowell had saved enough during his prosperous years to buy a plantation and slaves to work it in the true Southern style. During his middle fifties he retired there and, although sometimes called away to attend a particularly difficult case, lived the life of a country gentleman. He named his plantation Cambuskenneth after an abbey he had seen during his rambles in Scotland; this brief season in the Old World, not the adventures of the wilderness, seems to have supplied the romance of his life.

Ephraim was like his father a man of action and a convinced democrat, but he too found his ultimate critic in himself; the McDowells never cared for the opinion of the crowd. Since the surgeon knew he had lived usefully, neglect failed to make him bitter. Florid in complexion and a bit too fat, the aging man loved to sit before the fire with a glass of cherry bounce beside him and sing comic Scotch songs, accompanying himself rather unmusically on the violin. Although the vein of iron that had strengthened Samuel McDowell was built as strongly into his son, Ephraim had left the rigors of his Presbyterian childhood far behind. He enjoyed having his house filled with company and kept the best drinks on his sideboard to lure them in. He was happiest when his two sons, his three surviving daughters, and his squads of grandchildren were gathered around him for some family festival.

One evening during June 1830 McDowell went into his garden and ate freely of strawberries fresh from the vine. On his return to the house, his stomach was gripped by the most excruciating pain. Telling his wife to summon the family physician, he explained between paralyzing spasms that he must have eaten a deadly insect or some poisonous egg that clung to a berry. A servant, sent flying to the village, soon returned with the doctor. Realizing that McDowell was seriously ill, he asked for a consultation and treated the great surgeon for inflammation of the stomach. But medicine was helpless; after sinking steadily for two weeks, McDowell died.

His famous operation had paved the way for the cure of appendicitis. He probably died of a ruptured appendix.

Genius on the Ohio

DANIEL DRAKE

Daniel Drake

FROM A CONTEMPORARY ENGRAVING

GENIUS ON THE OHIO
DANIEL DRAKE

1

I SAAC DRAKE and his wife both came from a long line
of obscure New Jersey farmers. Poor, pious, and uneducated, they fled into each other's arms from the tyrannies
of two stepmothers. Isaac was earning a meager livelihood
by tending a grist mill when on October 20, 1785, his son
Daniel was born near Plainfield. It is according to the American
tradition that this infant, nurtured in ignorance and poverty,
should grow up to be the greatest physician of the new West.
Although almost illiterate at the age of fifteen, he became a
scholar of world-wide renown and the inspiration of generations of doctors beyond the Alleghenies. Teacher, founder of
universities, writer, scientist, and indefatigable crusader for
what he believed was right, he labored side by side with the
founders of cities, building medical institutions while they
built streets and factories, molding the physicians of the wilderness, who were isolated and illiterate as he himself had once
been, into a medical profession that could make the New
World with its strange diseases and novel problems as healthy
as the old. Every citizen of the Mississippi Valley who has
been sick and has called in a doctor owes a debt of gratitude to

Daniel Drake. A frontiersman of the mind, he was a leader in the second conquest of the West.

When Drake was two and a half years old, his father joined with two brothers in a plan to flee penury by migrating with some other Baptists to the territory of Kentucky, which had been opened up only a few years before. Although his daughter Elizabeth was still an infant at the breast, he loaded his family and his meager possessions on a two-horse wagon and, taking a younger sister with him, creaked ever westward for many laborious weeks. The roads were wild, rough, and deserted; wheels sank hub-deep in mud and sand. There were few taverns on the way, but had there been many it would have made no difference, since the Drakes had money only for the necessary food which they cooked over an open fire. Usually they slept in the wagon.

After they had crossed the Susquehanna at Harris's Ferry, now Harrisburg, the steep climb over the Alleghenies began. The baby had become restive, crying all the time, while little Daniel worked off his energy by getting into trouble. Once when the wagon clung perilously to a rocky mountainside, his terrified family was unable to find him anywhere. The vehicle, still pitching at a crazy angle, was stopped and a search instituted. Finally the child was found chirping merrily as he hung by his hands outside the front-board a few inches from the wheel. In telling the story to his own children, Drake commented: "Thus you see my disposition to leave a carriage in suspicious-looking places and take to my heels was an original instinct and not, as now, the result of experience."

At last the little cavalcade reached Old Red Stone Fort, where they waited until a flotilla of flatboats was ready to make the dangerous trip down to the Ohio and into Kentucky. As many families as possible were crowded with their horses

and goods onto each raft, for manpower was important in case
of an Indian attack. Beyond Fort Pitt they did not dare land
or even approach either bank. Their ears ever straining for the
sound of a war-whoop, their eyes for a canoe under the trees,
they drifted hundreds of miles across eddies, past sandbanks,
round snags that reared like white-maned horses from the
water. Despite all their precautions, one of the boats was ship-
wrecked, but no lives were lost.

On the Drakes' barge there was a most awe-inspiring pas-
senger. Although Dr. William Goforth was no older than
Isaac, he kept his hair powdered even in the middle of the
wilderness, and when he picked up an oar he first had to lay
down the gold-handled cane he always carried. Isaac was afraid
to speak to anyone so splendid, but Dr. Goforth treated him
with elaborate courtesy that soon put him at his ease. One
evening the physician enthralled the penniless immigrant
with a burst of impromptu oratory in which he shook the dust
of New York off his feet because a pious mob had broken up
the anatomy lectures of Dr. Charles McKnight and forced Dr.
Goforth, then a student, to scuttle for his life through a maze
of streets. Excitedly, Dr. Goforth brandished his gold-handled
cane in the face of the fascinated Drake.

Isaac, his son Daniel says, eventually summoned up the
courage to ask what must have seemed to him an almost impossible favor. We can see the flatboat, safe for a moment in
deep waters between distant banks, slipping down a broad
reach of the Ohio as the farmer in his torn shirt and faded
trousers sidled up to the magnificent doctor. He confessed
with much hesitation that it was the dream of his life that one
of his sons should be a gentleman. Urged on by the good
physician, he blurted out at last that perhaps, if it were not
too much to ask, he would eventually send Daniel, at the

moment an infant tumbling under their feet, to Dr. Goforth to learn medicine. We can visualize the humble pose with which the tattered farmer awaited a reply.

Smiling, Dr. Goforth agreed to the proposal. Probably he soon forgot his words that had sounded so portentous in the silence of the wilderness, but Isaac never forgot. Now that his vague dream of fathering a gentleman had taken solid shape, it became the comfort of his life. During happy moods, he called Daniel "doctor" in anticipation.

The flotilla reached Maysville, Kentucky, on June 10, 1788. "Before landing, father sprained his ankle and was unable to walk," Daniel told his own children in one of the long series of letters which minutely describe his childhood. "He had to be carried out of the boat, and then he could put but one foot on the land of promise. Who carried him I know not, but he was not very heavy, for he had in his pocket but *one* dollar, and that was asked for a bushel of corn."

Since there were no accommodations at Maysville and the danger from Indians on the other side of the river was great, the family moved on to Washington, where they lodged, all five of them, in a tiny sheep pen beside the cabin of a hospitable settler. Unable to afford any food that could not be brought down with a musket, they lived on game until they became so sick of meat it was almost impossible to swallow. Once Mrs. Drake called on a housewife who was churning butter. Watching the ladle suck through the rich cream, she set her heart on a drink of buttermilk, but when the fat had gathered into chunks her neighbor merely put the churn aside. Too proud to ask for what her neighbor did not think of giving, Mrs. Drake, in Daniel's words, "hastily left the house and took a good crying spell." Then she returned to the sheep pen and its multiple tasks.

The Drakes needed to secure provisions for a whole year, since it was too late to plant even had they possessed land. When his ankle was well again, Isaac joined with a friend in the desperate expedient of running a wagon-load of goods through the Indian-infested wilderness to Lexington, Kentucky, a distance of seventy miles. No sooner had darkness descended on the two nervous Easterners than they heard an unearthly whooping which could only mean savages were on the war-path. Abandoning the wagon, they dived into the underbrush and held their breath in terror as the sound bore down upon them. Finally it came so close they realized it could issue from no human throats; a pack of wolves ran by them in the dark.

They reached Lexington in safety and returned with such sorely needed luxuries as grain and tea. In the meantime, the older members of the group that had migrated from New Jersey bought 14,000 acres on the Lexington Road eight miles from Washington. This was divided among the colonists according to their ability to pay; although he sold his wagon and one of his horses, Isaac could purchase only thirty-eight acres. The five plots were laid out to come together at a salt lick, so that the cabins could be built close to each other for mutual protection. The men worked in a body clearing land and erecting their homes. Since they were too far from the village to return at night, they slept separately in the tangled cane, hoping thus to evade the savages. By fall the village of Mayslick was ready for occupancy.

The log cabin that was Daniel Drake's first memory had a floor of split logs and a roof of hewn clapboard, for sawing was out of the question. The one small room boasted a window without glass, a stout door built for defense, and a chimney made of small poles embedded in mortar. The rifle was hung on two pegs by the door, and the ax and scythe were kept under the bed at night in readiness for an Indian attack. Daniel's earliest recollections were tinged by the ever-present possibility of massacre, for the heavy door was never opened in the morning until some member of the family had climbed up a ladder to the loft and looked through the cracks to see if there were savages ambushed outside. Midnight butcheries, captivities, and horse-stealings were the topics of conversation that rang always in the shy child's ears; no wonder his dreams were haunted by the image of a savage triumphantly lifting in a bloody hand his own poor bleeding scalp.

When his Aunt Lydia was married in his father's house, a breathless horseman broke into the festivities with the report that Indians were attacking a wagon five miles up the road towards Lexington. The men had all brought their guns, of course; leaping onto their horses, they rode off in a swirl of dust. The alarm proved false, but the scene made a lasting impression on Daniel's mind. Although he never heard a war-whoop or the whistling of an arrow, the knowledge that the peaceful-seeming woods might at any moment disgorge a flood of savages made the world a hostile and uncertain place. If he was restless at night, his mother would tell him to lie still or the Shawnees would catch him. When Daniel was almost nine years old, General Wayne's great victory drove the shadow of the Indians from the forest, but this release from actual danger did not destroy the child's deep-seated terror of the world. The memory of the shyness and fear that haunted his boyhood was ever present to Daniel Drake when he was a man and famous; he refers to it with almost pathological insistence, trying to explain it in many ways.

As soon as his family was settled in the wilderness, Isaac destroyed single-handed the forest that had lasted for centuries and planted Indian corn in its place. The crop grew marvelously in soil now for the first time exposed to the sunlight. Watching it, the Drakes dreamed of bread and the few luxuries they desired, but their corn was killed by an early frost and for another year they lived on the game that already cloyed their tongues and their stomachs. After four years they were still so poor that they were almost ruined when a horse Isaac had rented died. Overcome by this misfortune, the frontiersman took to bed in acute physical suffering, and had to be comforted back to health by his wife.

The instant Daniel was old enough to be of any use, he was put to work around the cabin. Domestic economy was not the simple task that exhausts housewives today. Flax and wool, Drake remembers, were produced on the farm, dyed with natural colors obtained from walnuts or oak bark, and woven on a hand loom into the clothes the family wore. Meal was ground from corn or wheat in a hand mortar, sugar drawn from maple trees, brooms made by splitting saplings, soap rendered from discarded fat with the aid of ashes, candles poured before the hearth for state occasions when pine chips were not used. All the activities of a slaughter house, from making sausages to tanning leather, were carried on in the front yard. In fact, the home was a self-sustaining factory that supplied all its own needs except salt, whisky, and gunpowder, and in this factory Daniel labored from dawn to dark when he was yet hardly more than an infant.

The Drakes' cabin was on the main route from the Ohio to the interior of Kentucky; whenever Daniel could snatch a minute from his duties, he would hurry to the roadside. All the immigration that over night changed the wilderness into a flourishing State moved before the eyes of the ragged urchin who sat on a stone chewing grass, his thin, vital face concentrated with starved intensity on every sight that broke into his drudgery. He saw endless pack trains driven forward by cursing drivers; he saw poor immigrants struggling along behind their wagons on which broods of children swarmed; he saw gangs of slaves marching sullen or singing to plantations not yet hewn from the forest; but he loved most to see rich settlers ride by on fine horses with their women.

"I often saw ladies and gentlemen riding side by side," he wrote as an old man, "and I remember I thought the latter must be the happiest persons on earth, an estimate which nearly sixty years has not entirely over-ruled. From the reminiscence which I have just recorded, I find that an admiration for the sex was among the earliest sentiments developed in my moral nature. It has swayed me through life and will, I suppose, continue to govern me to its close. When that solemn event shall come, I hope to see female faces round my bed,

> And wish a woman's hand to close
> My lids in death, and say—'Repose!' "

Daniel's uncle kept a tavern opposite the Drakes' cabin. Whenever he could, the child hid himself in a corner of the public room and sat there grave-eyed for hours, listening and watching. Once a young couple from Virginia called him over to their table and gave him the first wine he had ever tasted. Memories of this adventure enlivened long hours at the washtub or mortar.

Like a true pioneer, Daniel's father did not care for people; by the time Daniel was nine, life in the growing village had become unbearable to Isaac Drake. He sold his few acres and bought a larger tract which, although only a mile from Mayslick, was buried in the forest. The lad helped his father clear away the primeval woods; armed with a small ax, he cut down saplings, burnt brush, and even girdled the big trees. Since his sister was now old enough to help in the cabin, Daniel continued to labor with his father in the fields. He rode a plow horse, planted, harvested first with a sickle and then with a scythe, built fences, sheared sheep; in fact, according to his boyish powers he did everything an adult frontiersman would do.

Although Daniel worked as long as there was daylight, he found time to be lonely. Now his world had shrunk to the little cabin and its cornfield, with the black forest bristling all around. However, youth is adaptable, the growing mind molds the world to its innate purposes. The riders with their ladies beside them whom he had found so romantic were merely counters in his personal dream. These counters taken from him, he found others; the flowers and trees, he tells us, became his companions, and the beasts of the field his friends. Like the savages who once had walked the paths he trod, he built up an anthropomorphic universe.

And Nature, the great goddess, was always present, sometimes kind, sometimes cruel, but always omnipotent; the Drakes confused her with the Baptist God they worshiped. During the thunderstorms which slashed like an archangel's sword at their solitary cabin, they fled from the fields to the family hearth. "God," Daniel remembered, "was present in the storm. Both Father and Mother became solemn, and the Bible was sometimes laid open and read. The children were admonished and instructed. We might have been destroyed, but another and purer emotion blended with our fears: a feeling of reverence converting terror into awe. We were in the midst of a great and sudden visitation of Divine power."

Daniel had been taught that the world might end in the eighteenth century. The Last Judgment filled his mind with fear as the shadows of the Indians had done. Once when a storm cloud appeared in the east whence storms never came, and exploded into cataclysms of lightning, he heard Gabriel's trumpet shouting in his ears. Terrified, he threw himself on the ground, and he could hardly believe his good fortune when the storm passed over.

Toiling among animals and plants, Drake received the training that was to make him a great naturalist. Of more formal schooling he had almost none. True, itinerant schoolmasters wandered through Mayslick, but they knew very little and Daniel could study under them only during the rare moments he was not needed on the farm. Even if he started school in the morning his father often appeared at the door before noon to say he needed his help with the plowing.

Daniel was taught reading, writing, spelling, and ciphering up to the rule of three. His proudest accomplishment was being able to repeat by rote a half-dozen lines of Latin poetry, the entire classical knowledge of the schoolmaster who taught them to him. Eagerly Daniel filled his starved mind with every book he could put his hands on; a new spelling primer was a marvelous acquisition, for it gave him more words with which to describe the exciting world around him. He was overcome with delight, he tells us, by a dictionary he procured somehow at the age of thirteen. His father's library consisted of a Bible, two books of hymns, *Pilgrim's Progress,* and a romance of the days of knight-errantry. However, Daniel was able occasionally to borrow other books. When he was twelve or thirteen, he secured a copy of Love's *Surveying* and immediately tried to teach himself this difficult science. He read Guthrie's *Grammar of Geography* and was even more delighted by the long words he did not understand than by the simple ones he did. For a week he went about his chores reciting triumphantly the phrase "brazen meridian," a magic charm that might mean almost anything.

Deprived of much association with school-fellows, Daniel had to rely almost entirely on the society of his parents. His memory of them in his later years was not flattering. His mother, he said, was more illiterate than his father and only tolerably clever. In her youth she must have been pretty. Till forty her health was good, her industry and endurance great. Although she was often frightened and frequently gave way to tears, she possessed more equable spirits than her husband, who rose to higher gayety and sank to deeper gloom; she had to nurse him through many fits of black despondency. He was not particularly able; his acquirements were moderate and his business enterprise small. He had physical courage when aroused, but he lacked moral courage; a hypochondriac who suffered from imaginary illnesses, he was afraid to engage in undertakings that were practical. His wife, however, always gave in to what she considered his superior knowledge.

This unconventional picture of two pioneers, showing them anything but rugged children of the forest, was penned by Drake when an old man. As a boy he worshiped his mother; he never forgave his father for making fun of her timidity. The perpetual motive of his childhood was to win the approval of the gentle soul who gave him love and a sanctuary from the world. There was never any hesitation in her praise or censure; things were right or wrong according to the word of God as she read it in His Book. It was wicked to treat anything alive with cruelty; it was wicked to neglect the cattle or forget the little lambs in winter; it was wicked to waste food; it was wicked to be lazy, to be disobedient, to work on the Sabbath, to tell a falsehood, to curse, to get drunk, or to fight.

Mrs. Drake passed her hatred of brutality on to her sensitive son; his memories of Saturday nights in Mayslick were tinged even in his old age with horror. He described "a pitched battle between two bullies who in fierce rencontre would lie on the ground scratching, pulling hair, choking, gouging out each other's eyes, and biting off each other's noses in the manner of the bulldogs, while a Roman circle of interested lookers-on would encourage their respective gladiators with shouts which a passing demon might have mistaken for those of hell." At corn-huskings or squirrel-shootings, Drake remembered, the whisky bottle was the most prominent guest; every man, woman, or child was supposed to take a swig on arrival and return to it periodically until before the evening was out there were fights and screams and a general drunken reeling. "When not twelve years old, I saw much at which my taste and moral sense revolted, and father and mother strengthened me in the aversion. On a calm survey in retrospect of the whole community, I am compelled to say that in purity and refinement it did not rank very high."

Indeed, Daniel's world was full of terrors. Going on errands was an ordeal unless he had his own dog with him to protect him from the neighboring dogs. The family ram, soon recognizing his timidity, loved to chase him across the pasture. Once when Daniel had the butcher's knife in his hand, he determined to stand his ground, and as the horned head neared with a tattoo of small hoofs, he stabbed the ram to death. When the animal appeared on the table the next day in pot pie, his murderer fled from the room and was ill. To this incident and to the care he lavished on the lambs and calves who slept with the family on cold nights, Drake ascribed the repugnance to meat which remained with him all his life.

The most delightful day of the week was Sunday and the most anticipated event was church, where his joy in society was not ruined by drunkenness. What a pleasure it was to have a clean face and clean feet, to put on a spotless shirt and "boughten" clothes on the Sabbath morning! What a pleasure to walk through cool and quiet woods beside his mother proud in a calico dress, with her black silk bonnet covering a newly ironed silk cap, the tabs tied beneath her chin with pieces of narrow ribbon! How nice as you moved under a rustling of leaves to meet other families, also bravely attired, and to gossip gently along until you reached the village temple, where horses were already hitched to the fence and more riders were arriving, their faces agleam with soap! What a chattering there was as the neighbors gathered in the enclosure or strolled among the graves, while squads of boys lay on the outskirts, swapping knives and teasing the girls who were bright in new ribbons! Deacon Morris was mighty in the pulpit, pounding out the truths of God, and the hymns were strong as sunlight in your throat. Then the service was over and there was more long gossiping while those who had come from far ate their lunches on the grass among the graves. How impressively all this contrasted with the revolting scenes of Saturday's sin!

Young Daniel was not unhappy. He wished he were less timid; he hated to grind corn with the hand mortar; he would have liked more time for school; but he felt none of the divine discontent we associate with the obscure childhoods of great men. Unlike city urchins who are continually confronted with people more fortunate than they, Daniel lived in a society so young it had not evolved into classes; although some of his neighbors exceeded him in prosperity, they all lived by the same menial tasks. Since he knew no other way of life, he accepted his hardships as inevitable and found pleasure in them. Isaac Drake, however, had lived in New Jersey; conscious that he was poor and underprivileged, he could not forget Dr. Goforth's promise. Had not the dream that his son would be a doctor and a gentleman comforted him through many years of toil and despair? When Daniel's older cousin studied with Dr. Goforth at Washington, Kentucky, it was agreed for economy's sake that Daniel should become the cousin's apprentice, but the cousin died before finishing his course and the old plan was revived.

Daniel was terrified by his father's scheme of sending him to study with Dr. Goforth, who was now in Cincinnati. When he had looked through his cousin's medical books, he had been unable to understand a word; obviously he was not clever enough or well enough educated to be a doctor. The world outside his father's cabin had always frightened him, and he had never spent more than a night away from home; now it was suggested he should go miles away to learn an impossibly difficult science among strangers. And how could he ever hold his head up among those majestic persons his father referred to as "gentlemen"? Pleading in an agony of fear, he pointed out that his family could not afford to dispense with his services or pay Dr. Goforth four hundred dollars. It would be much more sensible, he insisted, to apprentice him to Mr. Stout, a saddler with whom several of his cornfield associates had already studied. Isaac Drake, however, was not to be turned from his romantic dream; he arranged with the local teacher for Daniel to receive a few months of intensive schooling. But the corn had to be hoed, and seeding time required the wheatfield to be harrowed after the sower; Daniel rose before dawn and worked on the farm till breakfast, then ran the two miles to school, where the puzzled preceptor did his best by making him memorize the hard words in Webster and read in Scott's *Lessons*. Even this inadequate preparation did not last long, for three of the children came down with ague and fever, and a horse kicked Isaac Drake in the instep. Leaving the schoolhouse behind him forever, Daniel undertook all the labor on the farm.

That fall Isaac rode to Cincinnati, his foot still hanging pain-fully beside the stirrup, and completed his negotiations with Dr. Goforth. The whole family set to work on Daniel's outfit; they made him shirts from bought muslin and even some pocket handkerchiefs. On the morning of December 16, 1800, Isaac and his fifteen-year-old son set out on horseback. Daniel wept unashamedly to see the log cabin that had been his life disappear in the forest. Two days later they arrived at Cincinnati, a terrifying metropolis of a few hundred houses. Daniel pleaded with his father not to desert him there, but in vain. The farmer returned to the drudgery of the wilderness, leaving behind him the frightened boy whose feet he had placed on the path to fame.

2

DANIEL DRAKE was the first medical student in Cincinnati. The city was still an Indian mound in the wilderness when, about twelve years before, Israel Ludlow and his companions escaped the floating ice of the Ohio and reared half-faced camps on what is now called the quay. "Setting their watchmen round," Drake wrote, "they lay down with their feet to the blazing fires, and fell asleep under the music of the north wind whistling among the frozen limbs of the great sycamores and water maples which overhung them. The next morning they rose and began the survey of the town, and the lines were marked by blazes on the trees among which they passed."

As Fort Washington, Cincinnati became the headquarters of the armies that fought the Indians under Harmar, St. Clair, and Wayne. It remained little more than a military outpost until the peace of 1795 made it safe for settlers, and long after Drake came there the army dominated the society of this little village, whose richest inhabitants alone could afford frame houses rather than log cabins. Commerce and manufactures were, of course, unknown, and the rare mails were brought by pony express through the forest.

Daniel's new environment was really not so different from his old, yet its exterior aspects were terrifying. The uniformed army officers with their crisp manners were new to him, and Dr. Goforth, although only thirty-four, seemed at first the most frightening person he had ever known. Daniel's preceptor never left the house until his hair had been powdered by the itinerant barber and his gold-headed cane had been grasped by his gloved hands. His long face with its huge nose, popping eyes, and small firm mouth was usually clothed in dignity, but at any moment dignity might be cast aside in one of the gushing enthusiasms that were natural to him. Never had Daniel seen such elaborate courtesy as Dr. Goforth practiced towards even his poorest patients, but in a few days Daniel realized that his preceptor's intricate manners were a kind of play-acting; Dr. Goforth enjoyed them as much as the poor devil who was delighted to be bowed to by so fine-looking a gentleman. Indeed, the physician carried under his lace ruffles a heart as childish as Daniel's own. Dr. Goforth walked the world with a boy's delight; he was thrilled by flowers and Indian arrowheads and strange bones picked up in the wilderness. Soon he and his pupil shared their enthusiasms as if they were of the same age.

Nor did Daniel find medicine an impossibly difficult science. His first task, grinding mercury into mercury ointment, hardly differed from grinding corn in the hand mill, and memorizing Quincy's *Dispensatory* was only one step beyond memorizing the hard words in Webster. Had the fifteen-year-old boy been sent with his woefully insufficient preparation to a modern medical school he would have gone under in a week, but the things Dr. Goforth taught were not beyond his powers. For the most part his work consisted of putting up medicines and delivering them. When he accompanied Dr. Goforth on his rounds, he merely had to stand back and notice what the great man did. He studied Cheselden on bones without specimens, and Innes on the muscles without plates; if any hard words stumped him, the kind doctor was eager to translate; for the rest, he was not supposed to think, only to memorize. Then, without any knowledge of chemistry, physiology, or materia medica, he meandered through the humoral pathology of Boerhaave and Van Swieten, books full of exciting speculations and quaint reasoning it was hard to forget.

And what natural boy would not have enjoyed messing round in Dr. Goforth's apothecary shop? The most exciting smells rose, like incense to the god of physic, from brown paper bundles, bottles stopped with worm-eaten corks, and open jars of ointment. You mixed the delightful ingredients together with a metal instrument to make powders that you delivered to the sick, running full tilt down the streets of the little town, splashing through puddles rather than going round them because you had to be quick, like the pony express. And when you knocked on the door of some cabin, with what joy you were greeted by the anxious wife or mother, how eagerly the powder you had prepared was received by frightened hands!

Life at Dr. Goforth's was never dull, for the good doctor kept his imagination in a state of high and pleasurable excitement. Certain that there was gold in the woods behind Cincinnati, he financed adepts with the divining-rod and was particularly fond of a man named Hall who had a glass by which he could see a thousand feet into the earth. There were scenes of great rejoicing when the tattered ne'er-do-wells brought iron pyrites in a sack and proudly dumped the gleaming nuggets on the table. Nothing was too good for these adventurers while the worthless stuff was being analyzed by some silversmith; they lived in Goforth's house on the best food and wine. And when the sad report came in, the doctor was not discouraged, he had so many other marvelous schemes for making money. Someone convinced him that a valuable herb, East Indian columbo root, grew in the woods; Goforth enjoyed many dreams of wealth and laid out a goodly sum before he discovered the root was something else entirely.

For all his foibles, Goforth was an excellent physician. He had been well educated in New York before he began his migrations about the frontier, and he was the pioneer of vaccination in the West. A year after Dr. Waterhouse received the cow-pox serum from England, Goforth procured some which he immediately tried on his apprentice, Daniel Drake, who was thus the first person to be vaccinated beyond the Alleghenies.

Lying behind the greasy counter of the apothecary shop where he always slept, Drake hugged himself with excitement. He felt guilty sometimes to think of his family slaving away in the log cabin he had left so unwillingly a year before. Then he rose, lit the candle, and wrote long letters home. He explained that, although Cincinnati was dominated by officers who gambled and drank, he had not deserted his childhood principles. "Since I have lived here, I defy the town to impeach me with one action derogatory to my honor or reputation."

As a member of Dr. Goforth's household, Drake moved in the best society Cincinnati had to offer. While this was a joy, it was an embarrassment too; he was continually conscious of the inadequacy of his clothes, his education, his breeding. He struggled at improvement, and as he saw the gap between himself and his most cultured contemporaries close, his manner became self-confident; but deep down the old lack of sureness remained to plague him through all his years.

Meanwhile he was learning medicine so rapidly that his preceptor was amazed. He overcame obstacles with an ease and joy no well-stocked mind could know, for he found knowledge a series of revelations that opened up the world. Although Dr. Goforth considered himself a follower of John Brown's theories, in treating patients he followed his own common sense more than any textbook. Using purges even less than did Brown and relying greatly on stimulants, he naturally disapproved of Rush's depleting methods. Yet when Drake got his hands on one of Rush's books and became a follower, Dr. Goforth did not mind. Perhaps he thought it a good idea for doctors who practiced together to understand different systems; in any case, he made Drake his partner four years after the young man had emerged from the wilderness. At the age of nineteen, Daniel Drake, who had never witnessed a chemical experiment or the dissection of a human body, became Dr. Drake, and shared the leading practice in Cincinnati.

The leading practice in Cincinnati, however, was arduous and not very lucrative. Drake often rode thirty miles over wilderness trails to isolated cabins, carrying in his saddle bags a few instruments and some stock remedies: Glauber's salts, Dover's powder, strong paregorics, vermifuges, blisters, Peruvian bark for fevers, dragon's blood, gamboge, and nux vomica. The ordinary charge was twenty-five cents a mile, one-half being deducted if the horse was fed. Drake was a dentist as well; he asked a quarter for pulling a tooth, with an understood reduction if two or more were pulled at one time. In plugging teeth, tinfoil was used instead of gold leaf, and it had the advantage of showing less conspicuously. Most doses of medicine cost a quarter, although an ounce of the best Peruvian bark brought the princely sum of a dollar, the same sum as the doctor got if he sat up all night with his patient.

The two physicians were lucky if they collected a fourth of the two to six dollars a day they entered in their books; although a doctor at last, Drake still lacked money for necessities. He wrote his father that Dr. Goforth trusted everyone, as usual. "I have not had three dollars in money since I came down, but I hope it will be different with me after a while. An execution against the doctor for the medicine he got three years since was issued a few days ago, and must be levied and returned before the next general court which commences the first of September. This execution has thrown us all topsy-turvy. . . . I am heartily sick and tired of living in the midst of so much difficulty and embarrassment, and almost wish sometimes I had never engaged in practice with him, for his medicine is so nearly gone that we can scarcely make out to practice, even by buying all we are able to buy. In addition to this, it gives me great unhappiness to see him in such deplorable situation. I get but little time to study nowadays, for I have to act the part of both physician and student, and likewise assist him every day in settling his accounts."

Dr. Goforth tried to recoup his fortunes by wild speculations.

At great expense he exhumed from the sand of Big Bone Lick one of the largest collections of prehistoric fossil bones that had ever been found in America. These gigantic remnants now filled his attic; when the world seemed nothing but a vast caldron of creditors, the two doctors, Drake and his preceptor, fled to this sanctuary and, excitedly fingering vast jaw-bones and ribs like the ribs of a ship, speculated on the nature of the animals to whom they had belonged and dreamt of the huge fortune their sale would bring when they found money to ship them east.

A few years later a handsome and prolix Englishman who called himself d'Arville appeared in Cincinnati on what he announced was a scientific tour of the country to find fossils for exhibition in England. He won Dr. Goforth's heart at once by deducing from an Oriental-looking scrawl on an Indian mound that North America must formerly have been joined with China. Dr. Goforth acted as his guide over that part of Kentucky, filled his mind with stories of Indian teeth four times natural size dug up in Cincinnati, and finally intrusted the fossils to him. How was the physician to know that d'Arville, whose real name was Thomas Ashe, had been disinherited because of dissipation and forced to flee England because of fraud? Ashe was a plausible man; he so dazzled Thomas Jefferson that the President made him editor of the *National Intelligence*. Driven from this job too, Ashe became the father of all English lecturers who tell Americans what is wrong with them. Later, as was proper, he wrote a book for the English trade libeling the United States; he insisted that Kentucky had reached its maximum development, for it was too unhealthy to support the white race. The inhabitants of Lexington, he said, "show demonstrations of civilization, but at particular times, on Sundays and market days, they give a loose to their dispositions and exhibit many traits that should exclusively belong to untutored savages. Their churches have never been finished, and they have all the glass struck out by boys in the day, and the insides torn up by rogues and prostitutes who frequent them by night."

When Ashe got back to Liverpool with the bones he had collected, he was unable to pay the customs duties and was forced to sell them to a local museum; naturally he sent none of the money back to America. The catalogue he wrote for the Liverpool Museum gives us an idea of the speculations with which he delighted Dr. Goforth. He postulated the prehistoric existence of a gigantic lion, the megalonyx, sixty feet long and twenty-five feet tall. The ribs of this remarkable animal were constructed to shut up like an accordion; it could make itself small while waiting for its prey, and when it leapt it opened up like a jack-in-the-box to spring a prodigious distance. Ashe had two hypotheses to explain how so mighty a beast could become extinct. The megalonyx may have been killed off by the race of giants mentioned in the Bible, or God, remembering that He had promised Adam ascendancy over all the beasts of the field, may have struck down with thunderbolts the impious monsters who dared be more powerful than His darlings. Of course, there was a third possibility so awful that even Ashe trembled to suggest it; the megalonyx might not be extinct at all but was still roaming the unexplored West of North America.

It is extremely unlikely that Drake did more than listen to these theories with a tolerant smile; he was not given to theorizing. Conscious of his ignorance, he devoured all the books he could secure. In 1805 he borrowed enough money from his father to study in Philadelphia under his idol, Benjamin Rush. Before Drake left, Dr. Goforth gave him a diploma written out in his own hand and signed with the grandiose title, "Surgeon General, 1st Division, Ohio Militia." This was the first medical degree ever given in the West.

Drake was hampered in Philadelphia by lack of funds. After he had paid his tuition and board in advance, he had only a penny left. Living in a boarding house where he shared a room with a stranger, he studied till midnight and rose before dawn. Although he managed to get to the theater twice, his principal amusement was visiting churches of different denominations, where he watched with amazement the strange ritual of the Catholics and the silent worship of the Quakers. Since he did not have enough money to join the hospital library, he had to borrow textbooks at off hours. His funds gave out at the end of the first session, and, leaving without a degree, he started practice in Mayslick, his father's village.

In the meantime, Dr. Goforth had become so dazzled by the fine manners of some aristocratic French émigrés who had turned up at Cincinnati that after the Louisiana Purchase he decided to steep himself in this polite atmosphere by living among the French for the rest of his life. He floated in a flatboat to the bayous of the lower Mississippi, where he became a parish judge and a representative to the Louisiana constitutional convention. Although he soon found the manners of the Creoles not so fine as he had expected and wrote that New Orleans was "a hell on earth," he stayed for eleven years. During 1816 he made the arduous eight months' journey up the river to Cincinnati, where he died within a year.

When Goforth left for Louisiana, Drake took over his Cincinnati practice. At the age of twenty-two he married Harriet Sisson, the twenty-year-old poor relation of Colonel Jared Mansfield, who was surveyor general of the United States for the Northwest Territory. "Our courtship was not coy nor formal nor protracted," he wrote. "We conversed on the objections which each might find in the other and, while contemplating the obstacles to our union, our spirits imperceptibly commingled into one. . . . In person she was of middle stature or rather less, with a comely though not beautiful form, but erect, elastic, dignified; in countenance animated, forceful, expressive, free from affected looks and gestures, inclined to an aspect of honest and native pride. The great charm of her presence was simplicity. Her manner and appearance exhibited not less naïveté than her conversation. This was always marked with good sense and good feeling. Her opportunities for acquiring knowledge, particularly scholastic learning, had been limited, but her observation of those about her and of society was acute and discriminating. She saw with accuracy and judged with correctness. She expressed herself with that modesty which pervaded all her actions. In mixed circles she was silent."

The match proved to be a perfect one. Mrs. Drake, who had been humiliated by her dependency on the rich surveyor general, was just as eager for self-improvement as her husband. They spent their evenings sitting side by side, she reading literature, he science; whenever either found a striking passage, it was read aloud. Mrs. Drake accompanied her husband on his professional calls, and while the gig bumped over the rutted streets they discussed their ambitions, their friends, and later their children. When asked where was her home, Mrs. Drake playfully replied: "In the gig."

They always went out into the world together. "I had no separate social or sensual gratifications, no tavern orgies, no political club recreations, no dissipated pleasures nor companions. Society was no society to me without her presence and co-operation." What a comfort it was when he consorted with those who had been born gentlemen, to have by his side his attractive, competent, and loving helpmate. Soon the Drakes became leaders in a group of intellectual settlers who, although far from all the material means of learning, were well informed and eager for knowledge. During 1813 they organized a School of Literature and Arts which met to discuss original papers on such varied subjects as education, astronomy, chemistry, psychology, rural economy, and verse. Already they felt a grandiose desire to make their frontier outpost one of the intellectual centers of the world.

When Drake had come almost illiterate out of the wilderness, Cincinnati was a village. As he grew in mental stature, the town grew with him, doubling its population every few years until by 1810 it had 2320 inhabitants. Drake loved Cincinnati like a brother; he determined to write a learned hymn in his city's praise. Fighting ignorance at every step, for seven years he collected scientific data on every aspect of Miami County. He opened the Indian mounds on which the city had been built and exhumed rude sculptures of birds and fishes as well as some human bones which, comparison showed, differed little from those of living Indians. With the textbooks of these multifarious sciences beside him, he defined the physical topography, the geology, the botany, the meteorology, the political institutions, and the diseases of the new corner of the world which he was already beginning to regard as his own. Greatly interested in Cincinnati's material prosperity since he wanted the city to be a center of arts and sciences, Drake outlined a system of canals for the Middle West which was so practical that several were begun before the railroads put a stop to canal building. Again and again he jubilantly prophesied that Cincinnati would expand into one of the world's largest cities, the center of manufacture and commerce for the Middle West. Perhaps the "booster" spirit so repellent to the Old World, so typical of

America, is grounded on the intense personal identification with a community that is possible only to pioneers who themselves have changed forests into villages, villages into cities.

His book was a prodigious labor. Whenever he could spare a moment from his practice, he struggled over it, finding no time for amusements and little for sleep. Many a night he sat beside his wife till past midnight, rocking an infant with one hand while with the other he wrote by the light of a dipped candle. Although he completed his studies in 1810, he was too conscious of his limitations to publish them to the world; he brought out a privately printed pamphlet which he blushingly showed to his friends. After they had encouraged him to venture a public edition, he spent five more years checking every fact and adding others. In 1815 his *Picture of Cincinnati,* a volume of 250 pages, was introduced to the public by a modest preface in which the author apologized for his rough, untutored style. When, however, the book was enthusiastically received, his modesty dropped from him; he scattered copies far and wide with the pleasure of a small boy who has succeeded in doing what he feared was beyond his powers. In addition to giving Drake a national reputation, his *Picture of Cincinnati* acted like a real-estate prospectus, bringing thousands of new settlers.

Drake's famous battle with Dr. King showed that for all his hard work he had not lost the exuberance of youth. One winter, the following advertisement appeared in the newspapers: "Humble ones, my mission calls me among you. The Great Book, on being opened, announces my coming. Your pains, sufferings, and sorrows shall cease. Dr. King can look back through a vista of 3000 years and trace his descent from a continued line of great physicians. Wherever he has been, the blind have been restored to sight, the lame walked, the heartbroken made happy. . . . Dr. King cannot attend to any calls after

sundown as he is then engaged until morning dawn in consulting the stars and planets as to the proper treatment of his patients on the following day."

The great astrologer, who wore a turban and pretended to
be a native of India, so easily over-awed the pioneer population
that his success went to his head and he challenged the regular
doctors to a public debate. Drake immediately accepted.
Clothed in Oriental majesty, Dr. King spoke first in an absurd
gibberish which he insisted was the language of Farther India.
Since Drake was so wise, perhaps he would translate this
learned speech for the crowd. The young doctor, who had
guessed what his opponent would do, immediately introduced
one of his friends, whom he had dressed up in all the outland-
ish remnants of costume he could find in a dozen households.
Fedora, he said, was a native of Farther India; he would address the astrologer in his own language. When Fedora began
to bark and howl in a ridiculous manner, Dr. King could think
of nothing to do but keep up his pretense by barking and howl-
ing in reply. The two debaters screamed gibberish at each other,
and the crowd, who recognized Fedora as a local prankster,
rolled on the ground with mirth. After they had got enough
strength back, they made the unfortunate King admit that he
had recently graduated himself from tending a loom in a
Philadelphia woolen mill. Then they ran him out of town.

Although Drake was now recognized as one of the leading
doctors of the West, he was still conscious of his inadequate
education. In 1815 he made another pilgrimage to Philadelphia, where he finally got his medical degree. Since his
Picture of Cincinnati had carried his fame before him, he was
invited to meetings of the American Philosophical Society and
to the houses of its most distinguished members. This time,
however, he was not dazzled; he compared the intellectual

capital of the United States unfavorably with his wonder-child, the West. "I do not find in this great metropolis such an active literary zeal as I expected to meet with, and, having been very generally introduced to the savants, I must acknowledge myself somewhat disappointed."

While Drake was at Philadelphia, the first medical school west of the Alleghenies was organized at Transylvania University. The existence of a progressive center of learning in the frontier village of Lexington, Kentucky, is an amazing incident in American history, and when Transylvania decided to give the doctors of the region formal scientific training, the importance of the development could not have been overemphasized. Drake, as we have seen, despite his ambition and his unusually lucrative practice, was forced to wait more than ‑en years before he could afford to complete his medical course in the East. Naturally the vast majority of the frontier physicians had neither the means nor the ambition to leave their patients and take the several weeks' ride to Philadelphia, where they would have to remain for two expensive seasons in order to get a degree. Thus conditions beyond the Alleghenies were similar to those in the Colonies before John Morgan returned from England. For the most part doctors trained each other, handing down practical remedies from which the scientific background gradually sloughed away until nothing was left but a series of panaceas learned and passed on by rote. Of course a few doctors who had been trained in medical schools migrated from the East, but they were usually the unsuccessful ones. If the West was ever to be made healthy for large urban populations, it would have to begin training its own doctors in its own schools, and the medical department of Transylvania University was the first step in this direction.

When Drake was offered a professorship in the new school,

he was delirious with delight. A few years before he had emerged from the wilderness able to do little more than spell and cipher; professors had seemed God's elect, the hem of whose garments he was unworthy to touch. "I am now going to astonish you," he wrote a friend, "so cling hold of every support within your reach. *I am a professor!* Yes, incredible as it may appear to you and my other intimate friends, *I* am really and bona fide appointed a professor, and I repeat it on this side of the sheet to save you the trouble of turning back to see whether your eyes did not deceive you. I am, let me repeat, unquestionably a professor." Then he had a sobering thought. "But you must not suppose by this I am a great man. For a professorship to confer greatness it must be a professorship in a great institution. But this does not happen to be the case in this instance. In Lexington there has been for many years an incorporated seminary styled Transylvania University. It has ample endowments but very little celebrity. The trustees are, however, engaged in the erection of a large and elegant college edifice, and have established a faculty of medicine as well as a faculty of the arts. The professorship of materia medica and botany is the one they have offered to me, and five days ago I signified my acceptance. I am not, however, about to move thither, but calculate to be suffered to spend my winters there and the rest of the year in this place. . . . If the trustees should be displeased with my residing here, I shall resign, as I have no wish to exchange Cincinnati for Lexington."

Of course Drake could not bear to leave the city which he was certain would become the leading metropolis beyond the Alleghenies, nor did he believe that the great school which was destined to elevate the Western medical profession could be situated anywhere but in Cincinnati. What a marvelous achievement it would be to inaugurate and direct that school! During exalted moments, Drake wondered if he were the man for this glorious fate. It seemed impossible that one so humbly born and badly educated should make so important a contribution, but the impossible had happened to him many times; he had become a doctor at nineteen; his book had made him the outstanding doctor in his city; he was a professor. The destiny which had carried him so far might lift him to any height. For all his modesty, he could not put behind him the dream of founding the great medical school of the West. He would wait to see if he made a successful teacher, but in the meantime there was no harm in offering to instruct a few students during the summer months that he would be in Cincinnati. Drake published a card in the *Western Spy* announcing that he had taken Dr. Coleman Rogers into partnership and that the two physicians would receive any number of apprentices who might apply. It was a humble beginning, but perhaps it would lead to great things.

3

DRAKE'S desire for intellectual fame had become a monomania with him. Unable to forget the inferiority he had felt when he first met men better educated than he, he toiled at his books every moment he could spare from his extended practice; he could find no time for recreation or exercise. But when his labor seemed about to be crowned with a professorship at last, he was overcome with acute dyspepsia, a nervous illness caused by overwork. Violent dread of impossible happenings kept his mind in a continual state of horror while his body wasted away. His nerves became so tense that the slightest sound was agony; he could hardly get on with anyone, even the wife he adored. Although for a time he considered giving up his profession, a routine of exercise and no study restored him to a point where he could appear at Transylvania on schedule. However, his unhealthy nerves remained with him for the rest of his life; there is no telling how much they contributed to his subsequent difficulties and failures.

Drake soon discovered that he was a successful lecturer. His appearance was enough in itself to impress his students. He was nearly six feet tall, with a fine, expansive forehead, jutting nose, and deep-set eyes of vivid blue. His broad shoulders and powerful walk told of his youth as a backwoodsman, and his face had a rugged gravity in repose, but when he gave way to one of his recurrent enthusiasms it came alive with poetic fire. The intensity that was his outstanding trait showed in every line of his face and body. Speaking always extemporaneously, he expounded medical truths with the fervor of an evangelist. The great Dr. Gross describes Drake's oratory with typical hyperbole: "His words dropped hot and burning from his lips as the lava falls from the burning crater, enkindling the fire of enthusiasm in his pupils and carrying them away in total for-getfulness of everything save the all-absorbing topic under dis-cussion. . . . His gestures, never graceful and sometimes eminently awkward, the peculiar incurvation of his body, nay the very drawl in which he frequently gave expression to his ideas, all denoted the burning fire within, and served to impart force and vigor to everything which he uttered from the ros-trum. Of all the medical teachers whom I have ever heard, he was the most forceful and eloquent. His voice was remarkably clear and distinct, and so powerful that when the windows of his lecture-room were open it could be heard a great distance."

Certain by March that he was capable of founding a great medical college in Cincinnati, Drake presented his resignation from Transylvania. With his habitual inability to keep a tactful silence, he let it be known that he considered Lexington a town of inferior prospects and that he intended to found a rival school which would put Transylvania in the shade. Naturally Dr. Benjamin Dudley, the head of the faculty, was furious. His smoldering resentment flamed up over the body of an Irishman who had been killed in a drunken brawl.

Deprived of legal means for obtaining corpses, a group of students crept into the cemetery the night after the Irishman was buried and dug him up again. They were making their escape when a posse of armed citizens charged up the hillside. After a brisk encounter, the medical students were captured and led to court. A clever lawyer, however, quoted the Scriptural passage that from dust we came and to dust shall return with such telling effect that the judge let the students keep the body on payment of one cent damages for the amount of dust they had stolen.

Although the Irishman was dead, his pugnacious qualities lived after him. No sooner was his cadaver in the medical school than Drake and Dudley each insisted he had the right to make the dissection. The argument quickly became so bitter that they published pamphlets attacking each other, and finally Dudley challenged his rival to a duel. Drake refused to fight, saying duels were not Christian, but one of his partisans, Dr. William H. Richardson, accepted in his place. During the first exchange of shots, Richardson was seriously wounded in the groin. Dudley thereupon politely asked permission of his dying adversary to stop the hemorrhage. Permission being granted, he did so by pressing over the ilium, and then applied a ligature with such success that he and Richardson became life-long friends.

At the end of the session Drake returned to Cincinnati, which was gathering strength for its great expansion. Where of late on the river front there had been only the shouts of men and the noiseless movement of barges, escaping steam ripped the air, and in the dockyards there was a continuous sound of hammering. The days of the river steamboats were at hand; two had been built in Cincinnati during the last eight months and seven more were on the stocks. Soon the Ohio and Mississippi were to become populous highways northward from the Gulf; forests were to vanish before the magic sound of paddle-wheels, and prairies were to blossom with cities as naturally as they had once blossomed with flowers.

Drake delighted in these changes. A popular Fourth of July orator, he loved to tell churning crowds that until the Ohio Valley was discovered, "slow indeed had been the progress of society in the New World. With the exception of the Revolution," he would shout, "little had been achieved and little was in progress. But since that era society has been progressive, higher destinies have unfolded, and a reactive Buckeye influence, perceptible to all beholders, must continue to elevate our beloved country among the nations of the earth." When the crowd echoed his emotion in a roar of approval, a tremendous exultation swept through his long frame. He and the West were one; these people were his people; they were all marching together to a destiny so glorious it was dazzling to look upon. Once he went so far as to argue that no one but a citizen of the Ohio Valley could be a good President of the United States.

Trying to help on the destiny he foresaw, Drake labored to fill Cincinnati with progressive institutions. He was the leading spirit in founding a library, a debating club, a school in which were incorporated the advanced educational fads of his day, and a museum that was to "embrace nearly the whole of those parts of the great circle of knowledge which require material objects, either natural or artificial, for their illustration." He hired an unknown naturalist, John James Audubon, as one of his curators, and by 1822 the museum was the fourth largest in the United States.

Naturally, Drake, the booster, was as interested in a new kind of steamboat as in a new kind of flower; from the first his museum had a department of mechanics. He even went into business himself during the boom that followed the war of 1812, founding a grocery store and a drug store where he installed the first soda fountain in Cincinnati. However, Drake was so impractical that his business ventures always ended disastrously. Forced for a while to live in a log cabin a mile out of town, he humorously named this estate "Mount Poverty." His grocery store was taken over by his father, Isaac Drake, who thus escaped at last from the drudgery of the wilderness.

His other activities did not make Drake forget how sorely the West needed well-trained doctors. He lobbied in the Ohio legislature until it passed an act chartering the Medical College of Ohio and naming as the faculty Drake, his partner Dr. Rogers, Ephraim McDowell's old friend Dr. Samuel Brown, and a chemist, the Rev. Elijah Slack. Drake of course was president. Since he was full of revolutionary ideas for the improvement of medical education, he was determined to have no conservative board of trustees over his head. He induced the legislature to make the faculty self-perpetuating; professors could be hired or fired by a three-fourths vote. A year later he organized the first public hospital in Cincinnati.

Drake demanded unquestioning support for his reforms from the Cincinnati doctors, but to his amazement and outrage a storm arose that delayed the opening of the college. Since most of the local doctors had never been to medical school themselves, they feared that they would either have to study at Drake's institution or be cut out by whipper-snappers who could frame medical degrees for their waiting-rooms. They were afraid that distinguished physicians, brought in from the East to be professors, would take their patients. And they resented the financial advantage the new school would give Drake and his colleagues, for not only would the faculty keep their pupils' fees but, whenever the young graduates were faced with difficult cases, the professors were certain to be called in as consultants.

Absorbed in his idealism, Drake made no effort to circumvent the resentment of the medical profession at his pushing himself forward; indeed, he thought every criticism of his school, however slight, a sin against progress that had to be blasted with the most violent invective. By first starting the school as a personal venture, by having the power in what was supposed to be a State institution placed entirely in the hands of a faculty named in the charter, by renting lecture-rooms over his father's grocery store, he had opened himself wide to the charge that the Ohio College was a personal speculation of his own. Naturally the many enemies of the school insisted that the charter should be revoked, since it was an action by the legislature to increase the prosperity of one man. And it was an essential part of their campaign to prove this man unworthy by blackening his character.

Drake's principal foe was Dr. John Moorhead, a coarse and pugnacious Irishman whom Ephraim McDowell had persuaded to come to America. Drake the quick, the mercurial, was an exact opposite to his pedantic and clumsy adversary. A sentimentalist who was always prone to tears, Drake was repelled by Moorhead's invariable habit of asking, before he treated a patient, who was to pay the bill. While Drake sprang from mood to mood, from ecstasy to despair, Moorhead trod ponderously on in his knee-high buckskin boots, never going fast or slow, always dignified, always self-confident. When Moorhead married some years later, his medical class congratulated him during a lecture hour. "Just as the doctor was taking his seat," wrote an anonymous correspondent to the *Nashville Journal of Medicine and Surgery*, "at a preconcerted signal the whole class arose as one man when our orator, a very tall, gaunt man with enormous porter-house-steak whiskers, as red as blazes, fired away and in hot haste was up among the stars and walking the Milky Way as fearlessly as a conjuror dances on a tightrope. When he was through, we all sat down and so did the doctor, and leisurely taking out his old leather pocket book, he untied the string, took out a sheet, and commenced reading as if nothing in the world had happened." Drake would have been overcome with emotion. Naturally the two men disliked each other from the first.

Moorhead waged the battle to block the opening of the Medical College as a semi-political issue in the lay press. Although his letters were sometimes six columns long, they were read eagerly by the pioneer populace which always enjoyed a good fight. He called Drake "a calumniator," "a domineering coward" who had "a lust for quarreling" and proceeded "after the manner of a common assassin." In his replies, which were shorter and more epigrammatic, Drake gave as good as he got.

Once as Moorhead was waiting on the quay for an incoming boat, Drake happened by. As usual they shouted names at each other, but this time Drake, the pacifist, sprang on his adversary with such vehemence that before the ponderous Irishman could get started his eyes were blacked and his scalp laid open. Moorhead thereupon challenged Drake to fight with pistols and, when Drake refused, publicly announced that he was no gentleman. A few days later the unfortunate Moorhead met Drake's brother on the street and was given another severe drubbing.

While the uproar was at its height, Dr. Samuel Brown was offered a professorship at Transylvania. Since there was no telling when the Ohio College would get started, he resigned from its faculty to accept the new post. Drake could hardly believe that anyone could be so perfidious, and when his own partner, Dr. Rogers, admitted that he had advised Brown to go to Transylvania, Drake felt deserted by the whole world. These men were supposed to be his friends; they were supposed to be infused with his zeal to elevate the Western medical profession, and yet they stabbed him in the back.

His frustrated idealism came to a head in the fury with which he attacked Rogers; he demanded that his partner resign from the Ohio faculty. Naturally Rogers refused. In a few days the two men who had worked intimately together for years became fierce enemies. Drake recruited the Rev. Mr. Slack, the one remaining professor, on his side, but the two together were unable to expel Rogers, for according to the charter they needed a three-fourths vote. By this time Drake's emotions were so far aroused that it was impossible for him to compromise; like his mother, he knew things were right or wrong by definition, and Rogers was wrong. Putting off the opening of the college for a year, he traveled to Columbus, where he induced the legislature to amend the charter so that a professor could be expelled by a two-thirds vote. He and Slack then held a formal meeting and, with much regard for parliamentary procedure, voted Rogers out.

Afraid to trust any more of his friends, Drake secured the services of two Eastern professors, Jesse Smith and Benjamin Bohrer. He did not hesitate to promise them vast practices and tremendous reputations, for he had never lost his faith that, because he was working for the good of Cincinnati, everything was bound to come out right in the end. Often he admonished the citizens, telling them it was their duty to protect his school against every assault. "To suppose less than this would be to impugn the common sense, the feeling, and the liberality of the city." And if this holier-than-thou attitude annoyed the public, he was unconscious of it.

The Medical College of Ohio opened its doors during November 1820. Like all other American schools, it was merely designed to supplement what apprentices learnt from their preceptors. Although the course lasted two sessions, there was no division into grades; the pupils sat through the same curriculum twice over, on the theory that what they did not understand the first time they might understand the second. Sessions at most institutions were limited to three or four months, since many of the students were already practicing and could not afford to desert their patients for a longer time. Drake courageously lengthened each session to five months, but even this period was too short to cover his ambitious curriculum comfortably; the pupils had to work from dawn to midnight, and a professor sometimes lectured three times a day. Undergraduates paid twenty dollars a session to each professor, and three more as a graduation fee. They were expected to assist the faculty in raiding graveyards.

The school started auspiciously with a large enrollment.

However, the cabal that opposed medical education was busy fomenting trouble from the outside, and it was helped in its work of destruction by Drake's own temperament. His hypersensitive consciousness that he lacked early training and his self-made man's disdain for those who, despite their better advantages, were not as learned as he, made him incapable of taking criticism or compromising with ignorance. He demanded unquestioning obedience from the faculty of which he was president, and when he was opposed, the over-stretched nerves that had made him a sick man prompted him to strike out in a blind fury. "To give a full-length portrait of this *gentleman*," he wrote of one of his opponents, "would be a labor similar to that of dragon-making in the romances of the sixteenth century. It would be to combine all that is cunning and contemptible in the moral world. As it relates to his intrigues in the medical college, he is like his household idol, CASH, the root of all evil, like a general infection of the body everywhere present, corrupt and corrupting."

When Drake's new professors, already alienated by his dictatorial attitude, did not receive the vast practices his enthusiasm had painted, they accused him of misrepresentation and even trying to keep patients from them. Soon they made common cause with his enemies outside the school and won Slack over to the opposition. At the end of the second session Dr. Bohrer, unable to stand the backbiting any longer, resigned. Because of the two-thirds rule Drake had secured to expel Dr. Rogers, Smith and Slack, who with Drake now made up the faculty, were a working majority that could do as it pleased. Drake has left an account of their procedure.

"At eight o'clock we met according to a previous adjournment and transacted some financial business. A profound silence ensued, our dim taper shed a blue light over the lurid faces of the plotters, and everything seemed ominous of an approaching revolution. On trying occasions Dr. Smith is said to be subject to a disease not unlike Saint Vitus's dance; and on this he did not wholly escape. Wan and trembling he raised himself (with the exception of his eyes) and in lugubrious accents said: 'Mr. President, in the resolution I am about to offer I am influenced by no *private feelings* but solely by a reference to the public good.' He then read as follows: 'Voted that Daniel Drake, M.D., be dismissed from the Medical College of Ohio.' The portentous silence recurred, and was not interrupted until I reminded the gentlemen of their designs. Mr. Slack, who is blessed with stronger nerves than his master, then rose, and adjusting himself to a firmer balance, put on a proper sanctimony and bewailingly ejaculated: 'I second the motion.' The crisis had now manifestly come, and learning by inquiry that the gentlemen were ready to meet it, I put the question, which carried, in the classical language of Dr. Smith, *'nemo contradicente.'* I could do no more than tender them a vote of thanks, nor less than withdraw, and performing both, the doctor politely lit me downstairs. Dr. Smith immediately elected Mr. Slack registrar, and Mr. Slack in turn elected the doctor president *pro tempore.*"

Drake was no longer a member of the faculty which he had created in the conviction that it would bring both himself and Cincinnati fame. Unable to think of a single move he had made that was not for the good of the city he loved, he was inundated with bitterness. The West had been stupid, perfidious, and ungrateful; he determined to leave the West behind him forever. "Public unconcern in this city," he wrote, "has tolerated the sneers of the most insignificant and encouraged an opposition which in a well-organized society would have been promptly and indignantly subdued." What a fool he had been to think that the future of the country lay in the hands of these ignorant and quarrelsome exiles from a dozen civilizations! In a fury he asked his Philadelphia friends to prepare the way for his removal there.

Although the doctors who were afraid of trained competition consolidated their victory by making the Ohio College so insignificant that two years later it had no pupils to graduate, Drake's labors had not been in vain. He had placed an ideal in the minds of Cincinnati's better citizens that was to bear fruit surely, as all progressive ideals must, and he had trained a handful of young men, one of whom was to take a place beside him in the medical hall of fame. John Lambert Richmond, the pioneer of Cæsarian operations in America, would never have been great had it not been for Drake's Ohio College.

Richmond was born into a family of common laborers on April 5, 1787, near Chesterfield, Massachusetts. During his entire childhood he spent only two weeks in school, yet he acquired a passion for books. From the few pence he made as a farmhand, a woodcutter, and a coal miner, he managed to save enough to buy the primers that he learnt by heart, studying all night by the uneven flaring of pine chips. However, love trapped him into an early marriage, and the inexorable arrival of ten children, one crowding on the heels of another, reduced him to such dire poverty that he was forced to make money at night as well as by day. But even when every hour he could spare from sleep had to be employed in gainful labor, he did not give up studying; his wife sewed Latin and Greek exercises to his sleeves so that he might memorize them while he toiled. Through such desperate expedients he managed by the time he was thirty-five to earn a license as a Baptist minister. He had achieved his great ambition at last, but it made no difference in his worldly state, for no congregation would employ so rudely educated a man. Yet on Sundays he had his reward. On Sundays he put on his best clothes and, forgetting for the moment that he was the poorest of the poor, preached under the heavens to sinners as humble as himself.

At last he followed his destiny westward. After a decrepit farm wagon had carried him to the head of the Allegheny River, he loaded his numerous family and few goods on a raft he built with his own hands. The current bore him swiftly down to Cincinnati, where fate made him janitor to the Medical College of Ohio. Sometimes as the great Professor Drake lectured, he would see the janitor sidle through the door in his greasy clothes and stand there listening with a rapt attention none of the paying pupils could rival. Richmond would linger as long as he dared and, when he turned away at last, he would close the door with the utmost slowness as if trying to catch an extra word. Finally, forgetting his poverty and the needs of his children, he offered Drake half his janitor's pittance as tuition. Although this was much less than the usual fee, Drake remembered his own humble beginnings and agreed. Thus it came about that Richmond studied with the great medical teacher of the West. After his graduation, Richmond moved to Newtown, Ohio, where he added to his slender doctor's fees by preaching.

On the evening of Sunday, April 22, 1827, his church was almost empty, for it was storming. His sermon was interrupted when the door flew open and a drenched colored woman ran down the aisle, screaming hysterically. While his few parishioners stared in excitement, Richmond stepped down from the pulpit and calmed the newcomer until she could tell a coherent story. Her friend, she said, was dying in childbirth; the labor had gone on for hours and the midwives were able to do nothing.

Closing his Bible and picking up his pocket instruments, Richmond followed the messenger. They hurried on foot through the rain and then transferred to a boat, for the Ohio River was in flood and boiled in muddy turbulence around the hill where the patient lay. After a long row through blackness and storm, the skiff grounded in a tangle of bushes. Springing out, they ran up a jagged trail towards a log cabin, from which the wind brought them the sound of groans.

When Richmond threw open the door, he saw a tiny room lacking chimney or floor and in one corner a cot on which a huge colored woman lay uncovered, writhing in agony. Two trembling black midwives were holding up the blankets which should have been on the bed, pressing them against the log walls so that the wind which howled through the unchinked cracks would not blow out the candle in the dim light of which the whole scene flickered. Richmond hastened to the bedside of the sufferer. "She lay," he wrote later, "by spells comparatively easy; when her pains came on they continued for a short space of time nearly regular or natural, but in twenty or thirty seconds they were transferred to the stomach and immediately terminated in general convulsions which continued from three to five minutes. They were succeeded by alarming fainting which lasted ten to twenty minutes. The system was much exhausted, the pulse depressed, and not the least advantage had resulted from all she had suffered."

Richmond did everything he could think of to bring on the birth of the child. He tried to stimulate her system by giving her laudanum and sulphuric ether; he applied flannel wet with hot spirits to her feet. This mitigated her convulsions a little, but the child showed no signs of coming and the fainting spells grew longer and longer. Every few minutes he felt her pulse to make sure she was not dead. At his wit's end, he would have liked to call in some more experienced doctor, but flood and storm had effectively cut them off from the world. During four hours he paced helplessly up and down by his dying patient.

Although he had never heard of a modern example, Richmond knew that Cæsarian operations had been practiced in antiquity. When this expedient first occurred to him, he drove it out of his mind as impossibly dangerous, but as the hours passed and his patient only seemed more certain to die, his mind became firm with the resolution of despair. "I informed the patient and her friends of the only means by which I could conceive of relief; this was at once consented to as affording some hopes of life. After doing all in my power for her preservation, and feeling myself entirely in the dark as to her situation, and finding whatever was done must be done soon, and feeling a deep and solemn sense of responsibility, with only a case of common pocket instruments, about one o'clock at night I commenced the Cæsarian operation."

An incision revealed a deformity in the woman's pelvis that prevented a natural delivery. Although the baby was in such an unfortunate position that Richmond was forced to sacrifice it in order to save the mother, save the mother he did. The operation had been done without benefit of antiseptics or anæsthetics, yet in twenty-four days the patient was able to return to work, and seven weeks later she was strong enough to walk fourteen miles in one day.

Richmond's account of this case appeared during 1827 in Drake's medical journal. Since it was the first report of a Cæsarian section to be published in the United States, many writers have accorded him priority, although earlier authenticated cases have recently come to light. No one knows who really did the first Cæsarian in America, for not only do temporarily deranged mothers sometimes operate on themselves to stop labor pains, but such operations were part of the medical lore of Africa and there is every reason to believe that the slaves brought the custom over with them.

Richmond's life continued to be a story of heroism. When cholera broke out in Cincinnati, he fearlessly exposed himself to the contagion, coming down with the disease at last. His health permanently impaired, he sought milder climates and practiced whenever he was well enough. Although an invalid most of the time until his death in 1845, he helped found two medical schools: Dennison University in Ohio and Franklin College in Indiana.

4

DESPITE all his fury and heartbreak, Daniel Drake could not bear to leave the West. When he was offered his old professorship at Transylvania, he jumped at the chance, and again he refused to give up his residence in Cincinnati. The Transylvania to which he returned was no longer an obscure institution with "ample endowments but little celebrity." During Drake's short absence its president, Dr. Horace Holley, had by the sheer force of genius raised the frontier seminary into a university of world-wide renown that was earning for Lexington the title of "the Athens of the West." The medical department had grown with such mushroom rapidity that it was second in the United States to the University of Pennsylvania for size and distinction. Yet, despite their fame and prosperity, the professors were continually warring with each other, while the doctors of Lexington had not a good word to say for the institution that was bringing their obscure settlement international fame.

Indeed it would have been practically impossible to find a spot in the whole nation where the doctors were not at each other's throats. The more civilized East was no better than the wild frontier; even the University of Pennsylvania, that father of medical schools, was brawling hysterically with a newcomer in Philadelphia, the Jefferson Medical College. Nor were jealousies between rival faculties required to start the profession quarreling. Dr. Gross thus described his colleagues in a sleepy Pennsylvania town: "The medical profession of Easton at the period in question was in a decidedly mediocre condition, without science, without learning, without progress, and apparently without ambition. Every man seemed to live in and for himself. Hardly any two could be found willing to meet each other in consultation. Jealousy and ill feeling were the order of the day. Each physician had of course his little clique or faction. This poor fellow had this fault, that one that. . . . Very few of them ever read a medical book, and as to social intercourse [within the profession] that was of course wholly out of the question under the circumstances."

In an essay on the subject, Drake argued that the battles which racked his profession were due to rivalry, envy, and controversy over methods of treatment. Since their fees increased with their popularity, doctors tried to climb over each other's heads into public notice, while disagreements between different schools of medical thought—the kind that would today be settled by recourse to test-tube and microscope—immediately descended into personalities because, as Drake realized with amazing level-headedness, few methods of treatment were based on scientific facts that could be demonstrated. Doctors could support their methods only by boasting of their cures; naturally each clique tried to magnify its own and depreciate its opponents' triumphs. This situation, Drake foresaw, would continue until science acquired "fixed principles."

Realizing that medical schools were fought over because of the financial advantages they brought their faculties, Drake pointed out that "if professors withdrew from practice on being appointed they would be viewed with very different feelings," a startling prophecy of the full-time system that has been adopted by the most progressive medical schools within the last few years.

The only way to put an end to strife, Drake believed, was to set up some impartial body, some medical association, that would arbitrate disputes and protect ethical practitioners from quacks. In the absence of such a safeguard, medical feuds, he insisted, were unavoidable and to the public advantage. They originated "in the resistance of the good against the arts and encroachments of the bad," and were "the most efficient means of maintaining the purity of the profession." Indeed, he was unable to see "in what respect they seriously degrade the profession or injure society."

It is against the background of such warfare as Drake knew that we must evaluate modern medical ethics. There has been much criticism of the code which makes doctors, whatever their disagreement, present a united front to the public, and it has often been pointed out that by frowning on publicity the medical associations make it difficult for newspapers to find anyone who will sponsor the truth about public health, but we must remember that the alternative is continual internecine warfare, which makes an ignorant public the judge of matters beyond its comprehension.

Drake's own experience with the quarrels at Transylvania is illuminating. Since this was not the school he had founded, he had no desire to dominate the faculty himself. When his colleagues came to him with grievances much less trivial than his own grievance against Dr. Rogers had been, he listened to them in amazement. Unable to understand how such intelligent professors could become excited about such childish issues, he soothed them down. Soon the man whom Cincinnati regarded as impossibly cantankerous found himself in the position of mediator. By common consent, the different factions elected him dean.

Drake's ambition had been to head the school whose influence would raise the Western medical profession. As dean of the famous Transylvania faculty, he would seem to have achieved this ambition, but his new eminence meant little to him. Although he built up a magnificent consulting practice and his reputation grew to gigantic proportions in the Mississippi Valley, his thoughts continually turned to Cincinnati. He was sick with envy of the obscure doctors who headed the insignificant Medical College of Ohio.

During October 1825 his wife became seriously ill with "autumnal intermittent fever." Having prescribed quinine and calomel, Drake was haunted by the fear that the drugs he gave her were adulterated. With tears in his eyes, he begged the astonished apothecaries to give him the really pure articles, and he sat up late into the night making analysis. When her condition grew steadily worse, he rushed to the homes of his colleagues, importuning them two or three times a day to come quickly and do something, anything; his Harriet was dying.

After several nightmarish weeks, Mrs. Drake passed away.

"Wherefore," Drake wrote, "should I record that which now occupies my mind, seeing that she to whose scrutiny and approbation all my thoughts were exhibited is no more? For years the repository of whatever arose in my soul, the partner of every emotion, she is now withdrawn behind the curtain of death, leaving me at once rent asunder with feelings of grief and destitute of those sympathies which alone could afford consolation.

"What is the relation in which we now stand?" he asked himself. "Does her disembodied spirit take cognizance of me and mine? . . . Could I believe her still within my sphere, a witness of my actions, a listener to my expressions, frowning upon that which should be condemned and deriving satisfaction from that which on earth gave her joy in my conduct and conversation, I should at once be reconciled to her personal absence."

But the house was empty and silent; he could not believe that she was still by his side. He could only remember over and over again the immensity of his loss. "For eighteen years and more we have been coalescing in spirit. . . . Our hearts had become conjoined. They were conjoined on principles of equality. The relation of superior and inferior came not into the union. It excluded, it abhorred all despotism and servility. . . . It was deep and durable as life itself, but alas! how short is life."

Thus he wrote several hundred pages through the long night when his solitude had become unbearable, trying as his pen scratched over the paper to evoke even for a moment a sense that she was near. Indeed, he made a private religion out of the worship of his dead wife. The idea of remarriage remained abhorrent to him, and for several decades he wore on his arm a black band of mourning. Always he set aside the anniversary of her death for solitude, fasting, and meditation; always on that tragic day he wrote a poem in her honor.

Harriet Drake was, of course, buried in Cincinnati. At the end of that session, Drake resigned from Transylvania, where he had been three years. Leaving behind the glory of heading a great school and the prosperity of a vast consulting practice, he took his three young children to the city he loved with almost childish constancy; he would be less lonely there. For a while he languished in a lethargy, but then he noticed that the graveyard where his Harriet lay was in bad condition. He organized a movement to repair the fences and plant trees, and before he knew it he was back in the active life he enjoyed. He founded the Cincinnati Eye Infirmary and took over a newly founded journal which he soon put on its feet.

The *Western Journal of Medical and Physical Sciences* was the first medical periodical to become established beyond the Alleghenies. Until Drake recognized their plight, the Western doctors had no way of keeping up to date, since the Eastern journals were too erudite for their comprehension. Casting aside the temptation to strive for scientific eminence, Drake concentrated on educating his backward colleagues. His title page bore the motto, "A messenger to and from the woods." Naturally his journal circulated only on the frontier, but in that huge region it was the oracle which every doctor consulted. Traveling in the packs of the pony express, carried on snow-shoes to the far north, the *Western Journal* was read in log cabins while wolves or coyotes howled outside. Often the uneven glow of a campfire flickered across its pages. And the moccasined doctors of the wilderness, who had never seen a medical school or read a text not fifty years behind the times, stared at Drake's journal with amazement that so much was known of which they had never dreamed. Backwoodsmen whose arrow wounds had festered or who were stricken with mysterious fevers, pioneer housewives writhing in abnormal pregnancy, all these had cause to bless Daniel Drake that their physicians could consult the dog-eared pages of the *Western Journal* and apply the newest scientific technique there in the shadow of the pre-Adamite forest.

Drake wrote most of the magazine himself. From his articles on the treatment of disease we find that, as he grew more experienced, he reacted against the violent therapy of Rush and became a champion of moderate dosage. Himself a hypochondriac, he was better able than most of his contemporaries to point out the relation between states of mind and of the body. Although during his many years as editor he wrote on almost every disease that prevailed in the wilderness, he did not emulate Rush and the other great teachers of his period by formulating a philosophical system which attempted to explain all illness through the logical extension of one set of principles. Undoubtedly this was a great boon to the Mississippi Valley, as it enabled his journal to educate the doctors in the best that was taught by all schools of medical thinking.

Drake's position as editor further increased his reputation in the West. Laymen as well as physicians brought their difficult problems to him; once an obscure lawyer, Abraham Lincoln, wrote asking what to do about fits of melancholia. "I cannot prescribe in your case without a personal interview," Drake replied.

The Ohio College, which had taken Moorhead into the faculty, had remained an insignificant school without scientific standing. Still certain he could lift it to its rightful position as leader of the West, Drake returned to his old pugnaciousness; he intrigued continually to force a reorganization that would put him in the saddle. Naturally, the faculty had difficulty in distinguishing him from the devil.

At the beginning of every session all the professors sat around a large table while the students made the circuit handing each one individually his fee. One year Moorhead received six hundred dollars. He tied the mass of silver coins up in a bandanna handkerchief and, very pleased with himself, set out for the bank. On the way he came face to face with Drake, who stopped him and shouted that he was a thief extorting money under false pretenses, since he was incapable of teaching anyone medicine. In fact, he was a murderer; his pupils would certainly kill all their patients. The Irishman's square-jowled face darkened with the slow anger of a bull, and then suddenly he saw red. Whipping the heavy bundle of coins back over his shoulder, he brought it down on Drake's head with all the force he could command. Drake fell as if shot, and Moorhead walked ponderously on, leaving the West's greatest physician lying unconscious in the street.

When Drake's attempts to disrupt the Ohio faculty got nowhere, he changed his tactics and organized a rival school under the ægis of Miami University. A year's appointment as professor at Jefferson Medical College in Philadelphia enabled him to recruit so distinguished an Eastern faculty that the Ohio trustees realized their school would never be able to compete. After their attempt to have the legislature declare the new school illegal had failed, they were forced to beg Drake to combine the faculties under the name of the Ohio College. Drake had the pleasure of dictating the dismissal of his two old enemies Smith and Slack. When he could not make the trustees oust Moorhead as well, he threatened to cancel the merger, but his new professors had become weary of intrigue; they forced his hand. Much to his surprise he found himself sitting on the same faculty as his arch-enemy. Since Moorhead had the chair of theory and practice which Drake wanted, Drake had to accept a newly created professorship of clinical medicine. However, he comforted himself with the thought that he was back on the faculty at last; in time he would be able to maneuver Moorhead out.

Whenever Drake and Moorhead met in the halls, they indulged in Homeric quarrels; the session of the combined schools was one long battle in which all the professors were soon embroiled.

Haranguing their classes not on medicine but on the wickedness of their opponents, they circulated petitions demanding that a colleague be expelled or the trustees fired in a body. The students quickly divided into two factions, which rioted on the least provocation. It was rumored that the more timid thought it expedient to carry firearms for self-protection, and at least one professor never went to his lecture without a pistol in his pocket. In this civil war Drake continually lost ground; one after another the teachers he had brought from the East became convinced that the troubles of the school were due to his inability to compromise or take criticism. Before the end of the session, Drake was forced to resign.

However, there can be no doubt that the ideas for which he fought with so little guile were far ahead of his time. In the middle of this controversy he published a treatise on medical education which is considered a classic. Although he accepted the apprentice system as necessary, Drake insisted that a preceptor should keep his students from accompanying him on his rounds until they had learnt the scientific background of medicine. Once an apprentice had memorized his master's "infallible cures," Drake pointed out, he felt superior to studying dull matters like anatomy and pathology. "Of the different methods of generating quacks, this is the most prolific." Drake's list of the subjects apprentices should study sounds like the curriculum of a modern medical school, but he went further: he insisted that every pupil should have a first-class education in literature, classics, French, mathematics, mechanics, history, and geography. The almost universal lack of early training among physicians was, Drake insisted, the first great drawback of American medicine. Although he had begun his own studies as an illiterate youngster of fifteen, he inveighed against the conditions that had permitted him to do so; later he was to attack the Ohio College for lowering its fees so the poor could become students. "No devotedness to study," he wrote, "no intensity of ambition, no energy of intellect, not the whole combined, can make such a one what he would have been with early culture, nor raise him to that standard erected by his own vivid imagination. He may satisfy his friends, but must himself remain dissatisfied and unhappy." His book was published during a tremendous battle when he needed all the prestige he could muster, yet he dedicated it to the twelfth class of the Ohio College "in the hope that what I have written may contribute to preserve yourselves and your future students from some of the errors and defects of my own professional education."

His apprenticeship over, the young man, already proficient in many things, should, Drake believed, attend a medical school where a larger faculty than was then traditional should sit for longer sessions. Drake objected to forcing all the students to go to all the lectures whether they were ready for them or not. "I am not prepared to assert that it would be practicable to class our students of medicine into juniors and seniors and have lectures adapted to each division," but he would have the students observe an intelligent order in the courses they took. He even wished them to study for three sessions, a most revolutionary idea. As John Morgan had done fifty years before, he argued that medicine should be divided into physic and surgery, adding another specialty, obstetrics. He did not have to recommend that physicians cease being their own druggists, for this reform was already largely accomplished.

The cholera epidemic that made Richmond an invalid soon brought all progress in Cincinnati to a standstill for three years; then the city swept into a delayed boom that dwarfed all the others. Since the Mississippi steamboats which had fostered prosperity were in their turn becoming obsolete, the mind of every booster was rosy with dreams of railroads. Drake helped organize a half-dozen lines. During a meeting to project a branch as far as Paris, Kentucky, he was struck with a grandiose idea that brought him to his feet in a burst of oratory. A great southern railroad should be built to connect the Ohio with the tidewaters of Georgia. As Drake's loud voice filled the room, the whole meeting caught fire. A committee was appointed with Drake at the head, and the plan they drew up, although technicalities postponed its consummation for many decades, was immediately ratified by the nine States involved. This was only one of the many projects for civic betterment with which Drake filled the minutes he could spare from his practice.

Since his three children were just emerging into manhood and womanhood, he entertained a great deal for their sakes as well as his own. However, the ordinary gayeties of the city were not for him. "Public balls," he wrote, "have been abandoned by thousands who do not regard dancing as wrong, because of the dissipations connected with them; our theaters are shunned by the moral portion of the people on account of their licentiousness and buffoonery; our ninepin alleys are mere appendages of drinking-houses; our evening parties are scenes of midnight gluttony and drinking, etc., etc." Drake liked to gather a group of intellectual people around a bowl filled with lemonade and, having rung a bell to call the meeting to order, set a topic for serious discussion. Among his regular guests were Professor Stowe and his fiancée, Harriet Beecher; William Holmes McGuffey of the famous McGuffey readers; Judge James Hall, editor of the *Western Monthly Magazine;* and all the other intellectual luminaries of Cincinnati. His salon became so famous that few distinguished visitors passed through the city without appearing there.

Drake's repugnance to the gayeties of the world must have been based on early memories rather than on religious piety; unlike almost all his contemporaries, he belonged to no church. When his beloved wife, whom he followed in most things, had organized the First Episcopal Church of Cincinnati in his house, he had kept aloof. Too sincere a man to join a sect unless he believed wholeheartedly, he had been unable to resolve the conflict between the Baptist fervor of his parents and the greater formality of his wife's religion. As an old man he became an Episcopalian at last, but he immediately organized a society for the promotion of evangelical knowledge within the church.

Drake had by no means forgotten Ohio College, which had again sunk into insignificance. Under his urging, the local medical societies denounced the professors and trustees in resolutions which led to legislative investigations. On one such occasion, Drake wrote the Ohio representative: "I understand that you are about to attend the medical convention at Columbus. If such be the fact, let me advise you as a friend to curb your propensity for telling lies, so that you may not disgrace yourself among strangers and bring discredit on the conven-

tion. I do not of course suppose that you can refrain entirely—
but a strong resolution may enable you to hold in a little. I
hope this advice will not be lost upon you. Your obedient servant, Daniel Drake."

Harassed by such attacks, the trustees decided that the college could never exist peacefully while Drake was on the outside. They offered him a professorship, but when they refused
to dismiss Moorhead, he declined and realized the trustees'
worst fears by again founding a rival school, the Medical Department of Cincinnati College. Through his ability to recognize genius in young men, Drake managed to assemble the
most brilliant medical faculty that had ever taught in the
West. Samuel David Gross filled the earliest chair of pathological anatomy instituted in America. Other professors were
Willard Parker, the first in America to remove an appendix;
John Leonard Riddell, the famous botanist who later invented a binocular microscope; James B. Rogers, soon professor of chemistry at the University of Pennsylvania; and
Joseph Nashe McDowell, who had long since outgrown his
passion for Ephraim McDowell's daughter and married the
sister of his new patron, Daniel Drake.

The two Cincinnati institutions engaged in a free-style battle with no holds barred; even the students had fist fights. One
day Drake met an Ohio College professor on the street. They
both walked straight ahead until they faced each other chest
to chest. "I do not propose to step aside for a fool," said the
Ohio professor. "I will," replied Drake and stepped aside.

The most violent member of the Cincinnati faculty was
Joseph Nashe McDowell, whose tendency to bombast grew
on him yearly. He had garnished his narrow features with
tremendous walrus mustachios, which he hoped made him look
fierce; and whenever he stood on the lecture platform, his

high, hysterical voice rose in the most shocking epithets applied to the professors of Ohio College. "Give me one year's time and I'll blow the damned Ohio College to hell!" he would shout, scanning his audience with tiny, bellicose eyes, and woe to any student who dared smile. Yet it was common gossip that his mild-looking wife completely dominated Joseph McDowell, and he was known to hide under feather beds during thunderstorms. Since he amused his students and expounded anatomy with rare brilliance, he was a popular professor; it was said that he made the "dry bones talk," for he had a story to go with every bone, vein, and muscle in the body.

His desire to impress his pupils with his courage and virility made him go hunting and fishing with them, and he also borrowed money from them whenever it was convenient. During his lectures he boasted so much of his skill at target-shooting that some of the students offered to let him give them a demonstration. Having put up a target in a field, they secreted one of their number behind it who, after McDowell's first shot, leapt into the air screaming and fell down as if dead. Without waiting to investigate, the professor sprinted towards the boat-landing, his terrible mustachios flat in the breeze his own speed made. When his pupils finally overtook him and explained the joke, he was so relieved that with tears streaming down his face he repeatedly embraced the man he thought he had killed.

A superstitious man, Joseph McDowell would never lecture on Fridays. Since he believed robbing graveyards the height of bravery because of the ghosts that were certain to hover near, he loved to show off by leading the students in this eerie task. On one occasion a thunderstorm came up when McDowell was bringing a body home in a covered wagon. As the lightning came closer, his anxiety increased, and then suddenly he was terrified by the sound of a shot. Turning round, he saw that the corpse was sitting upright, a pistol clutched in its shriveled hand. Emitting a scream that drowned out the thunder, the professor leapt from the wagon, and he was not seen again until he appeared on the lecture platform the next day with a story of how ten armed men had tried to steal the corpse. With great bravery he had put them to flight and chased them for miles. As the students cheered him to the echo, he expanded with delight, not realizing that their applause was part of the hoax they had played on him.

After a girl had died of a very unusual disease, McDowell sneaked to the graveyard and exhumed her body so that he might find out what had killed her. No sooner had he got the cadaver back to the college than her relations and friends, who had discovered the theft, appeared round the building whooping it up in true Western style with guns and a nice strong rope. McDowell threw the corpse over his shoulder and hid it in the attic. That was all very well, but how was he to get out of the surrounded building? As he hesitated despairingly, his lamp went out and, according to his own account, he saw the ghost of his dear, dead mother whose halo lit up the dissecting-room. She pointed with a spiritual finger to the slab from which he had just removed the body; in a second McDowell had responded to this suggestion from the beyond by leaping on the table and pulling the sheet over his head. As the avengers searched the room for their dead relation, he tried to keep from breathing, and when they pulled the sheet back his fear gave him the waxy complexion of death. "Here is a fellow who died with his boots on," said one of them. "I guess he is a fresh one." "I thought," wrote McDowell, "I would jump up and frighten them, but I heard a voice, soft and low, close to my ear, say, 'Be still, be still' "; his mother's ghost was still watching over him. Finally the men went away and McDowell rose, jaunty and well pleased with himself, to boast of his exploit to anyone who could be made to listen.

During its second year Drake's school had a larger enrollment than its rival, but it was greatly handicapped by the law he had had passed fifteen years before, which gave the Ohio faculty exclusive right to use the public hospital for clinical instruction. Drake tried to expand his Eye Infirmary into a general hospital, but it was usually deficient in inmates. Ohio partisans asserted that Drake coached John, the old Irish nurse of the Eye Infirmary, to imitate all kinds of accidents and diseases so he might lecture on them.

Despite its brilliant faculty and large attendance, Drake's new venture lasted only four years. Since Cincinnati College lacked the public grants that had kept the Medical College of Ohio alive through so many tribulations, the ever-mounting expenses of the hospital, the continual need for books, apparatus, and repairs for the antiquated building, the necessity of making up the guarantees of $15,000 yearly which Drake had in his enthusiasm promised two distinguished professors he had brought from Baltimore, all these seemed likely to bankrupt the school. A bold attempt to induce the legislature to give his school all the Ohio College property, making it the State institution in the other's stead, failed by a miraculously close margin; two members of the investigating committee favored the plan, two opposed, and one abstained from voting. This last hope gone, professor after professor resigned from Cincinnati College until Drake alone remained. At last he too was forced to bow to the inevitable. For the second time he left Cincinnati in a rage.

5

Daniel Drake was now a man of fifty-four. Although his step was still elastic, his figure as straight as ever, his hair showed slightly silver at the temples. He had given the best twenty years of his life to his dream of founding a great medical school in Cincinnati and he had been defeated at every turn. For some time now he had fought back almost automatically, his mind falling into behavior patterns he had built up over decades, but the battle had not come easily to him, as it had when he was a young man full of hope. Even in his twenties the over-stimulation of his nerves had given him dyspepsia; now he found it still more difficult to hold his emotions in check. He wept at the slightest provocation. Reading fiction excited him so much that he had to give it up entirely. Perhaps he was relieved when Cincinnati College collapsed at last, for he could put the struggle behind him now, live at peace. Not that the Louisville Medical Institute, where he had accepted a professorship, was a particularly peaceful place, but its squabbles were not his squabbles. After a few years its founder, Dr. Charles Caldwell, was expelled as Drake had been from the school he started. And Drake, sitting quietly in a faculty meeting, voted for Caldwell's dismissal because he thought it would make for harmony; maybe he did not see the parallel.

The Louisville Medical Institute was an offshoot of Transylvania. His refusal to let sectarian dogma dictate the teaching of his professors had ended in the expulsion of Dr. Horace Holley from the presidency of that university. "The Gospel," his critics wrote, "is more valuable to the Western country and Lexington than all the science on earth," and when Dr. Holley died of yellow fever a few months later his fate was held up as "a solemn vindication of Divine Providence." Since the religious sects which had recaptured Transylvania fought over the spoils, the great school sank into obscurity as rapidly as it had risen to fame. The medical department managed to keep its distinction a little longer than the rest, but it was soon caught in the general downward movement. Observing that Lexington, once the metropolis of Kentucky, was being dwarfed by the new cities that steamboats and railroads had created, half the faculty resigned after a tremendous internal battle and moved to Louisville.

Transylvania lacked the vitality to recover from this desertion, and Ohio College still floundered ineffectively in a morass of backbiting and inefficiency; the Louisville Medical Institute became the great medical school of the West. Drake taught there for ten rich years. His reputation expanded, the old hatreds fell from him, but still he lacked the heart to give up his residence in Cincinnati. Although it had a bad effect on his practice, he returned every summer to the city which was his first love.

In mystical, patriotic ecstasy Drake had always believed that the new civilization which he saw being hewed out of the wilderness would be the greatest in history. Always his dream had been to identify himself with the growth of this wonder, and frustrated in one direction he turned to another. An undeveloped race, he knew, was forming in an unknown environment; its diseases could never be intelligently treated until doctors comprehended what that race and environment were. During the quiet of battleless years Drake returned to the project he had started with his *Picture of Cincinnati* and had dropped in order to organize the Medical College of Ohio. He determined to be the first scientific historian of the West.

Taking as his subject the whole central plain of America, the thousands of square miles between Lake Superior and the Gulf, between the Allegheny and the Rocky Mountains, he decided with the arrogance of a great mind to examine this region from the points of view of a dozen different sciences. He studied the topography, the meteorology, the oceanography, the geology, the anthropology, the history, the political institutions, the botany, and the diseases of the continent he had staked out as his own. Every summer, the instant his lectures were over, he embarked on extensive voyages of exploration. He sought knowledge, according to his own account, "in the cities and towns of the Middle West, in the villages and hamlets of the basin of the Mississippi, in the settlements of the colonist, in the reservations and wigwams of the Indian, around the campfires of the trappers, in the barracks of the frontier posts, in the mines of the unexplored West." Only a third of the region he studied contained permanent settlements. His blood alive with the restlessness of a pioneer, he was happy drifting in a canoe under the northern lights between dark pines; he was happy pushing aside with his oar the tangled undergrowth of fever-ridden bayous. Trappers in the farther wilderness warmed the tall, thin doctor by their campfires and pondered deeply over his questions while he took notes in the flickering light. Country doctors in remote settlements were overcome with awe when the great professor appeared on their doorsteps and listened with unrestrained eagerness to all they could tell him concerning the people and customs of their anonymous communities no one had ever inquired about before. Drake's mind, full of new thoughts and sights and inflamed always by the grandeur of his project, forgot the crowded disappointments of urban life, and his body became lean, strong, and brown with sun and wind. When at the summer's end he returned to his lectures at Louisville, he had a vast pile of notes to be correlated before next year's voyages began.

After ten years spent thus Drake published the first volume of his monumental *Treatise on the Principal Diseases of the Interior Valley of North America;* the second volume appeared posthumously. Although the third was never completed, the stupendous work contained several thousand closely printed pages. It was the most important contribution to medical geography since the days of Hippocrates. In fact, no work comparable to it exists in all medical literature.

Perusing his book, we are led to wonder what was the nature of Drake's genius. Although a doctor of great brilliance, he never made an experiment or attempted original scientific work. He himself regarded this as admirable self-sacrifice; had he not surrendered his chance for fame as a discoverer so that he might build up the medical institutions of the West? But when quiet descended on him in Louisville at last, he did not retire to his laboratory or his study; he set out exploring in the great world. "Medicine," he had once said, "is a physical science but a social profession"; always it was the social side that appealed to him most strongly.

Was Drake then a medical statesman, in his own sphere comparable to Isaac Shelby or Henry Clay? Perhaps, but certainly he was no politician. Never for a moment could he compromise with truth for political expediency. Although the reforms he fought for won out in the end, his love of medicine as a spotless goddess stood forever between him and immediate success. Medicine was to him what the muse is to a poet who writes as he feels regardless of the approbation of the world. Was Drake an artist then, a visionary hag-ridden by an æsthetic ideal? Certainly the youngster who came illiterate from the wilderness learnt to write with the pen of an angel. It would be difficult to find among the works of any other American physician passages more eloquent than many that Drake wrote.

Drake's treatise was in many ways a work of philosophical and ethical speculation. He believed that the intermingling of European, African, and Indian blood assisted by new conditions of climate, diet, and social institutions was producing the last new race on the surface of the globe. Eagerly he peered into the future, trying to discover what that new race would be. The great variations of temperature typical of the interior valley would, he decided, mold the faces of its inhabitants until they resembled the aboriginal Indians. In a thousand years most Americans would have sallow complexions, concave cheeks with high cheek-bones, and dark hair. Many influences would join to give them a "bilious temperament," to make them passionate and moody, bitter and irritable. Now that a century has passed since Drake's prophecy, we may wonder if we have traveled in the direction he pointed. Are we losing our blond Anglo-Saxon cast and the hopeful good humor we like to regard as a national attribute?

Anxious that the new race he foresaw should be as strong and moral as possible, Drake laid down rules to govern every angle of his neighbors' conduct. He discussed how houses should be built and heated, where shade trees should be planted, whether people should sleep on feather or hard beds.

He attacked the crack-brained reformers who wanted to liberate girls from corsets. Women's clothes, he insisted, did not protect them well enough; he wished more flannel were worn "next the surface. . . . For several years past an amelioration in this respect has been going on, and fashion, more governing in female apparel than in any other custom in the world, seems likely to render the use of muslin or flannel drawers universal. So many obvious considerations unite in favor of this addition to female raiment that the hope may be cherished that once introduced it will become universal." He thought women did not wear sturdy enough shoes, and wished to substitute wool for cotton or silk stockings. "The fashion of occasionally exposing the neck and upper part of the chest, which individuals ordinarily protect from the action of cold air, is injurious to the health of the lungs. . . . Thus, while the natural modesty of women is violated by this fashion, it is equally repugnant to sound physiology."

Many hundreds of pages are given over to minute geographical descriptions of cities, villages, mountains, and water-courses. A modern scholar trying to reconstruct some frontier settlement could do no better than to consult Drake's book; he would learn exactly on what hill the settlement was built, how far it stretched, what were its unusual features if any, and what diseases prevailed in it. He would be made to realize that America could never have become great had not malaria been conquered; on every page Drake testifies to its ravages. Or if our scholar were interested in the infant industries of the frontier, he would find them analyzed from a scientific point of view. Drake could hardly restrain his enthusiasm for the romantic careers of voyageurs and backwoodsmen, yet he described their lives minutely with notes on diet, physical surroundings, and occupational diseases.

Although he failed to admit the distinct individuality of typhoid fever which had just been pointed out by Gerhard and Pennock, Drake was far ahead of his time in his belief that most fevers are caused by germs. "Among visible plants and animals there are species which form no poison and others which secrete that which applied or inserted in our bodies produces a deleterious effect which is generally of a definite kind. . . . It seems justifiable to ascribe by analogy to microscopic animals and plants the same diversity of properties which we find in larger beings. . . . We may suppose that while many species of this minute creation are harmless there are others which can exert on our systems a pernicious influence." Opposing the use of violent drugs, he advocated treating fevers by the "expectant method" which relied on the healing processes of Nature to accomplish a cure, but stood ready to combat severe and unexpected complications. In this he was amazingly modern.

Since most doctors bought no medical books which were not handy guides to treating patients, the first volume of the treatise, which appeared in 1850, had a small sale. However, its critical acclaim was immense. That year the American Medical Association met in Cincinnati. When Dr. Alfred Stillé, chairman of the committee on medical literature, reported on the latest publications he gave most of his time to praise of Drake's work. The doctors stamped and cheered so enthusiastically that Drake was forced to rise. As the tall thin man stood up, stooping a little from age, his face alive with overwhelming emotion, even the Cincinnati doctors forgot their old enmity, and the applause rose to pandemonium. Drake tried to thank his colleagues but he could not get the words out. Suddenly he began to sway on the platform; friendly hands supported him to a chair. He covered his face with his hands and wept. To Dr. Stillé, who rushed up in anxiety, he managed to say at last through his tears: "I have not lived in vain, but I wish father, mother, and Harriet were here."

Drake's friends wanted him to run for the presidency of the association, the highest honor the American medical profession can give. Although he was almost certain of election, Drake refused. He was unworthy, he said, and no amount of arguing would dislodge him from that position; again the strange modesty that mingled with his arrogance had come to the fore. When Dr. Gross tried to persuade him to go to Europe, where he would have been accorded many honors, Drake answered: "I don't care to be brought into contact with the great physicians on the other side of the Atlantic, men of university education whose advantages were so much greater than my own. I think too much of my country to place myself in so awkward a position." Daniel Drake, the great traveler, never saw the Atlantic Ocean.

The Medical College of Ohio was battling along in its old, unregenerate way. During the session of 1849–50, there were twenty-five changes in a faculty of less than ten. When a scandalized public urged the legislature to abolish the college and distribute its property among the other educational institutions in Cincinnati, the trustees cast around for some distinguished professors to bolster up their prestige. After several had refused, they turned to Drake, who was having a minor squabble with his own trustees over the retirement age. Begged to save from extinction the school he had founded, the famous doctor, now in his sixty-fifth year, could not refuse; he had not forgotten the dream of his young manhood. Turning his back on the greatest medical school of the West, he left Louisville and returned to his prodigal son. Jesse Smith, Moorhead, all his old enemies were dead or scattered; surely now he could carry to fruition his life-long desire to make Cincinnati the medical capital of the nation.

Drake's inaugural address was a great triumph. As he appeared on the platform from which he had been exiled so long, pupils, professors, and trustees, all assembled to do him honor, rose reverently from their seats. His eyes misted, his body swinging in awkward, powerful gestures, he launched into his most moving oration. Reviewing the vicissitudes of his life, he declared that, wherever he had wandered, his heart had fondly turned to his first love, "your alma mater." A professor in many great schools, he had "lectured with men of power to young men thirsting for knowledge," but as he looked into the faces of four hundred students, behold! an image was in their midst; "it bade me stop and gaze upon the silvery cloud that hung over the place where you are now assembled." Even when he lost himself in the wilderness, the image was still his faithful companion and "whispered sweet words of encouragement and hope."

"I bided my time," he cried, his voice breaking with emotion, "and after twice doubling the period which Jacob waited for his Rachel, the united voice of the trustees and professors has recalled me to the chair which I held in the beginning. The first moments of reunion are always passionate and wisdom places little confidence in what is then promised; nevertheless, I must declare to you that I stand ready to pledge the remnant of my active life and all the humble talents with which the Creator has endowed me to her future elevation; and were I to put up the prayer of Hezekiah for length of days it would be to devote them to her aggrandizement, and for the pleasure of seeing her halls overflowing with inquiring pupils attentively listening to ardent, learned, and eloquent professors."

Drake quickly became disillusioned. John L. Vattier, the secretary of the board of trustees, had set up an espionage system by which he kept track of all that his professors did or said, and he tried to ruin the reputations of those whose actions did not please him. Before the session was out, Drake resigned, and the next winter he was back in Louisville.

Two years later the Ohio College, still in terrible difficulty, called him again. In his eagerness Drake managed to persuade himself that the old causes of dissension had been removed by another complete reorganization; again he resigned from the Louisville school to return to his ailing child. When the first faculty meeting degenerated into a free-for-all battle, Drake recognized the conditions that had frustrated his hopes so many times, and his disappointment, according to Dr. Gross, brought on an acute attack of the brain fever to which he had always been liable. After struggling against it for several days, he took to his bed dangerously ill. How truly he told his friends: "Medical schools have consumed me."

About midnight Saturday he called his daughter to say his headache was so great he would have to bleed himself although he realized bleeding prostrated excessively. Refusing to let her send for a doctor, he sat on the side of the bed and took a pint of blood from his arm. While he was applying the bandage, his daughter saw him slump suddenly backward; he had become insensible. When he returned to consciousness, he said his head was much relieved. In a few days, however, he became delirious, suffering great mental distress. On Friday, November 6, 1852, he died, a martyr to the dream of his young manhood that had hounded him to the end.

Two Men and Destiny

WILLIAM BEAUMONT

William Beaumont
FROM A CONTEMPORARY MINIATURE

Alexis St. Martin
FROM A PHOTOGRAPH

Two Men and Destiny

William Beaumont

1

"MY thoughts are nightly and every night and all the night constantly with thee, and faithful servants are they to the little divinity of love." So wrote William Beaumont in an ecstasy of loneliness, his pen galloping over the pages of his journal. "Morpheus sends them flying, fervent, faithful messengers of sleeping thoughts, to bear my love to you. Oh, could I come and go as easily, I would lay my glowing cheek where silently they rest upon thy swelling bosom and sweetly press those lips I love. Oh, how long doth seem our separation! Anxious indeed am I to know our final prospects. Were our present happy anticipations to be destroyed and our hopeful hearts, sustaining prospects, to be cut off, oh, how cheerless, difficult, and desperate would be the future scenes of life; A deadly banishment! A dark, benighted world! Could I not think of you by day and dream of you by night, there would be no zest in life, no stimulus. . . ."

With such adolescent phrases the thirty-five-year-old army doctor who was to become one of America's greatest physiologists heightened the excitement of his strange surroundings. Musings on the fiancée he had left behind him mingled romantically with the sounds of the Western night that made his native Connecticut seem part of a previous incarnation.

Although each evening the blackness outside his window was complete, it was alive with the noise of reveling Indians: scattered bursts from tom-toms, drunken war-whoops, the padding of moccasined feet. Then this alien cacophony would be drowned out by a melody equally alien; some provincial French ballad would explode from a hundred throats. The black square of window that had seemed part of the log wall would suddenly shine up brightly, and, looking out, Beaumont would see under the flare of torches a band of small, powerful Frenchmen, some pure Gallic, some bearing hawked Indian noses. They danced in scores, their feet, moccasined also, following the intricacies of a figure that had been danced across the sea for hundreds of years. Some were dressed like Indians —buckskin fringes, scarves, and feathers—but every face, swarthy and pale alike, was surmounted at a crazy angle by a stove-pipe hat.

As quickly as it had begun, the song would stop. Amid the gleeful shouts of spectators there would be the sound of a scuffle, and soon a knock on the door would summon Dr. Beaumont to treat some poor devil whose head had been bashed in.

The Island of Mackinac, that fortress at the juncture of Lake Huron and Lake Michigan where the army doctor had recently been stationed, was not only a border outpost of the Union in the Indian country, but also the headquarters of the American Fur Company. From these few square miles of mountainous land, named by the Indians "The Turtle," the most romantic business in all American history was carried on. Every fall some three thousand French-Canadian voyageurs set out in heavily laden canoes for the unexplored wildernesses of the West.

"The romantic scenery of the lakes and rivers, and the picturesque appearance of the savages and wild animals roaming
through deep solitudes, invested this new branch of commerce
with a charm that fascinated the Canadian imagination and
drew thousands into this peculiar service," wrote Daniel Drake
in his famous *Treatise*. "For a long time their voyages were
performed in canoes and pirogues of birch bark. Gradually the
adventurers became familiar with the western shores of Lake
Superior, ascended the River St. Louis, and, traversing a por-
tage, reached the highest waters of the Mississippi or spread
themselves over the distant Northwest. Others took their de-
parture from Green Bay, and descended the Wisconsin, floated
out upon the Mississippi at a lower latitude, while others still,
departing from the southern end of Lake Michigan, passed
down the Illinois and ascended the Missouri. Their evenings
were spent in smoking, garrulous talk, and singing. They
lodged under tents or beneath their inverted canoes. Many of
them spent the winter in those desolate regions, unwilling to
return without full cargoes of those furs which were the objects
they sought. . . . They mingled much with the native tribes
and adopted many of their customs; intermarried with them
and reared up a race of half-breeds to become, as already stated,
their associates and successors. . . . Free from care and alive
to the exciting novelties through which they passed, no despondency came over them, and the *gaieté de cœur* and vivacity
of the French never shone with finer radiance than on the
shores of Lake Huron, or the rivers which meander through
the boundless prairies between Lake Superior, Hudson Bay,
and the Rocky Mountains."

In the long winter months, when it was locked by ice from
Fort Dearborn, the nearest settlement, Mackinac had only four
hundred inhabitants, but when Beaumont arrived during the

spring of 1820, thousands of voyageurs were returning to its
shores, their *bateaux* intermingling with the canoes of some
fifteen hundred Indians who paddled up to exchange pelts for
trinkets and whisky, the benefits of civilization. After their
winter in the wilderness, where they had lived on water, corn,
and tallow, the voyageurs were in a festive mood; they had
stopped their boats, each of which contained eight to ten men,
at Pointe à la Barbe, so named some say because there every
man got his first shave since he had left civilization. From then
on they paddled with all their might, eager to make a gallant
entrance into gayety, and swept up to the island in a mist of
spray, every throat fully extended in song. Beaumont must
have shuddered during those first days with premonition of
accident as the heavy *bateaux*, decorated always with flowers,
rushed at the wharves under full speed; but just as all seemed
lost, the men backwatered simultaneously to stop within a foot.
Shouting wildly, they sprang on the beach and hurried to the
store, where they bought the high hats that, however battered,
never left their heads till again they set out into the wilderness.

Once their pelts had been appraised and paid for by the fur
company's clerks, they had money in their pockets to assuage a
whole season's thirst. The few months they remained in
Mackinac were a continual riot in which the Indians joined.
Every brigade had its champion who wore a black feather in his
hat, and whenever two champions met they fought. The winner
kept both feathers while all concerned repaired to the nearest
saloon to toast victory or defeat with equal high spirits.

The young man from Connecticut had entered a strange
world. Sometimes as he sat in a friend's house the room would
mysteriously darken. Springing up, he would see an entire
Indian family gazing in at the window, brave, squaw, and pa-
pooses equally intent, while they held a blanket raised behind

them to exclude the light so they might see better. When the doctor reached for his pistol, the older inhabitants laughed at him. Such peeping was correct according to Indian etiquette, he was told, and not to be resented. Since the savages would often stare for hours at a time, Beaumont learned to go about his business as if they were not there. Sometimes, looking at the dark, sinister faces, he must have felt that in this weird place he would find at last the destiny he sought; the thirty-five years of his life had been an endless quest for some consummation he could not clearly see.

William Beaumont was born November 21, 1785, at Lebanon, Connecticut, the third child of a small farmer. From the first he showed a desire for excitement and a love of bombast that the little village, which had sunk into an uneventful routine after the madness of the Revolution, could do little to satisfy. Religion was the great interest of the community, and the only memorable public event of all his childhood years was an acrimonious battle about the location of the Congregational meeting-house; every farmer wanted to have it near his land. Court writs were issued and workmen engaged to build the church were arrested. The boy, however, was bored by the whole quarrel, and would have preferred to have no meeting-house at all. He wrote in his later years that he had been driven to church so much in his youth that when he became twenty-one he swore never to attend worship again.

While the good boys in school read the Bible, Beaumont read the bloody epics of Ossian. Many a sunset found him sitting astride the revolutionary cannon mounted in the public square, dreaming of battles. The Fourth of July, when these relics were loaded and fired, was the banner day of his year; he boasted as an old man that he had bet his classmates he dared stand nearest the mouth of a cannon when it went off.

Gleefully, he almost leaned his cheek against the exciting tube and heard the ramrod pound in the powder and then the shot. When the loaders ran to get away from the muzzle, he stood still, his face tense with ecstasy. The explosion almost knocked him down. He won the bet, of course, but the ringing in his ears did not cease for hours and he never again heard well.

We may be certain that Beaumont was unhappy in the village of his childhood, for when he got away he never returned if he could help it. Probably his mind was so engaged in its own imaginings that he never saw the Connecticut countryside at all. Always, we infer from his writings, he dreamed of some marvelous and shadowy destiny that awaited him beyond the confines of his environment, some destiny without relation to the world he knew. But his ambition was the typical ambition of an adolescent, vague, undirected, more satisfying perhaps because it had no definite object. One day he could imagine himself a statesman, another a general, and if he ever thought of reaching fame as a doctor of medicine it could only have been in a rarely sober moment among his glorious moods.

His pious father, who by hard work had amassed a few acres of rocky, unfertile soil, looked with disapproval on this son who dreamed over the plow while the furrows ran crooked. Young William grew older and older, he became a man, but he never emerged from the adolescent fog in which he loved to wander. The time was long past when he should have settled on a farm of his own with a strong woman capable of bearing many children, yet still he mused on ideal flesh while the real farm girls plodded by.

During his twenty-second year, William told his father that he intended to leave home in search of fortune. When the old man asked where he planned to go, he replied ecstatically that he had no idea; like a true adventurer he would give the horse his head and allow destiny to pull the reins. There was a scene in the New England farmhouse. The Puritan elder, who knew that fortune was a hussy bent on no good, denounced his son as a fool and told him it was time he grew up. Anger unavailing, he tried persuasion; he walked the young man over to a fine field from which the rocks had been extracted, and told him he could have it for his own if he would stay and become a substantial, God-fearing citizen like his ancestors. But William replied in a flood of long words uttered with delight which made no sense to the shrewd old man.

The upshot, Beaumont used to tell his own son, was that he loaded all his possessions, a barrel of cider and a hundred dollars of hard-earned money, on a cutter he had somehow procured, and turned his horse's head northward. For several months he rambled through country lanes, watching winter turn into spring over fields that were beautiful because he had never seen them before. North and further north the slow wheels wandered until the cider was gone and all the money too. He found himself in the village of Champlain. Watching the sun play on the blue waters of a romantic lake, he decided this was the place fortune had chosen for him to stay.

He became the teacher of the village school, and instructed sixty to seventy pupils annually, but he was paid so little he had to work during vacations in a store. Selling turnips and applying the birch to sniveling youngsters was not the destiny he had imagined for himself; he took his dissatisfaction out in composing floods of high-sounding prose. "Let virtue and honor be your planetary guides," he wrote his younger brother; "temperance, justice, fortitude, and prudence your cardinal points; faith, hope, and charity your horizon; philanthropy, benevolence, friendship, and philosophy your atmosphere; and the elements of life will be smooth, transparent, and pleasant, gently gliding over your waving imagination like the eastern morning breeze across the swelling field of wheat."

Beaumont decided to study medicine. He borrowed texts from a local doctor and, when at last he had saved enough money, journeyed across Lake Champlain to St. Albans, Vermont, where he apprenticed himself to the most distinguished physician of the region, Dr. Benjamin Chandler. Like so many youngsters all over the land, he swept out the office, washed bottles, put up prescriptions, and accompanied his preceptor on his rounds. Since no cadavers could be procured, it was a gala day for Beaumont when a leg was amputated and he was allowed to dissect the severed limb. Dr. Chandler taught him the methods of Rush, in which he grew to believe implicitly; for many years he put his faith in depletion by bloodletting, purges, and sweat-causers, with "an entire disuse of tonic medicines."

The notebook he kept for his medical studies became the confidant of his moods. "She continued to fail faster and faster for about two hours," he wrote, "when to the heartfelt grief and inexpressible sorrow of her tender mother and affectionate brothers she expired, amidst the groans and lamentations of her sympathetic companions and congenial friends and associates, deluged in tears of grief for the loss of so amiable a daughter, sister, friend, and companion." But now that he had something real to put his mind on, such florid passages became rarer; most of the notebook was written not by the bad poet we know but by an accurate scientific observer. Case histories running to thousands of words show that the young man could, when he wished, use his mind as an instrument of precision. He copied down the following sentence as a maxim: "Of all the lessons which a young man entering medicine needs to learn, this perhaps is the first: that he should resist the fascination of doctrine and hypothesis till he have won the privilege of such studies by honest labor and a faithful pursuit of real and useful knowledge."

Perhaps he was helped in a dispassionate attitude towards medicine by a new excitement that had entered his private life. When he wrote: "The mind that can amuse itself with the love-sick trash of most modern compositions of novel reading seeks enjoyment beneath the level of a rational being," he was whistling in the dark. He lived in his preceptor's house and his preceptor had a daughter. That Mary Chandler was only fifteen probably increased her attraction for the young man, who, despite all his grandiloquence, was shy and afraid of people; in any case, the ideal female he had imagined suddenly became flesh and blood. But, alas, he disagreed with Dr. Chandler about politics.

The year was 1811, and the possibility of war with England the only subject of conversation. A stanch Federalist like most of his neighbors, Chandler thought such an adventure would be madness, but how could the young man, whose ears still rang from that revolutionary cannon, resist the fascination of fighting? Only cowards would allow the English to impress sailors unmolested, he shouted at the dinner table, while the frown on his preceptor's face grew deeper. No sooner was Beaumont graduated, than to his intense delight Congress declared war. Despite his preceptor's arguments and fury, he enlisted in the medical corps. A coldness ensued between Beaumont and the Chandler family.

Here was a situation after the young man's romantic heart; because of his bravery he was banished from the pure young girl he loved. He wrote his preceptor: "Therefore I go to meet the whistling messengers of death, encountering winter's inclement blasts, toil, fatigue, and painful abstinence to beguile a melancholy thought. Yea, I'd solicit the deadly weapon to pierce my heart sooner than justly incur your disesteem or general disapprobation. My chief interest, my happiness, my all is in your gift, yet God forbid that I should ever be induced unsuccessfully to ask them to displeasure of dissatisfaction. Dear sir, excuse an obscure sentence. It is a precious idea struggling for birth, though long constrained to remain enveloped in mystery, and must still so continue till future happy events shall have crowned my wishes with success."

In two separate diaries of his campaigns, Beaumont describes the war on the Great Lakes. He tells how the British, when they evacuated Little York, blew up their powder magazine, killing sixty Americans and wounding three hundred. "A most distressing scene ensues in the hospital; nothing but the groans of the wounded and agonies of the dying are to be heard. The surgeons wading in blood, cutting off arms, legs, and trepanning heads to rescue their fellow-creatures from untimely deaths. To hear the poor creatures crying, 'Oh dear, oh dear! Oh my God, my God! Do, doctor, doctor! Do cut off my leg! my arm! my head! to relieve me from misery. I can't live, I can't live!' would have rent the heart of steel and shocked the insensibility of the most hardened assassin and the cruelest savage. It awoke my liveliest sympathy, and I cut and slashed for forty-eight hours without food or sleep." Beaumont also took part in the Battle of Niagara and the siege of Plattsburg. He was cited for bravery.

Once peace was declared, he found the army dull. He amused himself for a while in a violent dispute with a fellow-officer whom he eventually challenged to a duel, coming out the victor when his adversary refused to fight and was therefore branded no gentleman in a broadside signed by most of the officers of the regiment. This quarrel over, Beaumont resigned from the service and set up in private practice at Plattsburg.

Modern doctors who complain of their fees should read the following list of fixed charges drawn up by the Clinton County Medical Society to which Beaumont belonged:

"Fee for each visit	$0.25
Riding per mile	0.20
Doctor in night	0.38
Consultation	1.00
Cathartics, viz. Sulphas Soda	0.13
All other cathartics	0.25
Emetic of Tartaris Antimonii	0.13
All other emetics	0.25"

To swell out his meager income, Beaumont and his partner ran a store where they sold liquor, tobacco, fish, window glass, powder, nuts, and groceries. He took apprentices, one of whom was his cousin, Samuel Beaumont.

No record remains that after his return from the wars the passionate physician wooed Mary Chandler any further. However, when she died a year later at the age of nineteen, he made a romantic pilgrimage to her grave and carved the words "My Mary" into the granite of her tomb. He soon forgot her budding charms in the riper attractions of a young widow, the daughter of the leading inn-keeper of the community. Although gentle enough to put Beaumont at his ease, Deborah Green had the assurance necessary to lead a shy man through the labyrinths of the world. Not only had she been married before, but as the hostess of the inn she had become adept at handling every kind of person. During the war, she had labored among the wounded as a nurse. There is a story, perhaps apocryphal, that when the doctors refused to let her tend small-pox patients because she was not immune, she purposely exposed herself to the disease so that after her recovery she might work in the wards.

Deborah Green's energetic character was clothed in a plump body surmounted by a pleasing dark head with a strong nose and a large, beautifully modeled mouth. A devout Quaker, she used thees and thous, and wore a white bonnet, not too austere, that brought out the softness in her face. She listened gladly to the suit of the ranting young physician, and before long they were engaged.

Although Beaumont soon secured so large a practice that he sold his share in the store, he was not content. Still he felt some shadowy greatness hovering over him that called on him to do he knew not what. His unsatisfied ambition did not drive him to medical school in search of scientific knowledge as ambition had driven so many an apprentice-trained doctor; instead, he dreamed of physical adventure. When Dr. Joseph Lovell, his friend and comrade in the war of 1812, became surgeon general, Beaumont accepted reappointment in the army accompanied with the promise of a romantic post. Ordered to Fort Mackinac, he set out in the spring of 1820, leaving Deborah temporarily behind him.

He passed through the Erie Canal and went by stage to Buffalo. Then he wrote in his diary: "Started this morning at four o'clock in the steamboat *Walk-in-the-Water* [the first steamboat on the upper lakes] for Fort Michilimackinac. Had on board General Macomb, Col. Wool, Rev. Dr. Morse, and many other gentlemen. Had a fine breeze and fair weather, a thunder shower between twelve and one o'clock. Adopted the following maxim this day: 'Trust not to man's honesty, whether Christian, Jew, or Gentile. Deal with all as though they were rogues and villains; it will never injure an honest person, and it will always protect you from being cheated by friend or foe. Selfishness and villainy, or both combined, govern the world with very few exceptions.' At sunset arrived at the lower end of Lake Huron, where the boat anchored for the night. Here stands Fort Gratiot, a handsome little fortification erected since the (Oh! D——, my heart a vacuum feels, your image only I can see, and wheresoever my body reels, my spirit wings its way to thee) war on a beautiful site."

After a year at Mackinac, Beaumont journeyed to Plattsburg for Deborah, who returned with him as his bride. They set up housekeeping within the walls of the fort that from its high cliff dominated the island. One of the twelve white women in the village, Mrs. Beaumont made her home a center for the local aristocracy, which consisted of the army officers and the executives of the fur company. Soon she had a daughter. Domestic life and the practice of a frontier post sank Beaumont into routine; even in this wild settlement, he had found no miraculous destiny. He was forced to take his restlessness out in quarrels with his neighbors. Then one spring afternoon there was the sound of a shot in the company store.

2

JUNE 1822 like every other June brought its flood of voyageurs and Indians to the shores of Mackinac. The silence of the long winter had been shattered by the shouts of many thousand men paddling in from the wilderness for their brief season of pleasure. Again the beach had become a fantastic parade ground. Indian braves in bright paint walked with grave and conscious pride, the strings of wampum heavy round their throats. And the French Canadians, those brown imps of the forest, were not to be outdone for grandeur; what money they could spare from liquor went for canes, and scarves, and gleaming jackets. The only soberly tinted citizens were the clerks of the fur company who appraised pelts by the thousands and grudgingly paid out a third of their value. Other clerks hustled behind the counters of the company store, taking the money back in exorbitant payment for trifles. But what if the voyageurs and the Indians were cheated; they were happy to have their hands on goods and liquor again.

The store was a joyous place. It was crowded to suffocation with men buying and men boasting. Here the voyageurs strutted, telling of unbelievable loads they had carried over portages, of rare pelts they had snared. Or the tone would change to horror and they would frighten each other with tales of vengeful *manitous* or dead Indians come back to reclaim their scalps. Suddenly a man gestured with too wild exuberance; the shotgun in his hand went off. And Alexis St. Martin, the nineteen-year-old voyageur who stood within three feet of him, fell to the floor, his stomach blown open. His shirt caught fire and burnt until it was quenched by the flow of blood. A shout went up for Dr. Beaumont.

"I was called to him immediately after the accident. Found a portion of the lungs as large as a turkey's egg protruding through the external wound, lacerated and burnt, and below this another protrusion resembling a portion of the stomach, which at first sight I could not believe possible to be that organ in that situation with the subject surviving, but on closer examination I found it to be actually the stomach with a puncture in the protruding portion large enough to receive my forefinger. . . . In this dilemma, I considered any attempt to save life entirely useless. But as I have ever considered it a duty to use every means in my power to preserve life when called to administer relief, I proceeded to cleanse the wound and give it a superficial dressing, not believing it possible for him to survive twenty minutes." Never had a case seemed more like a routine fatality, less like the triumphant knocking of fate.

"In about an hour I attended to dressing the wound more thoroughly, not supposing it probable for him to survive the operation of extracting the fractured spicula [fragments] of bones and other extraneous substances, but to the utter amazement of everyone he bore it without a struggle or without sinking."

Drake reported in his *Treatise* that voyageurs lived amazingly healthful lives, and St. Martin's recovery testifies to this fact. Under Beaumont's expert care, he rallied slowly although his body was still full of shot, wadding, and splintered bones. After four months his miraculous tissues began themselves to expel all foreign matter. First several shot and pieces of wad emerged from the wound. Then "there came away a cartilage, one inch in length. In six or seven days more another, an inch and a half long, and in about the same length of time a third, two inches long, were discharged. And they continued to come away every five or six days until five were discharged from the same opening, the last three inches in length. . . . Directly after the discharge of the last cartilage, inflammation commenced over the lower end of the sternum [breast-bone] which, by the usual applications, terminated in a few days in a large abscess and from which, by laying it open two inches, I extracted another cartilage three inches in length. The inflammation then abated, and in a day or two another piece came away, and the discharge subsided." A few months later, two more segments of bone appeared.

St. Martin's body could do everything but close up the hole into his stomach which remained so large that Beaumont had to cover it with a linen compress in order to keep the food from running out. Worried, the physician exhausted his skill during eight or ten months trying to excite "adhesive inflammation in the lips of the wound," but he had not the slightest success. Finally he proposed an operation which he believed might shut the aperture, but the patient refused to allow himself to be cut.

A year after he had been wounded, St. Martin was able to hobble around, but he was still very feeble. The poor fund of the town being exhausted, the authorities wanted to ship him in an open *bateau* the two thousand miles to his home in Canada. Beaumont objected, knowing the lad could not survive the trip; and when the authorities were adamant, he took St. Martin into his house, although he was paid only a little more than forty dollars a month. While Beaumont dressed the wound twice a day, the patient gained strength rapidly during another year. His body even constructed a valve for the fistula in his side, "a small fold or doubling of the coats of the stomach," that held the food in, "but was easily depressed with the finger."

Beaumont had long since realized that this wounded boy was the fate he had sought so many years. Despite his imperfect medical studies, he knew that digestion was a mystery no one had ever fathomed. Every man who had ever lived possessed a stomach; he could feel its motions sometimes with his hand and its pain with his nerves; he fed it several times a day; but what happened to the food once it slipped into this universal organ no man knew for sure. There were theories, of course, theories by the hundreds, but few had any basis in fact, and what imperfect facts there were dealt only with the digestion of animals. The gastric juice of man had never been isolated.

"I can look directly into the cavity of the stomach," Beaumont wrote, "observe its motion, and almost see the process of digestion. I can pour in water with a funnel and put in food with a spoon, and draw them out again with a siphon. . . . The case affords an excellent opportunity for experiment upon the gastric fluids and the process of digestion. It would give no pain or cause the least uneasiness to extract a gill of fluid every two or three days, for it frequently flows out spontaneously in considerable quantities; and I might introduce various digestible substances into the stomach and easily examine them during the whole process of digestion."

Beaumont had been given an opportunity that few men had received in the world before, but he felt inadequate to meet it. Why, oh, why, had he never taken the time to go to medical school? Without any self-confidence, he "suspended flesh, raw or roasted, and other substances in the hole to ascertain the length of time required to digest each; and at one time used a plug of raw beef, instead of lint, to stop the orifice, and found that in less than five hours it had been completely digested off, as smooth and even as if it had been cut with a knife." But he lacked the faith in these experiments to make them public or even preserve the records.

Instead, he wrote a description of the case, mentioning the possibility of experimentation, which he sent to his friend, Surgeon General Lovell, with the suggestion that he correct it for publication. Gone was the confident, bombastic prose style of the romantic officer; he wrote with sober accuracy now and was anxious to have others amend his sentences. Lovell made a few changes and had the article published in the *Medical Recorder* for January 1825.

Deprived of a formal medical education, Beaumont did not know how trained scientists experimented, and there was no other doctor within a week's journey of Mackinac to whom he could turn for assistance. He begged Lovell to station him somewhere in the East where he could get the advice of experienced men. In February he was ordered to Fort Niagara, but before he could leave, his hopes were shattered by a countermanding order. While the days of what now seemed an enforced exile rolled into weeks, the man with the miraculous stomach washed the floors and carried out the garbage, and Beaumont fidgeted in his office with anxiety lest his opportunity escape him. At last unable to wait any longer, he began his formal experiments.

However, lack of training was not the only difficulty he had to face. When deathly ill, Alexis St. Martin had been as easy to handle as a sick animal, but now he was healthy again except for the hole in his stomach, a lusty young man of twenty-two. Spring was returning to the Island of Mackinac, and with it the roistering rovers of the forests. Wistfully, the lad who had been convalescent for three years went down to the beach and joined his former companions. He sat silently while they told of the excitements he had known: rivers boiling white through black forests, deer coming down to drink and watching in awe-struck wonder as the *bateaux* glided by, buffalo lifting the dust of Western plains. Hearing such tales, Alexis must have smelled again the stuffy heat of Indian wigwams at the end of a long paddle, felt the bite on his tongue of a peace-pipe handed him by a friendly brave. He watched the bullies strut by under their black feathers and remembered that he too had once hoped for such an emblem of glory.

Usually the voyageurs hardly noticed that he was there, for he had no glorious tales to tell, but when they did notice it was even worse. Suddenly the whole brigade would turn on him with jeers. They knew that he made his living by letting a doctor poke things through an aperture into his insides; derisively, they called him "the man with a hole in his stomach," and laughed at such a freak. He offered to fight, but they only laughed the harder, and his heart was not in his challenge since he too thought it a disgrace for a young man to live as he did. His whole family came under the blight. His brother Etienne, also a voyageur, was continually taunted as "one of the St. Martins without a stomach," called "the little lard-eater from Canada, brother to a man with a stomach having a lid." Although Etienne promised to kill the whole brigade if they did not leave his brother's stomach alone, the teasing went on with heightened whoops of hilarity.

There was nothing for Alexis to do but get drunk. The liquor filled his veins with confidence until he could almost believe he was a complete man, a tough fellow well on the road to his black feather. At last, however, he had to return home. When Beaumont saw his experimental subject stagger up the hill, precious stomach obviously soured with liquor, his fury flowed in a stream of polysyllabic scolding, for he felt that Alexis was not only a dissolute servant but also ungrateful and a traitor to science. Such a renegade deserved no sympathy! Under the impact of violent words, the Canadian wilted to almost nothing, for he had no self-confidence left with which to fight. After he had sobered up, he docilely submitted to further experiments.

We may be sure that St. Martin was as relieved as Beaumont

when a new order to Fort Niagara came; perhaps in different surroundings he could forget he was not like other men. Back in civilization, Beaumont asked advice and began the series of experiments he later published. "At twelve o'clock, M, I introduced through the perforation into the stomach the following articles of diet, suspended by a silk string, and fastened at proper distances so as to pass in without pain—viz: a piece of high-seasoned à la mode beef; a piece of raw, salted, fat pork; a piece of raw, salted lean beef; a piece of boiled, salted beef; a piece of stale bread; and a bunch of raw, sliced cabbage." St. Martin continued his labors about the house, but every hour his master called to him and, making him lie on his right side, examined each piece of food to see how the digestion was going. After four hours, Alexis could stand it no longer. "The lad complaining of considerable distress and uneasiness at the stomach, general debility and lassitude with some pain in his head, I withdrew the string and found the remaining portions of the aliment nearly in the same condition as when last examined; the fluid more rancid and sharp. The boy still complaining, I did not return them any more."

However, a few days later the experimentation began again. As St. Martin lay on his side while Beaumont interminably determined the temperature of his stomach, surely his mind fled to his life as a voyageur. Again he paddled down the yellow Mississippi under a yellow moon in time to an old French boating song that rocked back from twin walls of trees unbroken for two thousand miles. All that territory belonged to him and his confreres; they shared it only with the Indians who were their friends, and with the wolves who shouted even as they at the glittering moon. "Turn over," said Beaumont curtly, and St. Martin was conscious again of the queer sensation in his stomach where the thermometer had been.

Although they spent hours together every day, Beaumont and St. Martin did not like each other. The army officer, who had difficulty getting on even with his equals, could bear association with so rough a character only if he treated him like the most menial servant. It is true that, when a voyageur, Alexis had been scolded and even beaten by the officers of the fur company if he could not avoid them during the few months at Mackinac, but once the wilderness had closed round him, he had been his own master. Now he found no relief from servitude; every day he was forced to cringe and surrender up his will. He became more and more dissatisfied.

Often his slow mind churned the wonder whether he was well enough to make his living again in the wilds if he escaped, but Beaumont was too indifferent to his servant's psychology, too absorbed in the experiments that had suddenly become the meaning of his life, to worry what so low an individual might be thinking. Eager for more knowledge with which to carry on his work, the physician took his subject on a trip through upper New York State, and haled him before several older scientists. He forced the embarrassed young man to exhibit his deformity to strangers.

When they arrived at Plattsburg, a few miles from St. Martin's native Canada, the temptation became too great; he tied his belongings in a bundle and, waiting until Beaumont was safely asleep, tip-toed out of the house. Awakening the next morning to discover his loss, the physician was amazed; it had never occurred to him that his servant might run away. He tried passionately to find St. Martin, but his efforts were useless; he had no clue. Fortune, who had suddenly smiled on her worshiper, had as suddenly withdrawn her gift. The heartbroken doctor returned to Fort Niagara, where he wrote up his experiments for the *Medical Recorder* and tried to forget his disappointment in one of the bombastic quarrels he had formerly loved.

Suspecting that a certain Lieutenant Griswold was pretending illness in order to escape his duties, Beaumont gave him a harmless-looking pill which was really a tremendous emetic and cathartic. Every few hours he visited his patient with mock solicitude on his face, and saw with growing delight that the young man continued to lounge by his window, "appearing very comfortable and undisturbed." Finally Beaumont announced that Griswold was malingering. "If Mr. Griswold," he said, "had taken the medicine as I directed him that morning, he would have had swelled jaws and a sore mouth for his imprudence."

A court martial dismissed Griswold from the service on Beaumont's testimony, but President John Quincy Adams, to whom the case was appealed, reversed the decision. "A medicine of violent operation," he commented, "administered by a physician to a man whom he believes to be in full health but who is taking his professional advice is a very improper test of the sincerity of the patient's complaints, and the avowal of it as a transaction justifiable in itself discloses a mind warped by ill-will."

Beaumont was in no mood to take back-talk from anybody, even the President. Failing in his demand for a court of inquiry, he published a pamphlet defending his conduct. Here we find all the fustian which was omitted from his writings about St. Martin: "Silence under the circumstances would be cowardice and submission meanness itself, suffering falsehood and error to predominate over truth and correctness, to the total subversion of good order and correct discipline, and the entire destruction of military pride and laudable ambition." He went on to say some pretty hard things about the President; it was lucky the surgeon general was his friend. Of course, his publication did not change the President's decision.

A short time later he was ordered to Fort Howard at Green Bay, Michigan Territory. This outpost on the Fox River, also a minor headquarters of the American Fur Company, was in most respects similar to Mackinac although it was even more isolated; in winter the rare mails were carried by foot from Chicago, and it was a routine matter for the postman to be chased by wolves. Beaumont's first taste of Indian fighting, the Winnebago War, did not make him forget his interrupted investigations. He begged those officers of the fur company who recruited voyageurs in Canada to find St. Martin for him. For two years they were unsuccessful; then W. W. Matthews wrote that he had located Alexis "twelve miles back from Berthier." He added that a Dr. Caldwell was negotiating to begin experiments. In terror lest his subject and his fame escape him, Beaumont made Alexis flattering offers to come to Green Bay.

3

St. Martin had returned to Canada determined to forget his accident and live a normal life. He had wooed and won Marie Jolly, a young Canadian girl, just as if he had no hole in his stomach. After he had fathered a child, he proudly enlisted as a voyageur with the Hudson Bay Company. Setting out again in a *bateau*, he must have felt that the past was forever behind him, but he soon discovered that long years of idleness had made him soft. The work that had been a joy to him once was now onerous labor, and he was so poorly paid that his family lived in poverty. Beaumont's offer, although it would make him a freak again, was a great temptation. For two years he struggled to preserve his manliness, but then he gave in.

In August 1829 the American Fur Company transported him, his wife, and his two children in an open *bateau* to Beaumont, who by this time was stationed at Prairie du Chien, a frontier fort on the Mississippi. The physician was delighted to find that his subject's "stomach and side were in a similar condition as when he left me in 1825. The aperture was open, and his health good.

"He now entered my service, and I commenced another series of experiments on the stomach and gastric fluids and continued them interruptedly until March 1831. During this time, in the intervals of experimenting, he performed all the duties of a common servant, chopping wood, carrying burdens, etc., with little or no suffering or inconvenience from his wound. He labored constantly, became the father of more children, and enjoyed as good health and as much vigor as men in general. He subsisted on crude food in abundant quantities except when on a prescribed diet for particular experimental purposes and under special observation."

Behind this matter-of-fact statement lies the drama of one of the strangest collaborations in history. Although Beaumont was fascinated by the stomach on which he worked, he grew to hate the stomach's owner; his letters are full of references to St. Martin's "villainous obstinacy and ugliness." Undoubtedly the young man, who had no interest in the work being done on him, often refused to be helpful. His lot was not easy. He had to remain interminably in certain positions, to fast for hours and then have his hunger assuaged not by the pleasant method of eating but the unpleasant one of having the food put directly in his stomach. Often he was forced to chew his meals lying down while Beaumont watched the food drop through his gullet. As he worked round the house, he was ordered to carry small bottles under his armpits, since Beaumont wished to demonstrate that animal heat was not different from ordinary heat. And many of the experiments made him feel sick.

Increasingly conscious of his importance to Beaumont, Alexis became less and less willing to be treated as a servant; he wished to be regarded as a friend of the family. He refused to obey orders unless they were phrased as requests for a favor, but Beaumont could not bring himself to make requests of such a man. And when the imperious physician stormed in fury, Alexis did not cringe as he once had done, for he now had an ally to back him up. Mrs. St. Martin encouraged him to evade unpleasant commands by pretending that he was needed at home. "You know," Beaumont wrote him many years later, "that the constant cares, anxieties, and vexations incident to you when your family is with you unavoidably embarrass and interrupt my observations and experiments upon you, and render your services to me about useless and dissatisfactory." We can see the indignant physician standing at the door of St. Martin's hut while his subject skulked inside and Mrs. St. Martin, her arms akimbo, gave him a tongue-lashing her husband would never have dared indulge in.

Beaumont complained at length about these difficulties, yet they did not seriously impede his experiments; Alexis, the laboratory notes show, managed to secure few holidays. And the Canadian's bad temper enabled Beaumont to observe for the first time in history the interrelations between emotion and digestion.

Having failed in his attempt to work in some center where he could get the advice of experts—Prairie du Chien was at least as wild as Mackinac—Beaumont was forced to rely on his own ingenuity, and strangely enough the ill-trained physician proved a brilliant experimenter. With no equipment but a thermometer, a few open-mouthed vials, and a sand-bath, he did a large part of the work that was to be the most important contribution to the understanding of digestion before Pavlov.

Although he was the first to isolate pure human gastric juice, Beaumont, who had never studied chemistry, could not even attempt to analyze it. Learning that the best physiological chemists were in Europe, he applied during 1831 for a year's furlough so that he might take Alexis across the ocean. He was helped in this scheme by Mrs. St. Martin's homesickness; she asserted that she could bear her exile from Canada no longer. Gleefully seizing this opportunity to get rid of his servant's troublesome ally, Beaumont gave him new clothes for his whole family and leave of absence to take them home. It was risky, he realized, to let his servant get out of his clutches again, but he had a bait to offer which he was sure would bring the young man back. The French Canadian had heard all his life nostalgic rumors of that mother city, Paris, which had painted itself in his imagination as the finest sight in the world. Whenever Beaumont spoke of going there, St. Martin's sullen face lit up with such unwonted eagerness that the physician let him go away without forebodings. "They started in an open canoe," Beaumont wrote, "via the Mississippi, passing by St. Louis, Mo.; ascended the Ohio River; then crossed the State of Ohio to the Lakes; and descended the Erie, Ontario, and the River St. Lawrence to Montreal."

Just as Beaumont was ready to travel east for his reunion with St. Martin, trouble sprang up with the Indians. Prairie du

Chien was one of the most important Indian agencies on the frontier. When the savages came in to sell pelts or finery their squaws had made, the agile agents got them drunk and kept them so until they had sold their lands to the United States for one more bottle of whisky. In the words of a contemporary observer, the red men returned to their villages "empty-handed, sans land, sans money, sans everything but a deep conviction of having been cheated." When such picayune methods did not serve to secure territory wanted by the whites, a pow-wow was held with whatever chiefs seemed most friendly, and whole States bought for a few dollars with little regard to whether the chiefs had a right to sell them. Naturally, the large Indian population that centered around Prairie du Chien became increasingly discontented.

They were weakened, however, by their tribal wars that went back to antiquity and could not be given up even under the menace of complete extermination by the white man. On one occasion, some Menominees and Sioux ambushed a band of Foxes near Prairie du Chien. Triumphantly they came to the walls of Fort Crawford, where Beaumont was stationed, to dance over the scalps. "They were painted for war," an eye-witness reports, "and had smeared themselves with blood, and carried the fresh scalps on poles. Some had cut off a head and thrust a stick in the throttle and held it high; some carried a hand, arm, leg, or some other portion of the body." Before Colonel Zachary Taylor could drive them away, Mrs. Beaumont had seen enough to receive a serious shock to her nervous system. Her husband had to nurse her through a deep depression.

Finally a Sauk chief, Ma-ka-tai-me-she-kia-kiak, or more simply Black Hawk, decided that the real enemy was the white man. Joining with the Foxes, he tried to form an alliance with the British in Canada. Although the British were unwilling, the situation became so grave that Fort Crawford was put on a war basis and Beaumont's leave canceled. For many months nothing serious happened, and then a band of Illinois volunteers fired on a delegation of Indians approaching under a flag of truce. This set off the Black Hawk War, a brief and bloody encounter in which the Illinois irregulars demonstrated their own method of scalping Indians; they removed a strip of skin from the back of the neck to use as a razor strop. Marching with the troops from Fort Crawford, Beaumont treated the wounded at the Battle of Bad Axe River, where Black Hawk's brave but hopeless insurrection was put down.

Beaumont returned to the fort full of eagerness to get away, but reinforcements from New York, who arrived too late for the fighting, brought an epidemic of cholera, the same epidemic that Drake and Richmond fought in Cincinnati. Ordered to stay and treat the sick, Beaumont turned to his notebook for solace. "Like a snake watching and writhing for its prey," he wrote, "the cholera lurks unseen through the pestiferous and malarious atmosphere, stealing upon human beings and thickly populated places, and gluts its cadaverous appetite more by the fears and dread it occasions than by its otherwise naturally fatal effects upon human life." The passage goes on for hundreds of words, getting more and more bogged down with misapplied adjectives.

Finally an order came granting his leave but cutting it to six months. In less than twenty-four hours he started east to meet St. Martin, who, after keeping him in suspense for a while, finally joined him at Plattsburg. Beaumont immediately made the illiterate Canadian put his cross at the bottom of a long contract which provided that in return for board, lodging, clothes, and one hundred and fifty dollars he would "submit to, assist, and promote by all means in his power such physiological or medical experiments as said William shall direct or cause to be made on or in the stomach of him, the said Alexis, either through or by the means of the aperture or opening thereto in the side of him, the said Alexis, or otherwise, and will obey, suffer, and comply with all reasonable and proper orders or experiments of the said William in relation thereto, and in relation to the exhibiting and showing of his said stomach and the powers and properties thereof, and the appurtenances, and powers, properties, situation, and state of the contents thereof. . . ."

Beaumont left his wife in Plattsburg and journeyed with his subject to Washington, where, finding the six months' leave too short for a European trip, he gave in to the request of patriotic doctors that he complete his work in the United States. Alexis must have been disappointed to learn that he would not see Paris after all, but when he expressed his displeasure, Beaumont certainly shouted him down, and the poor young man had no refuge now to which he could flee, no ally to aid him, since his family was in Canada. Unable by himself to stand up against his fiery and determined master, he was soon reduced to a cowering submission from which he fled into drunkenness. "St. Martin," Beaumont's case history reports, "has been drinking ardent spirits pretty freely for eight or ten days past." The physician fulminated, and was able to write a little later: "He has been restricted from full and confined to low diet and simple diluent drinks for the last few days, and has not been allowed to taste of any stimulating liquors or to indulge in excesses of any kind."

The experiments proceeded merrily, one or even two almost every day, for Beaumont was not seduced from his work by the attractions of Washington society; his growing deafness made going into groups of people difficult and he also missed his wife; both master and servant were deprived of the women who usually backed them up before the world. Beaumont wrote a friend in Prairie du Chien, contrasting the "ingenuousness and magnanimity of soul" typical of the frontier with "the commonplace, everyday, poorly disguised, cold, hollow-hearted affectedness of fashionable society of which this place is the seat and center, and than which nothing can be more discordant to the present state of my feelings."

Beaumont gave vials of gastric juice for analysis to two of the leading chemists in America, Professors Robley Dunglison of the University of Virginia and Benjamin Silliman of Yale. Stating that "the precise nature of the constituents of gastric juice may never be determined," Dunglison reported that the major active ingredient was hydrochloric acid. Silliman also found hydrochloric acid, but was so dissatisfied with his own analysis that he urged Beaumont to send a specimen to the famous Swedish chemist, Berzelius. The physician held up the publication of his book awaiting this savant's reply, but when it came it was the most disappointing of all. Beaumont himself was able to add to the work of the world's greatest chemists by the simple experiment of mixing some hydrochloric and acetic acid, diluting it with water until it tasted like gastric juice, and then putting some masticated boiled beef both in it and in the real juice. While that in the real juice dissolved, a jelly-like substance remained in the other vial; obviously the juice contained some undiscovered agent. Three years later, Theodor Schwann isolated pepsin.

Now, after several years of experimentation, Beaumont got his hands on physiology books which told him what was already known and postulated about digestion. Although not finding out what your predecessors have done until you have almost completed your own work seems a queer method of investigation, it probably was the best method Beaumont could have pursued. Indeed, St. Martin may well have done the world a favor by running away when his master planned to work under the supervision of the learned. Beaumont's character was hardly the kind you would associate with dispassionate, painstaking research; the desire for self-justification was a disease with him. Had he been enabled before he started his studies to identify his self-esteem with some theory that had especially appealed to him, he might easily have fallen into a major error which, as we have seen, was typical of his time; he might easily have sought truth not for its own sake but in order to prove a preconception.

Isolated at Prairie du Chien and conscious of his ignorance, Beaumont could only observe closely and record what he saw. He himself recognized the part his lack of training had played. He told the surgeon general that he had followed no favorite theory; "a mere tyro in science, with a mind free from every bias, I commenced them [his experiments] as it were by accident, and continued desultorily to prosecute them without regard to any particular arrangement or the confirmation of anything save plain and palpable truths and physiological facts."

Reading the books of the men who would have been his masters had he worked near a library, he was horrified by the spirit of speculation he encountered, and wrote the following paragraph that might well be memorized by every aspiring scientist: "It is unfortunate for the interests of physiological science that it generally falls to the lot of men of vivid imaginations and great powers of mind to become restive under the restraints of a tedious and *routine* mode of thinking, and to strike out into bold and original hypotheses to elucidate the operations of nature, or to account for the phenomena that are constantly submitted to their inspection. The process of developing truth by patient and persevering investigation, experiment, and research is incompatible with their notions of unrestrained genius. The drudgery of science they leave to humbler and more unpretending contributors. The flight of genius is, however, frequently erratic. The bold and original opinions of Brown for a long time unsettled the practice of medicine. . . . The gratification of a *morbid* desire to be distinguished as the propagator of new principles in philosophy, or as the head of a new sect, is not the only result to be expected from such heresies. New opinions or doctrines, whether true or false, will have admirers and followers, and will lead to practical results. And the errors of one man may lead thousands into the same vortex."

Indeed, Beaumont's great contribution lay in his unwavering pursuit of facts. Since the beginning of time every medical theorist, finding that the walls of the stomach barred him from real knowledge, had called on his imagination. We have seen that Rush thought digestion was acetous fermentation. Other brilliant thinkers believed that it was carried on by a spirit or archeus residing in the bowels; that the stomach was a stewpot which cooked, or a grinder which pulverized, or a mash barrel which produced alcoholic fermentation, or simply a vat in which substances were macerated and dissolved. Beaumont cut through this tangle and proved for all time that the active principle in digestion was the gastric juice, which functioned through chemical action involving hydrochloric acid.

True, other experimenters had step by step reached this conclusion before him. Réaumur and Spallanzani, having extracted the gastric juice of birds and other animals, showed that it digested and resisted putrefaction. There the work was taken up by John Richardson Young of Hagerstown, Maryland. Al-

though he died at the age of twenty-two and is today almost
forgotten, Young was the first American medical scientist ever
to use modern laboratory methods. Favored by the American
fauna, during 1803 he worked on bullfrogs, whose gastric juice
can be removed through their huge mouths with a spoon. The
acid in the juice, he demonstrated, was not a result of fermentation but an active chemical agent. Unfortunately, he identified
it as phosphoric, but in a few years the English scientist Prout
picked up the error, proving it was hydrochloric. This long
train of experimentation, however, was not generally believed
until Beaumont isolated human gastric juice in large quantities,
made it digest outside the stomach, demonstrated its properties
over and over.

Had this been his only contribution, his name would have
gone down in history, but he did infinitely more. His exact
descriptions of the interior of the stomach were the basis of all
knowledge on that subject till the discovery of the X-ray, and
even the X-ray has not been able to improve materially on
many of his observations. He showed that food does not remain
in the stomach, as was commonly believed, for a short time
before digestion starts, and his demonstration that gastric juice
is secreted only when the walls of the stomach are irritated refuted Spallanzani's theory that it accumulates in the cavity between meals. He charted the length of time the stomach takes
to empty, and cast much light on the mechanism of the pylorus,
the valve opening into the bowels. Although Alexis's fistula
made his organ act a little abnormally, Beaumont's account of
the motions of the stomach was the best up to that time. His
proof that the temperature of the stomach rises hardly at all
during digestion was the refutation of a popular belief.

Beaumont showed that the more finely food is divided, the
quicker it is acted upon, and his table of the length of time it

takes different aliments to be digested is the basis of the modern science of dietetics. True, he was wrong in stating that gastric juice dissolves fats and carbohydrates; probably he found in Alexis's stomach pancreatic juice regurgitated from the intestines and swallowed saliva which he did not differentiate from gastric juice. His belief that food is completely digested once it is changed into a semi-fluid homogeneous state also contributed to this error.

Far ahead of his time, Beaumont even discovered facts about the psychological aspects of digestion. He demonstrated that fatigue and emotion reduce the flow of gastric juice. While his contemporaries insisted that thirst was an "instinctive sentiment" that could not be explained, he showed that the sensation is due to dryness of the mouth caused by the respired air taking up the moisture faster than it can be supplied. Although he refuted the theory that hunger is caused by the sides of the empty stomach grinding together, he erred when he believed it due to an accumulation of gastric juice in the secreting vessels. Actually, hunger is caused by spasms of the stomach muscles; smoking stops them and tightening your belt retards them for a while.

Like so many great innovators, Beaumont had discovered a new method of investigation which completely altered the technique of subsequent workers in his field. No sooner was his book published than scientists everywhere in the world created artificial holes in the stomachs of animals. Even today variations of his method are producing miraculous results; Pavlov's famous experiments on dogs are lineal descendants of the experiments made possible by Alexis St. Martin's fistula.

Although Beaumont's association with St. Martin was a piece of wonderful good fortune, his achievement cannot be ascribed to luck alone. Alexis would probably never have survived the shooting had it not been for the physician's expert care, and Beaumont made magnificent use of his opportunity. Before his time, at least a dozen cases of gastric fistula were reported in medical literature, and not one was effectively experimented upon.

Such was the epoch-making work that Beaumont was now ready to compile into a book. After his furlough had expired, the surgeon general had stationed him at a succession of Eastern posts so that he might not be hampered in any way, but when the time came to put pen to paper an overwhelming modesty assailed him. He begged Lovell to write the book for him and, when Lovell insisted he do it himself, secured the help of his cousin and former apprentice, Samuel Beaumont. It was a slow and vexatious business, but at last the volume was published in Plattsburg at the author's expense. Sold by subscription, it appeared in December 1833, eleven and a half years after Alexis was shot. Although it was a clumsily printed volume and the text was not expertly arranged, its success all over the country was immediate. Newspapers gave whole columns to its praise, and medical journals were enthusiastic. A translation appeared at once in Germany. Beaumont's only disappointment was his inability to secure English publication. "I have returned Beaumont's experiments as I do not feel inclined to make an offer for it," was all one London publisher could make himself write.

Beaumont was inundated with requests from learned bodies to exhibit St. Martin before them. First making Alexis sign a new contract that ran for two more years, the physician browbeat him into allowing himself to be shown off. The former voyageur had all the modesty of simple folk; he hated to stand, naked to the waist, before an audience of strangers, and the embarrassment of this young man who longed to be normal must have been heightened by the feeling that he was being gawked at as a freak, like the fat girl who was so eager to sign her photograph at one of the "museums" where he sometimes tried to forget the loneliness of his Eastern exile. When he complained to his master, Beaumont, who regarded his scruples as due to "the natural obstinacy of his disposition," paid no attention. Certain that he was advancing the cause of knowledge, the physician dragged his trembling servant before classes at the Columbian Medical College in Washington. During a trip through New England, he exhibited him to the Connecticut Medical Convention and in Boston, where he gave a vial of gastric juice for analysis to Dr. Charles T. Jackson, the chemist who was later to claim the discovery of anæsthesia.

Finally Alexis became so obviously miserable that even Beaumont noticed it and felt a little pity for him; he gave him a two months' holiday to visit his family in Canada. Beaumont planned when St. Martin returned to take him to France, as the American ambassador, Edward Livingston, had agreed to secure an invitation from the learned societies there. Remembering that eagerness to see Paris had brought the French Canadian back from Canada before, Beaumont again tried to charm him with tales of the wonderful things they would see in that city. Pleased with his subtlety, he was not worried when Alexis set out for home; he was convinced that his servant would return without his family on the day set. It did not seem to have occurred to him that St. Martin, having been fooled once by such promises, might not believe him a second time.

4

DURING Alexis's leave of absence, Beaumont went to Washington, where he tried to induce Congress to reimburse him for the money he had spent on his investigations, and to grant him a sum with which to pay his subject in the future. Although his demands were modest in the extreme, only $10,000 in all, Congress turned the appropriation down because of theoretical objections to spending money for science or philanthropy. Beaumont then suggested that the army and navy buy a large number of his books to teach the men in the services "the true principles of temperance in both eating and drinking," but this effort also ended in failure.

He was ordered to St. Louis. When Dr. Jackson learned of this, without consulting Beaumont he persuaded some two hundred members of Congress to sign the following petition: "Being informed that Dr. Charles T. Jackson, an eminent chemist of Boston, is successfully prosecuting an analysis of the gastric fluid of Alexis St. Martin . . . and that the analysis cannot be satisfactorily accomplished without the presence of Dr. Beaumont and St. Martin . . . we request that the Honorable Secretary of War will station Dr. Beaumont at Boston." Since Beaumont had no desire to be kidnaped, Lovell quashed the petition.

Somewhat discouraged by the government's unwillingness to finance his experiments, the physiologist returned to Plattsburg for his rendezvous with Alexis. However, the Canadian failed to appear on the appointed day, and after that the days followed each other in dragging succession while Beaumont first hoped, then fumed, then gave way to despair. After two weeks of useless waiting, he was forced to go west to his new post.

He was overtaken by the following letter: "Dear Sir, My wife is not willing for me to go for she thinks I can do a great deal better to stay at home, for on my farm she thinks will be great deal more profit for me. I had started on the eighteenth of the month and went as far as St. Johns, and fell sick. On account of this my wife is afraid to let me go. Me and my wife joins in love to you and your mistress and all the family. Hoping this may find you all in good health, I hope you won't be angry with me as I can do better at home. I am much obliged to you for all you have done, and if it was in my power I should [do] all I could for you with pleasure. You will be good enough to give my love to Mr. Green and his family. No more from, Yours, Alexis St. Martin."

"Here we have his true character," Beaumont commented in a letter to Lovell. "His object was to induce me to come into Canada after him, and, knowing my inability there to enforce the conditions of his [contract] to any useful purpose, intended and expected to take advantage of my anxiety to extort a much higher salary. I know well his disposition and his ugliness, and hope rightly to [defeat] them. I have taken no notice of his communication, nor shall I make any demonstrations to get him again till I return in the fall (which I hope to be permitted to do without fail), by which time he will have spent all the money I advanced him to provide for his family for the year ensuing, become miserably poor and wretched, and be willing to recant his villainous obstinacy and ugliness, and then I shall be able to regain possession of him again, I have no doubt. Should it be decided by the Parisian committee to invite the case there, opportunity must be afforded and means used to regain control of him immediately before it is too late. I constantly fear he may lease himself to some of the medical men in Canada, and get his case into the hands of the English doctors. You can readily appreciate my anxiety. . . ."

Beaumont reopened the negotiations six months later, but they soon reached a deadlock. Remembering how lonely and helpless he had been without his wife to aid him, Alexis announced he would come only if he could bring her along. Beaumont, however, could not bear the prospect of putting up again with the humors of the woman who made his servant so difficult to handle; he refused to accept the condition. There the matter rested while the doctor, permitted by Lovell to carry on a private practice in addition to his army duties, was swept up in a flood of prosperity. As the leading physician in one of the fastest-growing cities of the frontier, he soon made six to eight thousand dollars annually, while successful land speculations swelled his income even more.

When he was offered the chair of surgery in the medical department of St. Louis University, then in the process of organization, the great physiologist, who had never received any formal scientific education, was terrified. He wrote the surgeon general explaining his lack of qualifications and requesting "a good excuse for non-acceptance," only to learn that Lovell had died two weeks before. Deprived of the shield that had protected him for so many years, he was unable to protect himself and reluctantly accepted the professorship. However, the school did not get started for some time.

In the spring of 1838, four years after Alexis had disappeared, Beaumont received a letter from the American Physiological Society in Boston asking whether they might not secure the services of the Canadian. "I presume," Beaumont replied, "no consideration whatever would induce him to engage himself to the American Physiological Society or any other society for the purpose of experimentation without my personal attention and direction. He is capriciously and foolishly obstinate in that respect and always has been. It has ever been my wish and effort to place him in some scientific physiological institution where greater and more extensive justice might be done the subject of experimenting upon him than has ever been in my power to do, but he has ever and determinedly refused his assent to such an arrangement."

This letter seemed to give the society permission to secure Alexis's services if it could, but when the Canadian threatened to go to Boston without Beaumont, the physician tried to prevent such a catastrophe by acceding to the demand he had so often refused before; he wrote St. Martin to bring his family with him to St. Louis. Alexis should have been elated at this sudden willingness to receive him on his own conditions, for he lived in poverty and squalor within a shack so tiny you had to stoop going through the door. He agreed to come, but instead of preparing for the journey, he fled to a saloon and stayed there. When his son, Alexis, Jr., died, that was another good reason for drinking; he failed to set out according to his promise. Disgusted and thinking better of his rash agreement to receive Mrs. St. Martin, Beaumont dropped the matter for several more years.

His mind was occupied with new troubles. Dr. Thomas Lawson, who had succeeded Lovell as surgeon general, had long disapproved of the favors his predecessor had showered on Beaumont; the physiologist soon heard rumors that he was to be transferred to Jefferson Barracks, a post so far outside St. Louis that he could not have continued his private practice. It was never officially established that the change was intended, but when Lawson refused to grant Beaumont a leave of absence he desired, the surgeon wrote his superior demanding to know if such a transfer was planned and implying that only a half-wit would consider stationing him at the barracks. "I cannot acknowledge just cause or even seriously anticipate an order of removal from this place." Beaumont obviously thought his composition, which was superficially couched in respectful language, a master political stroke; actually it was almost as insulting as it could be.

Lawson replied by commanding him to serve on a temporary commission in Florida; Beaumont threatened to resign from the army unless the command was rescinded. Soon we find him writing the adjutant general: "General order number two of twentieth inst. announcing the unexpected and ungrateful acceptance of my resignation 'to take effect on 31 December 1839' has been received—a most noble recompense magnanimously awarded to an old officer for duty efficiently performed and a life faithfully spent in the service of his country." Through letters to Congressmen and a memorial to President Van Buren he agitated with mounting violence for reinstatement. Although his intimate friends, Captain Robert E. Lee and Major Ethan Allen Hitchcock, worked for him in Washington, his resignation was allowed to stand. Fulminating against the "weak, waspish, and willful head of the medical department," Beaumont returned to private life after twenty-seven years in the army.

However, he did not find private life any more peaceful than Daniel Drake had done. St. Louis now had two medical schools to cause quarrels in the profession: the medical department of St. Louis University with which Beaumont was allied, although he never taught there, and the medical department of Kemper College, popularly known as McDowell's College, for its founder and leading spirit was Drake's brother-in-law and Ephraim McDowell's nephew, Joseph Nashe McDowell. In an address as president of the Medical Society of Missouri, Beaumont attacked the physicians who "seek to amalgamate themselves with our bitterest professional enemies, men rejected for their demerits, disappointed applicants for admission to our society, and vain, vindictive itinerants and egotistical characters called professors of a self-generated, ill-begotten institution yclept 'medical school' somewhere in the vicinity, which alike regardless of the common courtesy of medical communities and destitute of professional decency and etiquette obtruded itself into public notice like a swarm of ephemeral insects by the disgusting noise of its own creation in its sudden transit to decay and nothingness."

Joseph Nashe McDowell was not the man to take such an attack lying down. The passing years had brought his eccentricities close to the border of madness. Joseph wore a brass breastplate for fear of the Jesuits who were the incorporators of St. Louis University; he constructed his college building like a fort; he trained his students into an army with the idea of capturing northern California for the United States; and he melted the college bell down for cannon. Every Fourth of July he dressed himself up in a three-cornered revolutionary hat with a rooster feather in it, and buckled a huge sword round his waist under a blue swallow-tail coat with brass buttons. Full of zest and glory and patriotic fervor, he directed his students as they laid the cannon on saw-horses and fired them off to the extreme terror of the childen at the Christian Brothers Academy next door. These youngsters believed that Joseph was in league with the devil, and that if you searched his college you would find a passageway direct to Hades; no child or colored man could be induced to go within five blocks of McDowell's College after dark. The story went round that during a serious illness Joseph had made his friends promise that if he died they would hang his body, pickled in alcohol, from the roof of Mammoth Cave. He lived, however, to realize his military ambitions by leading his students on the battlefields of the Civil War and to represent the Confederacy on a mission to Europe. As an aged widower, he married a young woman who proved to be such a shrew that he fled to the Catholic Church from which he had protected himself with a breastplate for so many decades.

Joseph's valedictory addresses were famous; students from both colleges flocked to hear him attack St. Louis University, which at that time he called Pope's College. On one occasion, a former pupil remembers, he sauntered down the aisle of the amphitheater with a violin in his hand. Seeing some of the audience sitting sideways, which always annoyed him, he cried: "Gentlemen, I pray you, gentlemen, sit straight and face the music." After scraping away for a few minutes, he laid the instrument aside and burst into an eloquent farewell which ended with the picture of an old student returning after many years to visit his grave. "He will find amidst rank weeds and seedless grass a simple marble slab inscribed 'Joseph Nashe McDowell, Surgeon.' As he stands there contemplating the rare virtues and eccentricities of this old man, suddenly, gentlemen, the spirit of Dr. McDowell will arise upon ethereal wings and bless him. Yes, thrice bless him. Then it will take a swoop, and when it passes this building it will drop a parting tear, but, gentlemen, when it gets to Pope's College, it will expectorate upon it."

Such was the surgeon who in those wild days was called in consultation from the Alleghenies to the Rockies, who founded an important medical school and became vice-president of the American Medical Association. He was no mean opponent in the wars of Billingsgate so popular among doctors; twice his faction had Beaumont in court on charges of malpractice. But Beaumont too was an effective fighter; he won the case each time and continued to build up an ever larger clientele.

On leaving the army, Beaumont had bought a country estate where he lived with his children simply and pleasantly. They kept open house for their intimate friends; Captain Lee and Major Hitchcock stayed months at a time. Both were charmed with his daughter, Sarah, who was a very musical young lady. She played the piano while Hitchcock joined in on the flute and Lee, not dreaming yet of secession, turned the pages. Beside her sat the doctor, with his teeth firmly fixed on the casing of the piano, for he had become so deaf that he could hear only through bone conduction. This was a great trial to him, as music was his principal relaxation; he never entered a theater or permitted his children to do so. He danced, however, keeping time although he could not hear the music.

He was an indulgent father but a stern disciplinarian, especially towards his son, whom he inundated with good advice: "Discard the bewitching visions and flickering thoughts of passionate love and hymeneal blisses, during your professional pupilage at least. Relinquish all undue pretension to gallantry and obsequious attention to the girls, graces, or the muses. Consign them all to the entertainment and embraces of fops and fools. . . . Affiance your mind only to books, business, and professional studies and pursuit till you are a score and V or X or more, and then be cool and coy, as behooves a man, but not a boy."

Such letters were similar to the ones he had written his younger brother during his days of adolescent longing at Plattsburg. Indeed, his life had in some ways described a complete circle. He had met his destiny and done scientific work that was to make him forever famous, but destiny seemed to have moved on; years had passed since he had attempted any kind of experiment. But perhaps it was not too late, for St. Martin still lived.

During 1838, an edition of Beaumont's book had finally appeared in England. The next year the chemico-medical committee of the British Association asked the central committee for two hundred pounds to bring Alexis to England. Although this grant was blocked "by a noble member on the grounds that the subject was coarse, indelicate, and calculated to disgust," in 1840 the matter was brought up again and plans made for securing the Canadian. Warned by a former apprentice to "be watchful or those wily Englishmen will slip him over to London before you are aware of it," Beaumont began dilatory negotiations to have St. Martin brought to St. Louis, but again they effected nothing. Alexis stayed in Berthier.

Six years later the doctor made his former servant the usual offer of a few hundred dollars if he would come without his family. St. Martin replied through the local priest, who wrote his letters for him: "My wife will not hear of my going without her, and you can understand how hard it is for me to go off and see her and my four children in tears at my leaving them in that manner. I am happy where I am. I can earn sufficient to support them here. Money is no object to me alone. My only wish is to see my family satisfied. . . . My wife will be thankful to you for the balance that is owed to her for one hundred and fifty dozen of drapes, shirts, etc., that she washed for your family." He then ended, as usual, by threatening to allow some Canadian doctors to experiment on him if Beaumont would not receive him with his family.

So far, the dickering had proceeded according to routine, but suddenly Beaumont decided to send his son to Canada after St. Martin. This was his most ambitious attempt to regain the subject of his immortal experiments, yet he wrote Buddy the following instructions: "If he should obstinately refuse to come without his family, you will immediately return without him. . . . You will take him in charge as a private servant in traveling. Keep him in his place and strictly control his time and services. Allow no undue familiarity, or suffer him to take the slightest advantage of your age and inexperience to obtain indulgences. . . . If he should become obstinate and refractory and give you much trouble in getting him along, stop his traveling expenses and discharge him at once, and let him work his passage back or forward as he may choose and proceed on without him."

Beaumont's letter hardly seems that of a man who is moving heaven and earth to achieve a long-desired object. He behaved very differently in regard to things he really wanted; once he built barricades and hired an armed guard to repel the workmen sent by the city of St. Louis to continue a street through his property.

When Buddy reported that St. Martin had refused to come without his family, Beaumont dropped the matter. Even his friend and collaborator, Dr. Samuel Beaumont, was puzzled. "I am fully persuaded," he wrote his cousin concerning Alexis, "that he cannot be induced to leave his family to go so great a distance. I will not pretend to advise, as you know him better than I do, but would there be a great risk in advancing the amount necessary to carry his family to St. Louis? . . . If you think the object of sufficient importance to warrant the risk of the amount necessary to transport himself and family, I should feel it a pleasure and a duty to assist you in any way I can."

Ever since he had come to St. Louis, Beaumont had written a few letters every year or so negotiating for St. Martin on his own terms, but a careful reading of this correspondence indicates that he did not really want his subject back. This is a strange discovery! Who would suppose that a man whose fame rested on one series of world-shaking experiments would not be anxious to go on with them?

Obviously, the immediate cause of Beaumont's reluctance was his dread of further association with St. Martin unless he was sure he could control him completely; Beaumont's hatred for the Canadian shines from every word he wrote about him. But beneath this reason there must have been a deeper reason. Had he been convinced that he could further his fame and his usefulness to humanity, a man of Beaumont's positive character would never have let any personal dislike permanently block his way. Had his mind been full of ideas for new experiments, he would certainly have gone to Canada himself and brought Alexis back with two families if need be. For three years he had worked with rare ingenuity, making in all two hundred and thirty-eight experiments, and he had come to the end of the specific investigations he had planned. Even the most versatile and best-trained scientific workers exhaust at last their fertility on a particular subject, although there may be further steps to be taken that a man of less ability is able to see the instant their work is published. Beaumont, however, had not received an adequate scientific education, and he did not possess great mental flexibility; he never did any experiments except those

on his man, although the entire St. Martin episode took less
than fifteen years out of a long life. Are we not safe in assuming that Beaumont did not really want St. Martin back because
he did not really know what experiments he would perform
when he got him?

Beaumont was not the kind of man to make such an admission to himself or to the world. He had to absolve his own conscience by writing St. Martin periodically, gesturing as if he
really wanted him, although except in rare moments of enthusiasm he always put a joker into his offers which he knew
would keep them from being accepted. Sometimes, as in his
letter to the American Physiological Society, he made another
gesture: he pretended that he wished St. Martin to fall into
hands more able than his own. But how could he really wish
that to happen? No man who has reached fame after a long
and passionate quest, certainly no man as proud as Beaumont,
can willingly allow that fame to be taken from him by people
who had enjoyed advantages of education and position he
never had known. There was humility in Beaumont's character,
but it never brought him to the point of self-abasement.

As age descended upon him, weakening his pride and his de-
sires, that humility grew more and more intense. During his
sixty-sixth year, he received a letter telling him how much
Claude Bernard admired his researches and asking in the name
of the famous French physiologist for further information
about Alexis. Beaumont replied that the approbation of "truly
scientific investigators" filled him both with pleasure and with
regret that he had not made better use of his unrivaled opportunity. He hoped, he said, either to put St. Martin in the
hands of "others more capable than myself" or else himself
"to retrieve in a measure the neglected opportunity and my
own former inefficiency." The first step was to make another

try himself. He wrote to Canada, offering to receive Alexis with his family if need be.

Alexis had been reaching out in Beaumont's direction whenever his poverty made it seem madness not to try to secure so lucrative a position, but we may be certain that he too was glad of the disagreement about his family that kept him from really having to submit to unpleasant experiments under an unpleasant master. Now that this excuse was taken from him, he ran away from home. For months he was missing, and when he finally returned he decided he was too ill to make so long a journey. On hearing the frightening news that Beaumont himself might come up to Canada to get him, he leapt from bed and rushed off a letter saying he would be on his way at once. However, he managed to procrastinate until winter stopped all transportation.

Beaumont, conscious that his remaining years were few, continued his efforts. A letter he wrote his cousin Samuel expressed his undiminished hatred for St. Martin and then continued: "I have evaded his designs so far, but I verily fear that the strong and increasing impulse of conscious conviction of the great benefits and important usefulness of further and more accurate physiological investigations of the subject will impel me to still further efforts and sacrifices to obtain him. Physiological authors and most able writers on dietetics and gastric functions generally demand it of me in trumpet tones. I must have him at all hazards, and obtain the necessary assistance to my individual and private efforts, or transfer him to some competent scientific institution for thorough investigation and report. I must retrieve my past ignorance, imbecility, and professional remissness of a quarter of a century or more by double diligence, intense study, and untiring application of soul and body to the subject before I die.

'Should posthumous time retain my name
Let historic truths declare my fame.' "

He then explained that he had offered St. Martin a large sum to come by himself for one year with the understanding that he could bring his family the next year. "I think he will take the bait and come on this fall, and when I get him alone again into my keeping and engagement, I will take good care to control him as I please."

Alexis, however, did not take the bait, and Beaumont, despite all his fine resolutions, gave up his negotiations for all time. He sank contentedly into a peaceful old age. "Domestic affairs," he wrote his cousin, "are easy, peaceable, and pleasant. Health of community generally good. No severe epidemic diseases prevalent. Weather remarkably pleasant. Business of all kinds increasing. Products of the earth abundant. Money plentiful. Railroads progressing with almost telegraphic speed. I expect to come to Plattsburg next summer all the way by rail. Family all enjoying health, happiness, and abundance."

A year later, as he was returning home from visiting a patient, he slipped on some ice-covered steps and struck his head so violently that he wandered round in a daze until met by a friend who took him home. This accident gave him premonitions of an early death which were realized within a few weeks. On April 22, his old friend, William G. Eliot, wrote in his diary: "Have been with Dr. Beaumont who is near death. A carbuncle on his neck at the base of the brain is the proximate cause. He has suffered terribly and with the most manly fortitude. . . . He leaves me as his executor of a property of $150,000. This was arranged with great difficulty, for his deafness is so increased that it is almost impossible to make him hear one word at a time. Last Friday he directed me to place his name on our church record and partook of communion."

Having thrown himself at last into the arms of religion, Beaumont died on April 25, 1853.

St. Martin, who had up till then never allowed another doctor to experiment on him, was soon engaged in a tour of medical schools. Could his unwillingness to let anyone infringe on Beaumont's work during his benefactor's lifetime have been not entirely "villainous obstinacy," but also gratitude? If so, it casts a new light on the human guinea pig whose character medical writers, following Beaumont's own accounts, have universally reviled.

There are records of St. Martin's appearance at various places during 1856. Dr. Bunting, late of the British army in Canada, demonstrated his miraculous stomach at St. Louis. "In the exhibition which we witnessed," wrote the editor of the *St. Louis Medical and Surgical Journal*, "it is evident that the object was more to realize money than to promote science, but we hope that hereafter a different course will be pursued." This hope was realized by Dr. Francis Gurney Smith, who did a series of experiments in Philadelphia. Smith was no Beaumont, however; he decided that although hydrochloric acid was present in the gastric juice, the main agent was lactic acid.

St. Martin must have found his return to the medical faculties as unpleasant as he had always feared it would be; he never allowed another experiment to be done on him, although his family remained wretchedly poor. A move from Berthier to Cavendish, Vermont, did not help their financial condition. The old man lived in a hovel with four married children and a flock of grandchildren; he continually begged from Beaumont's son. After a time, he went back to Canada. The great disappointment of his life had been his failure to get to Paris according to Beaumont's promise, but as the years passed, his weakening mind made up for this deficiency by imagining he had been there. "I went to Europe with Dr. Beaumont," he wrote an inquirer from Rush Medical College. "I stay three months. I forget the year. I am so old that I could not remember the year."

The mellowness of his senile mind cast a glow over the past. "Dear friend," he wrote Buddy, "I am as well as can be expected and I received your kind and welcome letter which give me much pleasure to hear from you, and I would like to know how Sarah gets along and her family, and all my folks are well, send their best love to all of your folks. I am better here. To earn my living I chop wood by the cord. I have not done much work this winter because I have been sick, and I was much surprise to hear that your mother was dead because I had not heard about her death before you told me, and I have one more girl that is not married yet. No more at present. Write soon and tell me all the news that you know. I would like to hear them all. Good-by, kind friend. How I would like to be with you, but as I am not I will be satisfied as I am. My love to all of them that speaks well of me. I am your true friend."

And again: "Remember me as I remember you, because it is with a profound heart that I love you, never forgetting the days when I was in the company of your person, and I am bound to say that I regard you as a son and a true friend."

Alexis lived to be over eighty. When he died twenty-eight years after Beaumont's death, Sir William Osler, then still in Canada, offered his family a large sum for permission to do an autopsy and place the famous stomach in the Army Medical Museum at Washington. But the St. Martins, despite their searing poverty, were determined that their father's death should be what his life had never been; that he should rest in his grave like a normal man. In order to foil any doctors who might try to disturb him there, they delayed his funeral so long that the coffin had to be left outside the church during the service, and they buried him eight feet deep.

The Death of Pain

CRAWFORD W. LONG

and

WILLIAM T. G. MORTON

Crawford W. Long

FROM A CONTEMPORARY CRAYON DRAWING

The Death of Pain

Crawford W. Long
William T. G. Morton

1

DOWN all the long centuries of history whenever a
knife cut living flesh the result was agony. Then suddenly, within four years, a magic sleep was discovered two
separate times on a new continent, once by a rural Georgia
practitioner in his twenties, and once by a dentist not yet out
of Harvard Medical School.

A strange story this. The story of a discovery waiting for
half a century almost found, a discovery of overwhelming importance knocking continually at the doors of the scientific
great, begging to be taken in, only to be turned away until at
last, like the angel of an old fable, it knocked at the humbler
doorways of the inconspicuous and found a home. And astound-
ingly this great boon to mankind was a scourge to its inventors;
of the four men who claimed the discovery in the great ether
controversy that raged during the last half of the nineteenth
century, two died hopelessly mad, one by his own hand, and

a third starved, had a series of nervous breakdowns, and was finally killed by a stroke due to the pamphlet of one of his opponents. Only the fourth lived to an old age, and even he was embittered by a sense of injustice.

Before the discovery of anæsthesia, even as simple an operation as setting a dislocated leg turned the operating-room into a medieval torture chamber. The patient was stretched on a rack, his body attached to one set of pulleys, the offending leg to another, while muscular assistants tugged with all their force. As the heavy ropes inched tighter, the patient's muscles stretched until the sinews seemed about to tear. Despite all that opiates could do, perspiration of agony started out on his forehead. No longer able to stifle his screams, he struggled convulsively, vainly trying to escape from the tension that was inexorable as death. Surely the agony must stop now, surely no human being would submit another to such torture, but the surgeon stands helplessly by, for a long distance still intervenes between the ball of the leg-bone and its socket. The pull becomes stronger, the heavy men sweating at the ropes, until the pain passes human endurance, and the patient loses consciousness. Then the surgeon, who has been watching with a stern face of unavailing pity, springs into action. Taking advantage of the relaxation insensibility brings, he dexterously twists the head of the bone into its socket. Finally the torn and tortured sufferer is carried to his bed to recover from the operation as best he may.

If you were to dislocate your leg tomorrow, a whiff of ether would not only bring you sleep but relaxation so complete that the surgeon could snap the bone back into place easily and in most cases without the use of pulleys.

Anæsthesia was as important for the surgeons as for the patients; it gave surgeons the priceless boon of time. Before its development, they had to rush through operations at break-neck speed, although impeded at every moment by the struggles, both conscious and reflex, of the victims. He was the best surgeon who broke three minutes in an amputation or a lithotomy. William Cheselden, the friend of Alexander Pope, could cut out a bladder stone in fifty-four seconds. Since there was no leisure in these record-breaking operations for antiseptic precautions, had anæsthesia never been discovered Lister's methods could never have been applied. In the days of pain, surgery was limited to a few simple operations that could safely be done with lightning rapidity; the complicated operations that are one of the glories of modern science were out of the question.

Down the ages men have dreamt of relieving pain, and always something was known of narcotics. But drugs were not enough; "not poppy, nor mandragora, nor all the drowsy syrups of the world" sufficed to benumb the senses when the knife cut deep. The first step towards modern anæsthesia, and one that covered almost the whole distance, was made by Sir Humphry Davy during his experiments with laughing gas. In 1799 he wrote: "As nitrous oxide in its extensive operation seems capable of destroying physical pain, it may probably be used with advantage in surgical operations in which no great effusion of blood takes place." It is difficult to understand how this suggestion, so succinctly put in a book often consulted by men of science, could remain unacted upon for forty-three years. Yet such was the case.

In March 1800, William Allen, the lecturer on chemistry at Guy's Hospital in London, demonstrated the inhalation of laughing gas, commenting particularly on the loss of the sensation of pain. Astley Cooper, one of the pioneers of experimental surgery, sat in the audience; he heard the words and saw the demonstration, yet failed to make the obvious inference.

Besides pointing out the possible anæsthetic qualities of laughing gas, Sir Humphry Davy showed that its inhalation produced a most delightful drunkenness. The second part of his lecture was not forgotten. It became a routine diversion in medical schools to inhale the gas, have wonderful visions, and, when the effect wore off, laugh at the ridiculous antics of your friends who were still under the influence. Immediately the Yankee genius found a way to turn the amusing properties of the gas to profit. Those were the palmy days of traveling showmen, for the United States was fringed with an ever-widening fan of pioneers whose settlements offered them no amusements whatsoever. Soon there set out over the land a little horde of chemical lecturers who rolled sesquipedalian words from well-hinged tongues, who did experiments with liquids that changed colors and solids that exploded, but who depended principally on demonstrations of the drunkenness produced by laughing gas. Samuel Colt, the inventor of the revolver, was for a time a member of this motley band that all unwittingly sowed widely over the land the seeds of a great discovery.

In the winter of 1841, such a "Lyceum lecturer" approached Jefferson, Georgia. Although his name is lost to history, we can be sure he was not successful, for no successful showman would have played this tiny hamlet 140 miles from any railroad. We can visualize his long black beard that terrified the yokels flowing from beneath a broad-brimmed black hat of the type now worn only by Senators. As he rode in his brightly painted cart behind an under-fed nag, he could not have realized that he was making history; looking at the ramshackle houses of the little village, he must have wondered whether he would make enough for his evening meal. Listlessly, he drew up in

the public square and under the eyes of delighted urchins laid
out his apparatus.

That night the gayer young men of the town, most of whom
went to the village academy, gathered as was their custom in
the office of the local practitioner, Dr. Crawford W. Long. The
physician was a tall and handsome young man of twenty-six,
with a high forehead, blue eyes, and a large aquiline nose; he
was the center of every frolic and a terror with the young
ladies. Since he had been attending a patient in the country,
he had not known of the lecturer's visit, and he was heartbroken
to hear what he had missed. His friends described to him how
the showman had harangued his audience from the tail of his
cart and concluded his act by first inhaling laughing gas himself and then requesting the townspeople to do so. Several of
Long's friends had volunteered. They found the sensation delightful, more delightful than drunkenness even, for not only
were they happy, but they suddenly felt that they understood
all the mysteries of the universe. And it was fun to watch others
take the gas, for they went through the most ridiculous antics.
Some sang, some danced, some made impassioned orations or
engaged in imaginary arguments with invisible opponents.

"You're supposed to be a doctor and know something about
chemistry," Long's friends concluded. "Make us some gas and
we'll go on a fine tear."

While a medical student in Philadelphia, Long had attended
a chemical lecture during which the more up-to-date urban
showman had induced drunkenness not with laughing gas but
with ether. The young man had hurried back with his friends
to the house where they all boarded and, locking the doors so
his two Quaker spinster landladies would hear nothing, had
organized a private ether jag of his own.

He did not have any laughing gas, he explained to his friends in Jefferson, but he knew that ether would do just as well. Reaching into the cupboard, he brought out a bottle he always kept on hand. Ether was a common drug used for nervous ailments in minute quantities because it tasted so strong.

"The company," he told the Georgia State Medical Society many years later, "were anxious to witness its effects, the ether was introduced, and all present in turn inhaled. They were so much pleased with its effects that they afterwards frequently used it and induced others to do the same, and the practice soon became quite fashionable in the county and some of the contiguous counties. On numerous occasions I inhaled ether for its exhilarating properties." It is amusing to see peering from behind these respectable words the laughing face of a high old time.

Two or three evenings a week the young men of the town held ether sprees in Dr. Long's office. Hearing of the gay antics induced by the drug, the local young ladies developed a consuming curiosity to see for themselves. At a Christmas entertainment, a flock of them gathered round Long, begging and coaxing that he get some ether and inhale it for them. It would have taken a much harder heart than the one under the doctor's bright waistcoat to resist such entreaties. He demurred only long enough to receive a full broadside of the stamps and *moues* with which the armories of young ladies were well stocked in those days. Then he set off, whistling. Before he reached his office, he laughed out loud, for he had a wonderful idea.

It was a very grave physician who returned to the party ten minutes later. He said to the girls who crowded round him that although he had brought the drug he had decided not to inhale it after all, for there was no telling what he might do while under the influence, and Heaven forbid that he should forfeit the respect of even one of these fair charmers. At this the young ladies all expostulated at once, their eyes bright with eagerness. They wouldn't care what he did; they wouldn't even notice it; they would remember it was not his fault but the ether's. And please, please; they so wanted to see the sport.

"All right," said Dr. Long. "I'll inhale some if you all promise not to hold me responsible for anything I may do." Never had such a chorus of promises been heard under one roof in Jefferson, Georgia.

Still with the utmost solemnity, the handsome young doctor poured the liquid on a towel and put it to his face. Then, assuming the attitude of a sleepwalker, he marched gravely round the room and kissed every girl in turn. Telling of this prank as an old man, he would slap his thigh and roar with laughter. "The girls must have liked it," he said, "they were so anxious to try the drug themselves."

Long was something of a dandy in his youth. He was engaged to the prettiest girl in the town, Caroline Swain, the daughter of a local planter and niece to a former governor of North Carolina. When she was only fourteen, he had seen her on the main street of Jefferson, and been fascinated by the brilliant coloring of her white skin, sparkling eyes, and golden hair. Although he instantly decided to marry her, he waited until she was sixteen before he proposed. At the time of Long's Christmas escapade they had just become engaged, but we may be sure Caroline did not mind the prank he played on the other girls; she enjoyed having so dashing a young man for her fiancé. "I yet see him," she wrote in later years, "dressed in a light blue summer suit, collars and cuffs black, tan-colored silk gloves, wide-brimmed white hat, sitting superbly on his dapple-gray charger, firm, dignified—he rides like one to command."

However, it would be false to think of Dr. Long as nothing

but a handsome young fellow who loved to inhale ether for its "exhilarating effect"; he had a serious side too that led to his great discovery. Unusually well prepared for a country doctor of those days, he had graduated brilliantly from Franklin College, now the University of Georgia, at the age of nineteen, and studied medicine at both the leading schools of the nation, Transylvania and the University of Pennsylvania. Then he had spent a year and a half working in various New York hospitals.

During his childhood, he had been taught the importance of hard work. His father was a typically strait-laced Scotch-Irish elder of the Presbyterian Church who had much in common with Ephraim McDowell's father. James Long held family prayers every day and reared his children to recite the shorter catechism from beginning to end without asking any questions. He was a solid man who owned a plantation, a flour mill, and stock in the Georgia railway. An intimate friend of William H. Crawford and Henry Clay, he sat in the state legislature as a Whig, and attested to his intellectual interests by endowing an academy in his native Danielville, Georgia. All year round he wore a black broadcloth suit with a black satin waistcoat and a high silk beaver, in winter adding a voluminous black broadcloth cape. His granddaughter could not remember ever seeing him unbend.

Perhaps young Crawford inherited his tendency to be a dandy from his mother. Elizabeth Ware Long was a beautiful woman of Episcopalian stock who enjoyed fine clothes and the pomp of life. The other Presbyterian elders criticized her as worldly, but her husband did not seem to mind; indeed, he must have enjoyed his helpmate's pretty flutterings, for he supplied her with all the frills and gayeties she desired. And she, for her part, was able to settle down and run his complicated affairs when he was away. The plantation was a self-supporting community, and she spent her leisure hours teaching the daughters of her slaves fine needlework, hoping thus to assure her grandchildren beautiful clothes, for she never dreamed of abolition.

During the ether jags at his office in Jefferson, her son was the life of the party, but at the same time he was using his eyes and his mind. He noticed that, when his friends were intoxicated, they received without wincing falls and blows that should have produced pain. When he asked them about it afterwards, they assured him they had felt nothing. Sometimes he found bruises on his own body that he could not remember having received. All this seemed strange to him. He wondered about it, and one day he made the inference that thousands in the same situation had never made; he saw that ether was the death of pain.

At about this time James Venables, a dashing lad of twenty-one who went to the village academy and was very fond of inhaling ether, began to be bothered by two little tumors on the back of his neck. He was an intimate of Long's circle, and one evening, as that senate of good fellows sported in the doctor's office, he complained of his affliction. After a quick examination, Long said that the tumors would have to be cut out, and when Venables blanched at this statement, reached for his knife and jokingly offered to cut them out at once. But the patient made excuses—he did not feel very well that day—and for a long time afterwards he procrastinated until the boys teased him about being afraid.

Early on the morning of March 30, 1842, before the village academy opened, Long called on his friend. He had lain awake all night, worrying about the possibility of using ether to stop pain, and finally he had decided to make the test. Excitedly he suggested that if Venables would inhale the gas while the tumors were being removed, he would probably not be hurt. The idea was a strange one, but the doctor was able to back it up with so many incidents Venables remembered, when their friends had fallen and felt nothing, that he agreed at last to let Long try it on one tumor. The operation was scheduled for that afternoon as soon as school was over. Several of Venables's classmates begged to be allowed to see the experiment, and Long, who was always good-natured, agreed, but he insisted that the principal of the academy be invited as well to lend the proceedings an air of respectability.

The ether Long possessed had sat on his shelf for about a month. Here is the letter through which the first anæsthetic ever to be used in an operation was procured. It was addressed to Robert H. Goodman, a friend who had recently moved to the metropolis of Athens, Georgia.

"Dear Bob,

I am under the necessity of troubling you a little. I am entirely out of ether and wish some by tomorrow night if it is possible to receive it by that time. We have some girls in Jefferson who are anxious to see it taken, and you know nothing would afford me more pleasure than to take it in their presence and to get a few sweet kisses(?). You will please hand the order below to Dr. Reese, and if you can meet with the opportunity to send the medicines to me tomorrow you will confer a great favor by doing so. If you cannot send them tomorrow, get Dr. Reese to send them by the stage on Wednesday. I can persuade the girls to remain until Wednesday night, but would prefer receiving the ether sooner.

Your friend,
Crawford W. Long"

When this letter is quoted in medical histories, the reference to kissing the girls is usually deleted.

Simplicity, good fellowship, and joy of living mingled with intelligence to make Crawford W. Long a great benefactor of humanity. One may search the records in vain for any indications of self-conscious ceremony connected with the first operation ever done under anæsthesia, and as we shall see later, this lack of ostentation did damage to Long's reputation from which it has not recovered even yet.

After the village academy let out that March afternoon, three of the scholars accompanied their principal down the main street of the little town. Greeting everyone they met with the casual friendliness of rural communities, they came at last to the doctor's frame house. He received them at the doorway, a handsome young man of twenty-six, and motioned them in. No passer-by would have especially noticed this scene, which seemed part of the sleepy dullness of a small town.

The office into which Long showed his friends had no resemblance to the doctor's offices of today. There was a table, a few hard chairs, and a sofa on which young Venables nervously lay down. Long reached for the bottle which had been their companion in so many sprees, poured ether on a towel as he had done a hundred times, but this time his hand must have trembled a little for he realized that he was making an important experiment. The spectators, gathered in a knot at the back of the room, watched in frowning attention as with one hand he held the towel over his patient's mouth and nose, permitting him to breathe a little air as well as the drug, while with the other hand he felt his pulse. From time to time he pricked his friend with a pin, and when Venables did not feel the prick, he reached for his knife and removed the tumor. The entire operation took about five minutes. When the towel was removed from his face, Venables, after a moment of suspense, returned satisfactorily to life; he had to be shown the tumor to be convinced it was out. The relaxed tension set everybody joking and laughing. They discussed the operation for a while, going over it point by point as you might an exciting baseball game, and then went home to gossip with their families and friends about what had happened.

For ten thousand years men had sought to conquer pain; thus simply was the great quest ended. Nor was it entirely accident that a backwoods doctor had made the discovery. Although all medical men knew that ether produced insensibility when too much was inhaled, the faculties were unanimous in teaching that such stupefaction was dangerous to life. Ether parties were very common in those days. Innumerable times, of course, frolickers took too much and lost consciousness without injuring themselves in the least, but the doctors in urban centers had been taught to rely on authority and the words of the urban wise. Long, however, as he ministered to the scattered population of Jefferson County, fording streams, fighting storms, riding through unpopulated miles, had learnt to rely on his own eyes and his own ingenuity; there were no specialists he could consult, no medical libraries where he could read up on rare cases. The spirit of the pioneer who creates his own home from the wilderness brought about the discovery of anæsthesia.

If Long had immediately sent an account of his experiment to a medical journal and if the editor had condescended to publish so unorthodox and revolutionary a claim coming from an insignificant yokel in his twenties, the great ether war would never have been waged, for there could have been no doubt that Crawford W. Long was the discoverer. But this young man, who was so dashing with the girls, was a cautious and careful scientist. He had studied under Dr. George B. Wood, that enemy of premature publication, and he realized that an experiment done only once and without controls of any sort proves very little.

He soon learnt the need of certain proof. Although the youngsters from the Jefferson Academy and many of the simple people believed what he had done, the more distinguished doctors of the region, who had years and experience on their side, thought his claims ridiculous and were certain that he would kill a patient sooner or later. Their pompous pronouncements terrified even the people who had at first believed, until in a few months Long was changed from a hero into an object of terror. When he rode, jauntily as ever, through the lanes of Georgia that were now alive with spring, farm children scuttled indoors at his approach, while pious old crones reached for the Bible to protect themselves. Even the farmers working in the fields did not wave back when he waved. Word had gone round that this handsome, seemingly innocent young man could put people to sleep and carve them without their knowledge. Grave elders called on Long to warn him to stop his reckless madness before it was too late; they pointed out that if one of his patients died under ether he might be lynched. Sick people became afraid to come to him, and his practice dwindled.

Although Long was not secretive about his discovery but rather broadcast it to the world, there was no danger that another doctor would steal the credit; no other doctor would have anything to do with such madness. A strange document is the affidavit sworn to years later by one James Caman, M.D.: "This certifies that in the month of May 1843, I was present and assisted Dr. R. D. Moore in amputating a leg. He said to his three students, I being one: 'If I had thought of it before leaving home, I would have tried Dr. C. W. Long's great discovery producing insensibility by inhalation of ether.' "

It is hard to imagine what Dr. Moore was thinking. If he had really thought that Long had made a great discovery, he would not have been so casual about it, and if he had really forgotten, he would have done his next operation under ether. Perhaps he knew that he should give his patient the boon of sleep, yet dared not go against established medical opinion, and, ashamed of his own cowardice, pretended he was not afraid but absent-minded.

Long showed an inquiring spirit from the very first. When he removed Venables's second tumor, he experimented by stopping the ether before he began cutting, for he believed that, if ether were to be used in lengthy operations, it might be dangerous for the patient to continue inhaling the whole time. Since his friend's tumor had formed adhesions to the adjoining parts, the excision took a good many minutes, and towards the end, Venables showed slight signs of suffering. "Since that time," Long told the Georgia State Medical Society, "I have invariably desired patients, when practicable, to continue the inhalation during the time of the operation."

Faced with a rising gale of criticism, Long reacted in the manner of a true scientist; he tried to find possible flaws in his proof that ether killed pain. Perhaps Venables's nerves had been deadened not by ether but by suggestion. The medical great were at that time busily squabbling as to whether patients could be thrown into hypnotic trances before operations and thus made insensible; perhaps Long had inadvertently mesmerized his friend. The way to eliminate this possibility, he decided, was to use ether on many people, since not all individuals could be mesmerized.

It could also be argued, he knew, that a few persons were

immune to pain and that his patients were among these. To prove that this was not the explanation, when he amputated two fingers from a Negro boy, he did one operation with ether and one without. The poor child slept satisfyingly under the drug and screamed satisfyingly when deprived of it. Some time later, Long cut three tumors from the same patient in one day, the second with ether, the first and third without, and he was delighted to find that the pain came only when he expected it.

His practice had shrunk because of his experiments. Few surgical patients dared come to him, and even these would not let him use ether. Although he reasoned with stolid farmers as they squirmed in his chair, pointing out that pain was a nasty thing and he could stop it, during four long years he was able to use his drug in only eight minor operations. Above all things he wanted to prove his case by a successful major operation, but when no opportunity arrived he did not worry. He was not the worrying kind, and his days were full, riding miles to minister to the far-flung sick of Jackson County. In any case, he was young, with tens of years before him. Religiously he tended his country practice while the precious months that constituted the priority of his discovery massed into years.

One winter evening four and a half years after he had operated on Venables, Long rode up to his house after a busy day. He dismounted wearily and handed his horse's reins to the colored boy. Soon he was settled before the fire, slippers on feet that ached from the riding boots. He allowed his thoughts to wander nebulous as the nebulous flicker of flame until a prick of conscience arose in the back of his mind and fought forward against the inertia of exhausted nerves. His spare hours were few and he was behind on his reading of the *Medical Examiner*, the journal that kept him up to date. Sighing, he found the December number and returned to the fire, but he could hardly

keep his tired mind on the words he read. Suddenly he sat upright. His eyes had struck the following headline: "Insensibility during Surgical Operations Produced by Inhalation."

The article said that "a certain Dr. Morton, a practicing
dentist in Boston," had secured a patent for a substance which
he asserted would prevent pain. The preparation, it was reported, smelt of ether and was probably an ethereal solution of
some narcotic substance.

"From a paper by Dr. H. J. Bigelow, one of the surgeons of
the Massachusetts General Hospital . . . we derive the astonishing information that Dr. Warren and Dr. Hayward, men at
the top of our profession, have allowed Morton to administer
his 'preparation,' a 'secret remedy' for which he has taken out
a patent, to patients on whom they were about to operate! . . .
We are persuaded that the surgeons of Philadelphia will not
be seduced from the high professional path of duty into the
quagmire of quackery by this will-o'-the-wisp; and if any of our
respectable dentists should be tempted to try this new *patent
medicine*, we advise them to consider how great must be the
influence of an agent over the nervous system to render a person unconscious of pain; the danger there must necessarily be
from such an overpowering medication, and that if fatal results
should happen to one of their patients, what would be the effect
upon their conscience, their reputation and business, and how
the practice would be likely to be viewed by a Philadelphia
court and jury. We cannot close these remarks without again
expressing our deep mortification and regret that the eminent
men who have so long adorned the profession in Boston should
have consented for a moment to set so bad an example to their
younger brethren as we conceive them to have done in this instance. If such things are to be sanctioned by the profession,
there is little need for reform conventions or any other efforts

to elevate the professional character: physicians and quacks will soon constitute one fraternity."

In great excitement Long called his wife, showed her the article, and then sat down to compose a letter to the editor of the *Medical Examiner*, saying that ether was enough by itself to produce insensibility, and that he had used it for several years. But he had hardly written a few lines when there was a knock on the door, and a frantic man rushed in, crying that his wife was "taken very bad" and begging the doctor to come at once.

Although as his horse stumbled over frozen mud in a hundred country lanes he composed his letter to the editor again and again in his mind, seeing the words against bare trees, gray hills, and deserted stubbly fields; although as he knocked at the ramshackle doors of distant farms strong phrases pounded through his mind and struggled with the swell of heat as the doors opened; although he thought of little else for the next four or five days, he could not find a minute to write another word. And then the postman brought the January *Medical Examiner*.

This issue gave an entirely different picture. The substance used was announced as pure ether and its usefulness accepted as a fact. There was even an indignant communication saying that Morton's discovery had been anticipated by another dentist named Wells. Long must have noticed that Wells's first experiment was two years after his own, yet he merely tore up the beginning of his letter; there was no further need to point out that pure ether, without any admixture of narcotics, sufficed to deaden pain. Although more than ever there was need to claim the credit for the discovery if he were not to be cheated of his due, he did nothing about bringing his experiments before the world during three more years.

Many scholars have speculated on the reason for Long's delay. They have usually regarded as ridiculous his statement that he was waiting to see if some other doctor would make a claim even prior to his, but this is not so ridiculous as it may seem. It must have been very difficult for a simple country practitioner only thirty-one years old to believe as he went his routine rounds, purging babies and delivering farmers' wives, that he really was a great man, that a simple experiment which had grown naturally from his carousals with the gay boys of the village could revolutionize the medical world. Of course he said to himself that, if such an inexperienced youngster as he could observe the anæsthetic quality of a common drug like ether, surely a dozen older and wiser men must have observed it first. And Long was no Yankee trader who believed that the devil took the hindmost; he had been taught that all ostentation was ungentlemanly; to his dying day he told his womenfolk it was a terrible sin to wear artificial jewelry or machine-made lace. Gentlemen, he believed, do not push themselves forward. And perhaps he had the faith of the simple in heart that a just cause, whether publicized or not, wins out in the end.

But was his cause just; was he really the discoverer of anæsthesia? Such distinguished physicians as Dr. William H. Welch and Sir William Osler say: "No." Although they admit that Long was the first man to use ether as an anæsthetic, they insist that the credit for the discovery should go to William Thomas Green Morton, the Boston dentist.

William T. G. Morton

2

Aʟᴍᴏsᴛ three years after Long's first operation on Venables, an obscure dentist in Hartford, Connecticut, sat in his office reading the *Hartford Courant*. Dr. Horace Wells was a young man of twenty-nine, with a round, soft, handsome face and bushy side-whiskers. Turning the pages idly, he reached the following advertisement:

"A grand exhibition of the effects produced by inhaling ɴɪᴛʀᴏᴜs ᴏxɪᴅᴇ, ᴇxʜɪʟᴀʀᴀᴛɪɴɢ, or ʟᴀᴜɢʜɪɴɢ ɢᴀs! will be given at Union Hall this (Tuesday) evening, December 10, 1844.

"*Forty gallons of gas* will be prepared and administered to all in the audience who desire to inhale it.

"*Twelve Young Men* have volunteered to inhale the gas to commence the entertainment.

"*Eight Strong Men* are engaged to occupy the front seats to protect those under the influence of the gas from injuring themselves or others. This course is adopted that no apprehension of danger may be entertained. Probably no one will attempt to fight. . . .

"N.B. The gas will be administered only to gentlemen of the first respectability. The object is to make the entertainment in every respect a genteel affair."

Dr. Wells called to his wife and suggested that they go to the show. Had he foreseen the future, perhaps he would have stayed at home, for this seemingly innocent evening's entertainment brought him not only immortality, but madness, and prison, and death at last by his own hand.

When night came he was sitting next his wife in Union Hall. Having delivered a short lecture on laughing gas, Dr. Gardner Q. Colton administered some to himself from a rubber bag through a wooden faucet similar to those used on cider barrels. Then he declaimed most wonderfully, his words glowing in the air. Finally he stopped short, put his hand to his head, and announced solemnly: "The effect is now nearly gone."

Dr. Colton invited volunteers to come on the stage, and Wells filed up with the others. After watching those before him go through ridiculous antics, he sniffed the gas himself and behaved rather foolishly, his wife thought. He had returned to his seat before Sam Cooley inhaled from the spigot. The brawny drug clerk broke into a cross between an Irish jig and a Hopi war dance, but when he noticed that a little man in the front row was laughing at him, his high spirits turned into fury. Leaping from the stage, he made for the man, who fled in terror. Although smaller than Cooley, the fugitive was fast and shifty; it was a good race that brought the audience to its feet. For an instant, the pursued was cornered at the end of the hall, but he doubled like a rabbit, vaulted a settee, and sprinted down the center aisle. When Cooley struck his leg in following over the hurdle, he did not seem to notice. On the straight stretch, he almost overhauled his quarry and his hands reached out to clutch; then the gas-madness left him. He stopped, looked about him with a foolish smile, and amid shouts of applause slid into a seat near Wells. Presently the dentist saw him roll up one of his trousers and gaze in a puzzled way at the bloody leg which had struck the settee.

Wells used to tell in later years how he fidgeted on the edge of his chair until the lecture was over, and then rushed to Cooley. "How did you hurt your leg, Sam?" he asked, trying to hold his voice calm, not to seem excited.

When Cooley told him that he did not know, that he must have hit his shin against something while under the influence of the gas but had felt nothing, Wells turned and tried to charge through the crowd to the stage. Would these people never get out of the way? Reaching Dr. Colton at last, he talked so excitedly that the lecturer could not understand what this young man with the flushed face wanted. But at last Wells managed to make Dr. Colton agree to give him gas the next morning when he was to have a tooth pulled.

Mrs. Wells was irritated at having been kept waiting so long, and on the way home she told her husband in no uncertain terms what a fool he had made of himself while drunk with the gas. But he did not listen. For a long time he had realized that dentistry would be more profitable if clients were not kept away by the fear of pain, and perhaps he had found the solution.

The next morning Dr. Colton administered gas to him while a fellow-dentist pulled a deeply rooted molar. Wells awoke with his famous remark: "A new era in tooth-pulling!"

There was no hesitancy in Wells's nature; he went at things slapdash, in a rush of inspiration, and if they did not pan out immediately he was likely to drop them altogether. His single experiment having been successful, he at once began the manufacture of laughing gas, and in a short time he had administered it to fifteen patients, but only with varying success. Since the gas worked sometimes, he did not bother to discover why it did not work always. When Dr. E. E. Marcy suggested to him that ether might be preferable to gas since it was easier to handle and had the same exhilarating effect, he allowed himself to be put off by his next informant who told him that it was unpleasant to take and less safe.

Still in the full tide of enthusiasm, he hurried to Boston and through Dr. William Thomas Green Morton, a former dental partner who was now studying medicine, arranged to give a demonstration of painless tooth-pulling before one of the classes of the famous surgeon, Dr. John Collins Warren, at the Massachusetts General Hospital. Unfortunately, Wells had been taught to give only the exhilarating dose of gas Dr. Colton used in his lectures; he had never taken the time to find out that more was needed to produce certain anæsthesia. Since on this occasion he failed to administer enough, the patient not only felt pain but was very vocal about it. His agonized screams filled the lecture hall. The students laughed and jeered at the "humbug" who had promised not to hurt him, and Wells returned to Hartford as precipitously as he had come, convinced there was nothing to the great discovery he had been so enthusiastic about a few hours before. Dropping all interest in laughing gas, he absorbed himself in arranging a panorama of natural history for the city hall in Hartford, and in selling patented shower baths. However, the excitement of great hope followed by abject failure brought on an illness from which he never completely recovered.

Luck had been against him. When Wells administered his gas, it worked perfectly half the time; had it only worked the day he demonstrated before Dr. Warren's class, he would undoubtedly have been hailed as the discoverer of anæsthesia for the same reasons Morton was. As it happened, Wells's demonstration merely fertilized the mind of the man who was to be his triumphant rival.

Morton had been born at Charlton, Massachusetts, on August 9, 1819, the son of a well-to-do farmer and shopkeeper. So great was the father's ambition for his son that, when William was only eight, he sold one farm and moved to another in order to be nearer the village school. From the first the boy wanted to be a doctor; he dosed his playmates with pills made of bread and leaves. But after he had almost killed his baby sister by pushing some weird compound down her throat as she lay asleep in her cradle, his parents were forced to disbar their infant practitioner for malpractice.

At the age of thirteen, he was sent to the academy at Oxford, where he boarded with the local doctor and spent much time pretending to read leather-bound books he could not understand. To the rhapsodies on medicine of this intense, nervous child the old physician would reply grumblingly: "Young man, you hardly know what you talk about or how hard I have to work."

In his second year Morton ran away from the Oxford Academy because of a punishment he considered unfair; the injustice affected him so deeply that for a long time he was ill, "unfit," one of his friends tells us, "for thought and action." Nor could he remain at the next school to which he was sent; this time he was homesick. Then he went to Northfield Academy, where he managed to stick, but his classmates remembered him as a strange, shy lad who would rather search the hills for rare minerals than play with the other boys.

Just as he was ready to begin studying medicine, his father lost his money; Morton found himself working in a Boston publishing house. However, he felt he was not appreciated, and in a few months returned home to stand behind the counter of his father's store. A little later he decided to become a great merchant. He set up in business on his own account, only to be duped by his older partners and have his dreams of wealth come tumbling down in a disastrous failure.

Morton thereupon returned to science; he resolved to become a dentist. During the first half of the nineteenth century, the care of teeth was a very backward art. Every physician had to be a dentist too, but he was expected to do no more than pull teeth and fit in an occasional set of false ones if he could make or procure them. Although in the larger cities a few men specialized in dentistry, most of them were ignorant charlatans who knew only what they had been able to learn by their own efforts. When they pulled teeth, for instance, they were satisfied to twist off the crown and leave the roots to fester. Yet, since nothing cries so persistently for cure as a toothache, dentistry became increasingly important until in 1840 the leading practitioners resolved to make it a respectable branch of medicine. Meeting at Baltimore, they formed the American Society of Dental Surgeons. In his address, Dr. Chapin A. Harris said: "The calling of the dentist has been resorted to by the ignorant and illiterate, and I am sorry to say in too many instances by unprincipled individuals, until now it numbers in the United States about twelve hundred, of which I think it may safely be asserted that not more than one-sixth possess any just claims to a correct or thorough knowledge of the pursuit." In order to remedy this condition, the association organized the Baltimore College of Dental Surgery, the first dental school in the United States.

Morton was in the initial graduating class. After practicing in a small town for two years, he formed a partnership with Wells and set up an office in Boston. Now a city practitioner, he soon became conscious of ignorance, for the new dental school had taught him very little. Since there were no textbooks, the only way he could increase his knowledge was by associating with his more experienced colleagues. Fighting a constitutional shyness which had forced him to grow fierce mustachios, Morton tried to make friends with the older dentists. They were glad enough to joke with him, even to stand him a drink, which he did not particularly enjoy, but when he brought the conversation around to their profession, they glanced at their watches and remembered pressing engagements. Every dentist regarded any improvements he might work out as his particular stock in trade that brought him patients and must be kept from his colleagues at all costs.

Deciding that, if no one would tell him anything, he would have to work matters out for himself, Morton paid Dr. N. C. Keep five hundred dollars for the use of his laboratory. The young man had the practical gift which is a part of the American genius; although he knew no mechanics and practically no medicine, he soon worked out a superior way of putting in false teeth. He had learnt the lesson of secretiveness from his colleagues, and it never occurred to him, as it would have to a physician, that he should give his discovery to the world. Instead, he told Wells that they would no longer have difficulty getting patients since they now had their own specialty to offer.

Jubilantly the two young partners advertised their new method in the papers, promising your money back if you were not satisfied, and waited for a rush of business. Sure enough, hundreds of people began to shuffle up their stairs that had been silent so long, but most of them shuffled down again in a few minutes. Morton's system required the removal of the evil-smelling roots that had been left in patients' jaws by incompetent dentists, and the process was so painful that practically no one would submit to it. Even the few who remained had to be treated at a low price that left no profit. Wells, incapable of waiting for anything, resigned from the partnership in disappointment and returned to his native Hartford.

However, this failure brought home to both young men

what a vast fortune could be made by alleviating pain. We have seen the slapdash rush of inspiration by which Wells sought to reach this end; Morton's was a more roundabout way. All that he did was accompanied with doubts and self-torture, with suspicion of the world yet need for the world's confirmation at each step. However, behind his hesitations was the strange persistence of a man who expected everything to go wrong and was therefore never completely discouraged, the confidence of a man who, because he always doubted himself, knew that in any individual case his self-doubt was meaningless.

More ignorant than most physicians were even in those days, a fledgling dentist, Morton set out to abolish pain. He tried every method he could think of. He got some of his patients drunk on brandy, and when that failed, on champagne; others he drugged with opium in vast doses. He attended all the lectures on mesmerism he could find, and even tried it on his startled patients himself without success. Determined to make his mark in the world, to become rich by advertising some method other dentists could not rival, he left himself no time for the frivolities of life; and his nervousness made him glad to flee from drawing-rooms to the laboratory.

Like so many men who are afraid to face the world alone, Morton fell in love early with a girl even younger than he. Elizabeth Whitman was only sixteen and a student in Miss Porter's school at Farmington, Connecticut. During the year before her graduation, she remembered, "Dr. Morton had paid me attentions which were not well received by my family, he being regarded as a poor young man with an undesirable profession. I thought him very handsome, however, and he was very much in love with me, coming regularly from Boston to visit me."

By promising to give up dentistry and become a doctor, he

finally won the consent of Miss Whitman's parents. The young lady must have been long-suffering and understanding, for when she induced her shy and ambitious fiancé to escort her to a party, he would sit in a corner and meditate on new ways to make false teeth or alleviate suffering. Answering with grudging monosyllables all attempts to draw him into conversation, he acquired the reputation of a morose and stupid man.

In 1843 he married, but he could not forget his scientific researches even on his honeymoon. He brought a skeleton along in a bag and sometimes when his bride awoke on the pillow next to his she discovered that he had the bones out and was busily studying anatomy. For Morton had decided that he must know more about the human body before he could deaden pain. He had apprenticed himself to a physician who was also a distinguished chemist, the same Dr. Charles T. Jackson who had tried to kidnap Beaumont and St. Martin.

Jackson told him what was at the time common knowledge, that ether applied to the outside of a sore tooth lessens sensitivity. Having tried it with reasonable success, Morton wondered how the effects of the drug could be made more general. Perhaps he could have the patient take a bath in it, but that, he had to admit, was a little impracticable. When Jackson said that riotous medical students inhaled ether for their amusement, Morton rushed to the library to discover what effect such inhalation had. He was deeply disappointed to read that ether administered in large enough quantities to produce stupefaction was dangerous to human life. Of course, the books might be wrong, but Morton could think of no experiment to prove them so, that might not also prove fatal to the experimenter. For hours he sat in his laboratory with the ether bottle beside him, staring at the colorless liquid and wondering. Once he had a sudden paroxysm of courage. Quickly, before he had time to change his mind, he poured a few drops in his handkerchief. His arm trembled convulsively as he lifted the handkerchief to his nose. But the amount of ether he had dared inhale was so small that the only result was a fiendish headache.

He was soon taken ill and forced to retire to his father-in-law's house at Farmington. However, he could not get his mind off his obsession; he would scoop a goldfish out of the ornamental spring and try as it struggled in his hands to put it under the influence of ether. "He used to bottle up all sorts of queer bugs and insects," his wife remembered, "until the house was full of crawling things. He would administer ether to all these little creatures, and especially to the big green worms he found on grape vines. . . . I was only a girl of eighteen at this time, and had not the least idea of what he was trying to do, nor would I have understood the importance of his experiments had he told me. I only knew that his clothes seemed always saturated with the smell of ether, and I did not like it." When his friends found out what he was doing, they teased him unmercifully, and in this teasing his wife gleefully joined. "I was mortified and vexed," Morton tells us, "and bottled up the subjects where they remain to this day." He dropped his experiments on anæsthesia.

The next winter he matriculated at the Harvard Medical School, and his dental practice occupied all the time he could spare from his studies. He became so famous for mechanical ingenuity that he was in demand as a plastic surgeon too. A contemporary biographer, Dr. Nathan P. Rice, solemnly described as follows his treatment of an unfortunate lady who had lost her nose. "Having taken an accurate mold from a dwarf in the city who was noted for the beauty and symmetry of her nasal protuberance, an exact copy was made by Dr. Morton in platina and enameled. This, colored as nearly to life as art could make it, was attached to her spectacles. With this accessory appendage well adjusted, and a piece of court-plaster placed as a beauty spot upon her forehead to act as a foil and attract the attention of those who saw her, the defect was hardly to be noticed."

Morton also established a factory where false teeth were manufactured by the mass-production method Henry Ford was to find so useful later on. Dr. Rice tells us that the receipts from this as well as his practice and his private dental pupils came as high as $20,000 a year.

Early in 1845 he sponsored the demonstration of laughing gas Wells had rushed up from Hartford to give. Pitilessly ragged concerning that disastrous failure by his fellow-students at the Harvard Medical School, the lanky dentist postponed his experiments on the inhalation of ether for yet another year.

While studying medicine, Morton taught dentistry. In the spring of 1846, Thomas R. Spear, Jr., a gay lad who had become one of his apprentices, told him how much he had enjoyed getting drunk on ether at Lexington Academy. Excitedly, Morton asked Spear innumerable questions, repeating them over and over to make sure he had heard aright.

After several sleepless nights, Morton grimly set out for his country place at West Needham. Under one arm he carried a glass bell-jar, under the other a bottle of ether. His heart failed him when the family spaniel greeted him with a wagging tail and yelps of delight. But he told himself that science was important and that the discovery would make him rich. Taking two witnesses with him, he led the trusting beast far from the house to the banks of a deserted lake. The dog cringed but submitted when Morton put his head in the bell-jar that had ether in the bottom. Instantly, he wilted down in his master's hands. With a beating heart of dread, Morton removed the jar and waited to see if his pet would revive. He pinched and poked the dog to no purpose. For three awful minutes the animal lay there breathing convulsively; then he emitted an ear-splitting yelp and with one bound leapt ten feet into the water, or so it seemed to Morton's excited imagination.

Sure now that he was on the way to wealth and fame, Morton could no longer be bothered attending to his medical studies or his practice. Although his lawyer insisted it was the first step to financial ruin, he employed another dentist to treat his patients. Immediately he tried to persuade his new partner to inhale some ether; the man replied coldly he had not understood that that was to be part of his duties. Thus thrown back on his own resources, Morton mixed some chloric ether and morphine in a jar surrounded by hot towels, and sniffed at it gingerly himself. Again he did not dare breathe enough to do more than give him a headache.

Experimenting on the dog was easier; he took the next train to the country. But as soon as the spaniel, who had learnt his lesson, smelt the reminiscent, sickish odor, he struggled so effectively that he broke the bell-jar and spilt most of its contents. In a fury of disappointment, Morton hurried back to Boston, resolving to inhale what remained if it killed him. Nightmares and apprehensions tossed through his mind all night, but the next morning he shut himself in his office with the bottle beside him. For the third time, he did not take enough. "I inhaled from my handkerchief all the ether that was left, but was not completely lost, yet thought myself so far insensible that I believe that a tooth could have been drawn with but little pain or consciousness."

As Morton approached step by step nearer his goal, a new apprehension assailed him; perhaps someone would guess what he was doing and beat him to the discovery. From now on, all his subtlety was employed to avoid such a mishap. Afraid that his own druggist would suspect if he asked him for any more ether, he sent his apprentices across the town to purchase a demijohn under an assumed name.

The next day Morton ordered his pupils to try to lure from the wharves of South Boston a stevedore who would let him pull a tooth under ether, "a big Irishman, a full robust man" capable of absorbing a large quantity. The tough denizens of the waterfront must have been amazed when the two young-sters came into a saloon and, talking unnaturally from the corners of their mouths, tried to pretend they were regular fellows. As long as the boys stood drinks all round, they were gratifyingly popular, but when they promised five dollars to anyone who would allow himself to be experimented on while in an unnatural sleep, a horrified silence must have arisen round the bar. When the enormity of the proposal finally sank in, we may be sure that the drinkers took off their coats and spat on their hands. The apprentices hurried back to their preceptor, glad to escape with no bones broken.

Morton thereupon summoned all his eloquence to persuade his pupils to inhale the ether themselves. Spear finally agreed, but instead of going to sleep as the spaniel had done, he be-came pugnacious and offered to fight the company. He had to be held down in his chair. However, when he came to, he "expressed himself delighted with his sensations." Hearing what fun it was, the other student agreed to inhale, but only if the sportive Spear were banished from the room; he wanted no practical jokes. The ether also made him violent. Later Morton blamed these results on impurities in the drug, but at the moment he was discouraged, telling his partner that he "feared there was so much difference in the qualities of ether that in so delicate a matter there would be great difficulty in bringing about any generally useful and reliable results." His nervousness affected his companions; when he offered Spear five dollars to inhale again, the young man, who had gone on ether jags often and thought them pleasant, hesitated, consulted his family, and finally refused to take the risk.

Disconsolate, Morton fled the hot weather to the country, but in a month he was back in town with a new idea. Thinking that ether might work better if inhaled through some apparatus, he determined to borrow the India rubber bag from which Jackson administered laughing gas. And perhaps his preceptor might be able to suggest some appliance that would be still better. Morton realized that consulting him was a dangerous business; he knew that Jackson had publicly claimed the discovery of the telegraph because once in a conversation with Morse he had given the real inventor some hints upon which he himself had never acted. However, Morton was sure that he was wily enough to get the information he wanted without letting Jackson know why he wanted it.

Although no two witnesses agree concerning what happened when Morton called on his preceptor, by comparing conflicting stories we may reconstruct the scene with reasonable accuracy. Wrapping subtlety around him like a conspirator's cloak, Morton asked, in as bored a voice as he could affect, for the gas bag. After he had taken it from the closet, Jackson laughingly remarked: "Well, doctor, you seem to be all equipped minus the gas."

Morton managed to laugh too and, his face alternately red and white, said there would be no need of having any gas if the person whose tooth he pulled was made to believe there was gas in the bag. With too much detail and emphasis, he told a long story of a man who died because he was made to believe he was bleeding to death, while in reality it was nothing but water that trickled over his leg.

"You'd better not try any trick like that," Dr. Jackson said, "or you'll be set down as a greater humbug than poor Wells was with his nitrous oxide." And then, horror of horrors, he suggested the use of sulphuric ether.

"Sulphuric ether?" cried Morton. "What is it? Is it a gas? Show it to me." The two medical students who were listening to the conversation filed in their memories Morton's admission that he had never heard of ether until Jackson told him of it.

The subject having been brought up, Morton inquired about the different forms of the drug, a subject he had never understood, and learnt that highly rectified sulphuric ether was the kind to use. Saying he had something better than a gas bag for the inhalation of ether, Jackson gave his pupil a flask with a tube inserted in it.

Morton left the laboratory in an agony of apprehension; he had let Jackson get so near the truth he was afraid his preceptor would take the final step before he did. He hurried into a drug store, bought highly rectified sulphuric ether, and ran home. Desperation gave him the courage that for almost two years he had lacked.

"I procured the ether from Burnett's," he wrote, "and taking the tube and flask, I shut myself up in my room, seated myself in the operating-chair, and commenced inhaling. I found the ether so strong that it partially suffocated me, but produced no desired effect. I then saturated my handkerchief and inhaled from that. I looked at my watch and soon lost consciousness. As I recovered I felt a numbness in my limbs, with a sensation like nightmare, and would have given the world for someone to come and arouse me. I thought for a moment I should die in that state, and the world would only pity and ridicule my folly. At length I felt a slight tingling in the end of my third finger, and made an effort to touch it with my thumb, but without success. At a second effort, I touched it, but there seemed to be no sensation. I gradually raised my arm and pinched my thigh, but I could see that sensation was imperfect. I attempted to rise from my chair, but fell back. Gradually I regained power over my limbs and full consciousness. I immediately looked at my watch and found that I had been insensible between seven and eight minutes."

Morton rushed out into his office screaming: "I've found it! I've found it!" He danced round the room with explosive joy, laughing, slapping his pupils on the back. All his doubts and hesitations were destroyed at last. Eagerly he waited for some patient to come on whom he might demonstrate his discovery.

Towards evening fate sent him Eben Frost, a burly young man with a very swollen face whose bicuspid pained him terribly. He explained that he had postponed for days coming to the dentist because he was afraid pulling the tooth would pain him even more. He blanched at the sight of the doctor's instruments and he begged to be mesmerized so he would feel nothing.

Telling Frost he knew a better trick than mesmerism, Morton poured some colorless liquid on a handkerchief. "Just breathe this."

Frost struggled against the heavy drug and then lay still. With a trembling hand his partner held the lamp while Morton reached into the patient's mouth and pulled the tooth. During the painful operation, Frost did not stir. That was all right, but after the handkerchief was removed he did not stir either. The two men leaned over him, one with the lamp in his hand and the other still clutching the bloody tooth. Was Frost asleep or in a fatal coma? Silence descended in choking waves, time stood still as the two men leaned over their victim, motionless as he. They were drawn upright by a groan; was it a death rattle or the return of life? For a moment the dentists waited in heightened anxiety, and then the limp man began to swear. Never had profanity sounded so grateful to human ears. Morton and his partner gazed at Frost with the delighted stare of lovers as he spat blood and awoke to see his tooth lying on the floor.

There was a general jubilation. The patient remained with the doctors, repeating over and over for their enchanted ears the tale of how he had felt nothing until he came alive to see his tooth lying on the floor. Before he left, Morton carefully made him sign an affidavit attesting what had happened.

But Morton's troubles were not over. His next patient was a boy on whom the ether had no other effect than to make him very sick, with vomiting. His furious parents swept him out of the office, took him home in a coach, and consulted a doctor, who said he had been poisoned. Within an hour the irate father was back, threatening to sue Morton for trying to murder his child. It is interesting to speculate what would have been the effect on Morton's cautious experiments if this youngster, not Frost, had been the first patient. Perhaps the ever-doubting dentist would have given up as Wells did; certainly his discovery would have been much delayed. Again the long hand of luck appears as a determining factor in our story.

A little later Morton gave ether to a lady who grew very

drowsy but refused to go to sleep. When he changed his method of administering the drug, she got over her drowsiness in an instant, became flushed and excited, and talked with such alarming steadiness that Morton could not get the forceps into her mouth. He respectfully asked her a half-dozen times to be quiet but she only gossiped faster. Finally, he offered her a few dollars. This had the desired effect; she said not another word and he drew the tooth without her feeling a thing.

When Miss L——, a demure young lady of twenty-five, minced in, she seemed a perfect patient, but a whiff of ether changed her character at once. She leapt into the air screaming like a red Indian, and wrestled with the embarrassed dentist as he tried to hold her in the chair. On coming to, she instantly became demure again and said she could not remember what had happened. Taking a few deep breaths to restore his courage , Morton gave her the ether once more. This time she slept peacefully and he extracted two molars with no difficulty whatsoever.

These cases were exceptions, for the ether usually worked perfectly. Finally the press took notice of what was happening; the *Boston Daily Journal* published the following squib: "Last evening, as we were informed by a gentleman who witnessed the operation, an ulcerated tooth was extracted from the mouth of an individual without giving him the slightest pain. He was put into a kind of sleep by inhaling a preparation the effects of which lasted for about three-quarters of a minute, just long enough to extract the tooth." As a result of this, the first notice of anæsthesia ever to appear in print, the curious flocked to Morton's office.

When Dr. Henry J. Bigelow, the famous surgeon of the Massachusetts General Hospital, also appeared, Morton must have received him with mixed emotion. It was fine to have the countenance of the great, and Bigelow's influence might help him put the discovery over, but supposing Bigelow guessed that the magic substance was ether and stole the credit! Morton, though interested in helping mankind by killing pain, felt he deserved to make a fortune from so important an advance. Following the tradition of dentists that continues even today, he planned to patent his discovery rather than give it freely to the world as a physician would be expected to do. He allowed Bigelow to watch the operations, to give advice, and to take notes, but he never allowed him to examine the substance he used or get near enough to guess its nature.

A few days later, perhaps at Bigelow's advice, Morton asked the same Dr. Warren who had permitted Wells to demonstrate laughing gas whether he might not administer his secret preparation during a surgical operation at the Massachusetts General Hospital. That Dr. Warren considered this proposal without first determining the nature of the substance to be used, seems remarkably courageous if not foolhardy; probably he was assured by Dr. Bigelow that it was safe. In any case, after ten days of suspense Morton received a letter inviting him "to be present on Friday morning at ten o'clock to administer to a patient who is then to be operated upon the preparation which you have invented to diminish the sensibility to pain." As the day approached, Morton's old apprehensions descended upon him with redoubled force; they have been described by Dr. Rice, who wrote his biography of Morton under his subject's critical eye.

Morton had learnt that when he administered ether the effects were not uniform, and he realized that, if Dr. Warren's patient got drunk and violent, he would be laughed out of the amphitheater as Wells had been; he would become a public fool for all Boston to point at. Or perhaps the patient would be a hardened drunkard who would breathe down a dram of ether as if it were gin and show no effects whatsoever, or a "tender female" who would swoon and weep and not really give him a chance to administer the drug. If only he dared call on Dr. Warren and insist he be given a healthy man like Eben Frost! But no; he must control himself.

Supposing, he thought, as he paced up and down his office, supposing the patient, already weakened by disease, should die under the knife as patients sometimes did? Would he not then be tried for murder? Would not all his hopes of fame and riches end in jail, on the gallows even? He had a vision of his body hanging from a rope, the head pulled unnaturally to one side.

This helpless waiting around was unbearable; Morton sped out to ask Dr. A. A. Gould, the distinguished naturalist, if he could think of a better apparatus with which to administer the drug. Although Dr. Gould obligingly sketched an appliance with valves to keep the patient from breathing back into the globe, he advised against the use of anything untried during the crucial experiment. But Morton's nerves cried for action; he took the sketch to an instrument-maker.

When the hour of the experiment approached, the new apparatus was still uncompleted. In an agony of apprehension, Morton stood over the instrument-maker, pleading, suggesting, getting in the way. Finally he snatched the appliance from the man's hands and started to run towards the hospital. When he had covered only a few blocks, he remembered that he wanted to take Frost with him to testify, if worst came to worst, that he had succeeded before. Turning, he sprinted towards Frost's house.

In the meantime, a large audience awaited him in the amphitheater of the Massachusetts General Hospital. Boston's most distinguished surgeons sat in the front seats; behind them rows of medical students stretched to where the mummies and skeletons of the medical museum reposed in glass cases against the wall. At the dot of ten, the time when the demonstration was supposed to start, a young man of twenty was brought in and placed on the operating-table. Then Dr. Warren arose, clad in all the majesty of years and fame, to announce that a "test of some preparation was to be made for which the astonishing claim had been made that it would render the person operated upon free from pain." There was a sound of incredulous whispering which grew louder as Dr. Warren stood there scowling, swinging his watch around on its gold chain, impatiently eying the door for Morton to appear.

After fifteen minutes, Dr. Warren put his watch back in his pocket with a determined gesture. "As Dr. Morton has not arrived," witnesses remember that he said, "I presume he is otherwise engaged." The tension relaxed in a derisive laugh, and Dr. Warren ordered that the patient be prepared for the operation. Just as he picked up his knife, there was a sound of tumultuous footsteps in the hall. Morton hurried through the door, out of breath and very pale, followed by a very red and flustered Frost.

Dr. Warren stared at the couple disapprovingly. "Well, sir," he told Morton, "your patient is ready."

Having stammered an apology for being late, Morton walked over to the patient, who, he was relieved to see, was male, young, and sturdy-looking. Now that the crisis had come, he felt surprisingly deliberate. Taking the patient by the hand, he assured him he would partially relieve, if not entirely prevent, all pain. He pointed out Eben Frost, who was perspiring in a corner, as one of his successful cases. "Are you afraid?" he asked.

"No," the patient replied. "I feel confident and will do precisely as you tell me."

Morton adjusted his apparatus and commenced administering the drug. For one awful moment, the man showed signs of becoming violent; then he fell into a deep slumber. The confused rustle of feet and voices lapsed into silence while the spectators leaned forward, motionless as the skeletons and mummies behind them. Morton's low voice filled the hall when he told Dr. Warren: "Your patient is ready, sir."

The operation was for a congenital tumor of the neck, extending along the jaw to the mouth and embracing the margin of the tongue. As Dr. Warren gathered in his hand the veins under the patient's skin, the famous surgeons in the front row were on their knees, leaning over to get a better view. Behind them not a medical student moved a muscle. The patient neither winced nor made a sound at the sharp stab of the knife; only towards the end of the operation, when the veins were being isolated, did he move his limbs a little and murmur deliriously. After the tumor had been removed, the wound sewed up, and the blood washed from his face, he was allowed to regain consciousness. Dr. Warren asked: "Did you feel any pain?"

At first the patient was dazed and did not seem to know what was being said to him. When at last he understood, he answered: "No. It didn't hurt at all, although my neck did feel for a minute as if someone were scraping it with a hoe."

Turning to the audience, Dr. Warren drew himself up to his full dignity. "Gentlemen," he said, "this is no humbug."

3

Morton's difficulties were not over. Although he succeeded whenever the Massachusetts General Hospital allowed him to administer ether, they suddenly stopped calling on him. "The surgeons," he was told, "thought it their duty to decline the use of the preparation until informed what it was." Planning to patent his discovery, Morton found himself in a quandary; if he admitted the drug was ether he might lose his exclusive right, and if he kept the secret he would certainly alienate his only professional patrons. The newspapers which had carried accounts of his successes brought him comfort no longer, for they were suddenly full of articles by physicians that derided his claims as ridiculous. He felt himself alone, deserted by the world in what should have been his moment of triumph. When Jackson dropped in to say he wanted five hundred dollars for the advice he had given, Morton was so anxious to have at least one well-known person associated with his discovery that he agreed to take out the patent in both their names and give Jackson ten percent of the proceeds. The application renamed ether "Morton's Letheon"; it was Oliver Wendell Holmes who coined the term "anæsthesia."

After the papers were safely filed in Washington, Morton divulged his secret to the surgeons at the Massachusetts General Hospital. Dr. Bigelow thereupon wrote up the discovery for the *Boston Medical and Surgical Journal;* despite his distinguished reputation, his article elicited violent criticism like that Long read in Georgia. A group of Boston dentists, terrified by the sudden prominence of one of their number, held a mass meeting and drew up a manifesto warning the public. It contained touching tales of tender virgins who, after receiving ether from Morton, became delirious and remained so for days, with bleeding at the lungs, melancholy, and other dreadful symptoms. These atrocity stories gained easy credence among the thousands of doctors who had been taught that large doses of ether are deadly.

In addition to such professional objections there were religious objections. Evangelists preached impassioned sermons to demonstrate that anæsthetics interfered with divine justice; had not mankind been doomed to pain as a punishment for its misdeeds? Relieving the agony of childbirth was considered particularly wicked, since on that subject the curse in the Garden of Eden had been specific. "In sorrow thou shalt bring forth children," the Bible said; what could be more heretical than to circumvent consequences of original sin? This prejudice still crops up today, sometimes in the most unexpected places. During 1936, a psychologist told the American Medical Association: "Childbearing is so essential an experience for a woman that the thwarting of its normal course by the excessive use of analgesics may cause great damage to her personality. If she is carried through delivery in an unconscious state, she is deprived of the experience of giving birth to her child and in some cases will pay for this escape from reality with nervous disorders." Perhaps the old prejudice has discarded the outworn robes of fundamentalism to wear the more modern dress of psychology.

Against a storm of criticism, Morton worked unsparingly

to perfect his invention and build up an organization of sales-
men to distribute it all over the world. According to his lawyer,
for three months he "hardly knew a full night's rest or a regular meal"; he was forced to abandon his dental practice
completely to assistants. He offered ether free to charitable
institutions, and published a periodical in which he combined
attacks on his critics with persuasive sales talk. When he tried to
sell rights to the army and navy for use in the Mexican War,
the dentists' calumnious circular, which had been distributed in
Washington, barred his way. "The chief of bureau," the Secretary of the Navy wrote, "reports that the article may be of some
service for the use of large hospitals, but does not think it expedient for the Department to undergo any expense for its
introduction into the general service, in which the Department
concurs." The army's reply was similar.

This temporary setback did not greatly depress Morton,
for the Massachusetts General Hospital was putting his discovery over. Since Dr. Warren, Dr. Bigelow, and the Hay-
wards were solidly behind the use of ether, the clamor against
it in the medical journals died down. And when word came
back from Europe of its enthusiastic reception there, most
physicians were convinced, although a few die-hards refused
to believe for another twenty years.

The general acceptance of anæsthesia put the army and navy
doctors in a difficult position; they had no legal right to use
the drug, and yet it seemed impossible inhumanity not to do
so. Reluctantly, they violated the patent. This emboldened
the myriad physicians who were annoyed by paying tribute
for a common drug like ether, and soon no one bothered with
Morton's claims. His agents all over Europe and America demanded their salaries and their fares home, while physicians
who had bought licenses insisted they should be reimbursed,

since they had received no privileges others did not have. In the meantime, Morton had run up a huge debt for the manufacture of inhaling apparatus which became worthless when a sponge proved to be more effective. Instead of putting money in Morton's pocket, his discovery was draining it out.

He consulted his friends at the Massachusetts General Hospital. Since they had never enjoyed being involved with a patent medicine, they suggested that he forgo his rights under the patent and appeal to the United States government for compensation. They gave him a thousand dollars in a silver casket, and in order to start him off correctly drew up a petition to Congress which many leading Boston doctors signed. However, no sooner had Morton presented the petition than two rival claimants appeared in Washington; Wells and Jackson both insisted they were the real discoverers of anæsthesia.

After he had secured his patent, Morton had written to Wells offering to make him one of his agents. "Your letter dated yesterday is just received," Wells replied, "and I hasten to answer it for fear you will adopt a method in disposing of your rights which will defeat your object. Before you make any arrangements whatever, I wish to see you. I will be in Boston the first of next week, probably Monday night. If the operation of administering the gas is not attended with too much trouble, and will produce the effect you state, it will undoubtedly be a fortune to you, provided it is rightly managed."

Wells made no claim for himself in this letter, but less than two months later he wrote the *Hartford Courant* that his experiments with laughing gas had given him priority. However, he did not seem deeply interested even yet, for he sailed abroad almost immediately to buy cheap reproductions of Louvre pictures which he hoped to sell at a huge profit to the new rich of the West. In Paris, he came under the influence of a dominant American dentist who persuaded him to notify the French learned societies that he was the discoverer. Soon he was swept away by the excitement of being a great benefactor of mankind; he attended meetings, made emotional appeals, accused Morton of stealing his idea. He could hardly sleep at night, his mind was so busy throwing up images of glory. When he sailed back to America to press his claims there, the fire in his brain was already burning dangerously high.

One gentle spring evening a prostitute was strolling up Broadway in New York when a strangely agitated man sidled up to her and, whipping his hand out of his pocket, threw some liquid in her face. The liquid burnt frightfully. As her screams resounded down the street, the culprit was easily caught. Thus it came about that Wells was sentenced to prison for throwing acid on a street-walker. Unable to bear the disgrace and confinement, he cut his radial artery at the wrist and bled himself to death in his cell.

His death added to Morton's troubles. Mrs. Wells petitioned Congress to recognize her husband's claims, and the rumor gained credence that Morton was a fiend who, having stolen the credit for anæsthesia, had persecuted the real discoverer into madness and suicide.

Meanwhile, Jackson had not been idle. The day after the patent was granted, he had sent a sealed letter to a member of the French Academy of Sciences in which he asserted he was solely responsible for anæsthesia. He did not, however, give the Frenchman permission to break the seal until January 1847, when there could be no more doubt that the new method was really of great importance. Although Morton saw him several times a week, he heard nothing of Jackson's claim until word came back from Paris.

Jackson's story was as follows: During February 1842, while delivering a chemical lecture, he accidentally inhaled some chlorine gas. He resorted to the antidote prescribed in textbooks, the alternate inhalation of ammonia and ether. Since his throat was still sore the next morning, he seated himself in a rocking chair and inhaled some more ether from a towel. Noticing that while under its influence he was immune to pain, the story continues, he decided then and there "that I had made a discovery I had so long a time been in quest of: a means of rendering the nerves of sensation temporarily insensible to pain." Since the idea had occurred to him, the discovery was of course accomplished. Having no medical patients of his own, he did not bother to prove his theory by actual tests until 1844 when he requested Morton to undertake experiments as his agent. Morton, he insisted, deserved no more credit than a nurse deserves for carrying out a doctor's orders.

Amazingly, many people believed Jackson, although his contention that Morton was merely his subordinate during the demonstration at the Massachusetts General Hospital seems today completely untenable. Not only was Jackson absent from this crucial test himself, but he kept away from the hospital for a long time afterwards, and he was careful to disassociate himself from Morton's experiments, saying, according to sworn testimony, that Morton was a rash man to use ether as he did and would kill someone sooner or later.

On the other hand, Jackson enjoyed a much greater scientific reputation than his rival, and he possessed one trump card: reliable witnesses stated that on the morning before he pulled Eben Frost's tooth Morton had said, when Jackson suggested ether, that he had never heard of it. And the fact that Morton had taken out his patent jointly with his preceptor was construed to mean that they had collaborated in the discovery.

Before the question of ether had come up, Jackson had given Morton a testimonial to his zeal and skill, but the moment they became rivals the older man could think of nothing too outrageous to say about his former friend. "It has often been asked," he wrote, "how I happened to commit the execution of my early verification experiment to an ignorant and wholly uneducated person like the quack doctor Morton. This I will now explain. I was not aware of the infamous character of that man when he came to solicit the privilege of entering his name at my office as a medical student. . . . I soon found that he was too ignorant to be capable of learning enough to become a surgeon dentist. He was a well-dressed, plausible man, and although I knew him to be an ignoramus in all matters of science, I thought he could perform the very simple operations I was about to commit to him, namely the administration of ether to some of the patients whose teeth he was about to extract. His office, I knew, was frequented by the lower and credulous class of people such as were attracted by his quack advertisements with which he filled our daily newspapers."

"We have proofs," Jackson wrote a few months later, "that Morton is a swindler, and that he has tried to bribe his workmen to certify falsehoods. . . . He is accused of swindling with forged letters of credit on persons in St. Louis, New Orleans, etc." When the French Academy of Sciences presented Morton with a gold medal, Jackson insisted that the medal was a forgery made without the academy's knowledge, and, strange to say, this story, so easily disproved, circulated in American newspapers for years.

Jackson's accusations received such credence that in Morton's own home town the dentist was burnt in effigy. No new patients dared come to his office, and the assistants to whom he had entrusted his practice became afraid to be publicly associated with him and resigned, taking most of his old patients with them. Finally the *coup de grâce* was given to what remained of his practice by the manufacturer whose inhaling apparatus had never been paid for; getting an attachment on the dentist's property, he wrote all Morton's patients, even by error those who had settled their bills, threatening to hale them into court for non-payment of arrears.

Morton gave way to a persecution complex that culminated in alarming physical symptoms. "I have become," he wrote a friend, "a perfect sensitive plant. . . . My nervous system seems so completely shattered that a trifling surprise or sudden noise sends a shock all over me. I am so restless that I cannot lie or sit long in any position by day or night. Then convulsive pains seize me suddenly without any premonitory warning or apparent cause, and my limbs are instantly drawn up by the intensity of the cramps which rack me so that I cannot prevent screaming until I fall exhausted. I can compare my sensations at such times only to the appearance of the curling up of a piece of leather subjected to a high heat. . . . This disorder has not diminished for the last four years, but seems rather to increase in the frequency and severity of the attacks."

In 1849 his friends took up a collection that enabled him to urge his claims before Congress, where, of course, he had to compete with the claims of Jackson and Wells. While in Washington, Morton hid himself away except when he had to go out on business, and he refused all formal invitations. Bills appropriating a hundred thousand dollars for the discoverer of anæsthesia were presented to three sessions of Congress, but they always got side-tracked in long committee hearings and Congressional debates on the question of who was the discoverer. It is not amazing that no conclusive results were reached, for in the thousand pages of printed testimony it is difficult to find any fact concerning which witnesses have not sworn to two or more different versions.

The battle among the adherents of Morton, Jackson, and Wells was wallowing in its usual morass of litigation and Billingsgate eight years after Morton had patented his discovery, when a quiet voice was heard speaking from Georgia. During 1854, Senator Dawson received a letter from one of his constituents, by name Crawford W. Long, in which Dr. Long asserted that he had operated with ether as early as 1842, that he had published an account of his experiments in the *Southern Medical and Surgical Journal* in 1849, and that the Georgia Medical and Surgical Association had in 1852 unanimously passed a resolution naming him the discoverer of anæsthesia. He was not seeking any pecuniary reward, Long wrote, but at the urgent insistence of his friends was putting his claim before Congress so that the credit for the discovery might not be entirely taken from him. Puzzled by this new aspect of the ether controversy which had already raged so long, Senator Dawson showed the letter to Jackson.

In the years that had intervened since his work on anæsthesia, Long had moved from Jefferson to the metropolis of Athens, where he became a leading practitioner and the proprietor of the largest wholesale and retail drug store in northeastern Georgia. The passage of time and the responsibility of a growing family had changed him from a gay dog to a jovial Southern gentleman of the old school. No longer did he sport light-blue suits and tan silk gloves; now he wore a frock coat made by the best tailor in town, lightened in the summer by an endless succession of spotless white waistcoats. He still enjoyed dancing and whist. He attended every play or opera that came to his neighborhood, and laughed as uproariously at a good minstrel show as the children did. He was fond of hunting and fishing and, naturally, of good horses. His children were permitted to ride only the best Kentucky breeds, and at country fairs, although he never allowed himself to bet, his frock-coated figure was often seen leaning over the barrier as he cheered on the horse whose high-stepping beauty had particularly caught his fancy. When his judgment was vindicated by victory, he was as pleased as if he had won a hundred dollars.

His house was continually crowded with guests who came for weeks and stayed for months, increasing the atmosphere of gayety which the doctor liked to find at home after a tiring day. "About sundown, when papa usually returned," his wife remembered, "we were out on the veranda watching for him. A shout went up when he appeared, then such racing to meet him. Of course, he waited patiently for all [the children] to climb in the buggy, with two or three clinging on the outside. If on horseback, he strung as many on Charlie in a row as could safely be put astride, while those less favored trotted in as near him as possible. Then comes the time for a kiss for 'little wifie,' and then he grasps the baby, tosses it in the air, crowing and reaching out its little arms—and papa dearly loves babies."

Domestic life suited Dr. Long. He liked to sit by the fire and read Homer aloud to his daughters. When he was away from home, he wrote his wife innumerable letters, of which the following extract is typical: "Restless and uneasy as I am yours must be a severer trial than mine—you sick, our dear children sick, and then the other trials added. I do hope that the good and great God who has been so kind and gracious hitherto will preserve and protect you in all your trials and afflictions and make these trials a blessing to us. They are sent for some wise and good purpose. May we see their intent and profit by them."

Into the drug store of this genial Southern gentleman there hurried on March 8, 1854, a spare, angular stranger with dark hair and eyes, whose swarthy face betrayed signs of agitation. He demanded the doctor so urgently that the apprentice who was in charge thought he must be sick and offered to help him. But the man said his business was not medical and sat down by the fire to wait. When Long returned, the stranger presented a card on which were engraved the words, "Dr. Charles T. Jackson." He explained that, as they both claimed to be the discoverer of anæsthesia, he thought that perhaps they could compare notes and come to some understanding.

Long showed Jackson into the office at the back of his store, but insisted that his apprentice be present. Then, the young man remembered, he unlocked his desk and with loving care brought out affidavits concerning his early operations which had been sworn to by many witnesses. Jackson had his documentary evidence in his pocket; for several hours they examined each other's papers with slow, cautious exactness. It was, in the opinion of the apprentice, "a weary day's work." As the interview went on, Jackson became increasingly glum. Finally he left, saying he would get in touch with Long later.

In a few days he was back in the drug store with the proposal that they lay their claims jointly before Congress, Jackson to claim the theoretical discovery and Long the first practical use. This would have the effect, he pointed out, of completely undermining Morton, but Long indignantly repudiated the scheme, stating that his claim to the discovery of anæsthesia "rests upon the fact of my use of it on March 30, 1842."

Unable to persuade him, Jackson took his leave. To everyone's surprise, he notified Senator Dawson that he withdrew his own claim, since Long was the real discoverer. He could not help asserting, however, that he himself had conceived the idea first, although he had failed to apply it, and that Long had agreed this was the case.

If Jackson's honest acceptance of Long's claim was not an attempt to defeat Morton, motivated by a hate so strong he was willing to defeat himself as well, it argues that he may have been sincere during the entire ether controversy in which he seems to have played so disgraceful a part. Undoubtedly, his mind was unbalanced; he spent the last seven years of his life, 1873–80, in a sanatorium. The consistency with which he claimed discoveries that were not his own suggests a pathological obsession. Not only did he try to get credit for the telegraph and for ether, but he later asserted that Schönbein had stolen the invention of gun-cotton from him. Since even stable minds tend to paint their rivals in the blackest colors, as every jealous lover knows, Jackson may easily have convinced himself that Morton was the fiend he publicly accused him of being.

Whatever Jackson's motives, his admission of Long's priority ruined Morton's chances of getting any money from Congress. Having long since given up all pretense of practicing dentistry, Morton spent his winters lobbying in Washington and his summers on a farm near Boston, where he tried to forget his troubles by nurturing prize pigs and raising vegetables that carried away the honors at the county fair. However, all this was expensive, and the small sums occasionally granted him by grateful civic societies supplied his only means of support. He was forced to borrow on his dental instruments and finally even on his gold medal. After each new defeat in Washington, his creditors, fearing for their money, descended upon him; naturally Jackson's alliance with

Long ruined him completely. All his property went under the hammer. If one of his friends had not bought his house and allowed him to stay in it, he would have had no place in the world to lay his head. Once when his family had for a week been unable to buy food, he borrowed back his cart that was under attachment at the sheriff's and loaded it with wood from his own pile which he exchanged for half a barrel of biscuits. Not the blackest poverty, however, could make him descend to taking a job; he sued the navy in a belated effort to enforce his patent. This action, hopeless in any case, was interrupted by the Civil War.

Down in Georgia, Dr. Long used his influence against secession. He was an up-country Methodist who believed that the providence of God had permitted slavery in order to Christianize the Africans, and that once this object had been achieved they should be gradually emancipated; he disapproved of the tidewater plantation-owners and their aristocratic ways. When his children wanted to see the torchlight parade with which the young men of Athens celebrated secession, he gruffly refused to let them go. "It is the saddest sight of my life," he said. However, he served the Confederacy as head of a military hospital at Athens.

One morning when the physician was in town attending his patients, a wounded young captain galloped up to the Long house with his crutches across the saddle-bow. Reining in with a bandaged hand, he called the ladies out on the veranda to tell them that General Stoneman and a division of federal cavalry were nearing Athens with orders from General Sherman to burn the town, take all the mules and horses, destroy all the provisions, and decoy away all the Negroes. He brought a message from the doctor ordering his eldest daughter and her younger brother to drive the silver and valuables in a carriage to the wounded captain's house, which was away from the line of march, while the coachman hid the remaining horses in a swamp.

Just as the carriage was ready to start, Long came running down the road with a glass jar that contained two huge gold watches and a roll of papers. His daughter tells us that he pointed to the papers and said: "These are most important and under no circumstances must be lost; they are proofs of my discovery of anæsthesia. Promise me that when you reach your destination you will bury them in a secluded spot, but if overtaken by the raiders you may be frightened into giving them the jar if ordered to do so."

"I'll die before I do," cried his daughter as she leapt into the carriage. Long watched anxiously as it joined the press of vehicles streaming out of Athens. When the girl arrived at her destination, she found the secluded house already packed with the valuables of the entire community. The captain's sister, whose husband was away in the army, helped Miss Long lengthen her dress down to the ankles. They suspended the jar with its precious papers under her skirt by a cord tied round her waist. That done, the two young ladies set out for what was apparently an afternoon stroll, but the jar, banging against Miss Long's knees, made it impossible for her to walk naturally. "An ugly black old Negro man," fascinated by her strange gait, followed the girls, but eventually they managed to lose him. When they were deep in the woods, the captain's sister produced a shovel from under her dress; digging a hole, the young ladies buried the jar and covered the place with sticks and leaves. Then by a circuitous route they made their way back to the house.

The next day they received the joyful tidings that the Yankee raiders had been captured by Colonel Breckinridge twenty miles outside Athens at Jug Tavern. The girls hurried back to the woods and exhumed the proofs of Dr. Long's discovery.

During reconstruction, Long tried to mitigate the miseries of Athens by serving under the hated federal government as health officer. His fortunes, wounded by the war, gradually mended until he owned two plantations and at his death left an estate of $40,000. His claims to the discovery of anæsthesia, however, had been completely obliterated by the excitement of war and hatred of the South. Disappointment made the subject so painful to him that his children were instructed never to mention ether in his presence. They knew that he kept the proofs of his priority in a green traveling trunk in the attic. When their usually jovial parent came into the house with a preoccupied look on his face and after a curt greeting to his family stamped upstairs to the attic, they knew that the old fever was upon him and that he would spend several hours poring over the affidavits on which his claim to immortality rested. Each new child, when it came to an age where it could understand, was instructed that the most unforgivable sin was to open or even touch the green trunk. "Some day," their mother told them, "it will make your father a great man."

During the war, Morton had administered ether to the wounded after several battles, but peace found him back at the ever more hopeless task of trying to make a fortune from the discovery that had reduced him to poverty. His days and nights were uneasy with pamphlets, litigations, and appeals to medical societies. Again and again friends or scientific bodies had to give him small sums to keep him from starving on the streets.

In July 1868, while a subscription was being got up for Morton's benefit in New York, a magazine article appeared objecting on the grounds that Jackson was the real discoverer. It was a long time since any such claim had been made, and the article agitated Morton, his wife tells us, "to an extent I had never seen before." He rushed to New York, but immediately became so ill with his nervous ailment that his wife was forced to join him. When he felt better, he suggested that they drive to Washington Heights for the night in order to escape the heat of the city. Almost cheerfully he whipped up the horse, but soon he returned to wondering whether the article would endanger his subscription. He became more and more excited.

"Just as we were leaving the park," Mrs. Morton wrote, "without a word he sprang from the carriage, and for a few moments stood on the ground apparently in great distress. Seeing a crowd gathering about, I took from his pocket his watch, purse, and also his two decorations and the gold medal. Quickly he lost consciousness, and I was obliged to call upon a policeman and a passing druggist, Dr. Swann, who assisted me. We laid my husband on the grass, but he was past recovery."

After an hour wasted in trying to secure a suitable carriage, Morton was finally transported to St. Luke's Hospital. He was dead, killed by apoplexy. "At a glance," his wife continued, "the chief surgeon recognized him, and said to me: 'This is Dr. Morton?'

"I simply replied: 'Yes.'

"After a moment's silence he turned to a group of house pupils and said: 'Young gentlemen, you see lying before you a man who has done more for humanity and the relief of suffering than any man who has ever lived.'

"In the bitterness of the moment, I put my hand in my pocket and, taking out the three medals, laid them beside my husband, saying: 'Yes, and here is all the recompense he has ever received for it.' "

Long outlived his rival by a decade and had the pleasure of seeing his claim reasserted before the world during 1877 by the famous Southern surgeon, Dr. J. Marion Sims. A year later, while delivering a lady in childbirth, he too suffered a stroke. His last words as he expired in his patient's guest-room were inquiries about her condition and directions for her treatment.

4

THE story has been told and the facts lie before us; nothing remains but to judge who was the real discoverer of anæsthesia. Not that it makes much difference any more. The men are all dead, pursued to the end by their tragic destinies, and each in his own way deserves credit. They have all attained immortality.

Yet, since the world pretends to recognize discoveries, since statues are erected and textbooks written, it might be interesting to see where this review of facts has led us. Certainly we can begin by dismissing the claims of Wells and Jackson. Wells did nothing that Long did not do first, and as for Jackson, whatever brilliant ideas he may have carried about in his mind, they hardly went any further than Sir Humphry Davy's speculations had gone more than forty years before.

The controversy between the adherents of Long and the adherents of Morton will probably continue until the history of anæsthesia is no longer written, for the argument hinges on a definition of what constitutes discovery. It is impossible to deny Long's priority in time. Nor is it possible to refute Dr. William H. Welch's statement that we cannot assign Long "any influence upon the historical development of surgical anæsthesia or any share in the introduction to the world at large of the blessings of this matchless discovery."

It can, of course, be argued that, if the medical profession of Georgia had been as progressive as that of Massachusetts, Long's discovery would have been accepted and publicized while Morton was still dosing his patients with narcotics. Certainly Long brought his work to the attention of the local profession, which is really all that Morton did; the Massachusetts General Hospital put his discovery over, and the first scientific paper on anæsthesia was written not by Morton but by Bigelow. It can be argued further that, if Morton had never lived, Long would surely have published his discovery in the end. Many medical heroes who are hailed without controversy waited longer to publish than the Georgia doctor did. Ephraim McDowell is an example; his account of ovariotomy appeared eight years after his first operation, while Bigelow's article followed the experiment on Venables by only four and a half years. Yet all this reasoning does not change the fact that it was Morton not Long who introduced anæsthesia to the world.

A flood of irrelevancies is usually brought in to cloud the issue. It is asserted, for instance, that Long was an incompetent youngster who did not realize the importance of what he had done; we have seen that this does not agree with the facts. On the other hand, Long's supporters point out that he was much more admirable than his rival, who picked many brains to achieve what Long achieved single-handed, who patented his discovery and tried to levy tribute. Although we are not concerned with the evaluation of character, it is difficult to resist the sentimental appeal of supporting the simple country doctor against the power of the Massachusetts General Hospital and the organized Boston medical profession. Morton's adherents like to regard Dr. Bigelow and Dr. Warren as impartial judges, forgetting that these gentlemen owe their principal fame to their admirable and courageous co-operation with Morton. We find such statements as the following by Dr. Warren quoted as gospel: "It is probable that Long performed three or four minor operations with primary anæsthesia and then abandoned his claims. As Dr. Keen says, he is deserving of nothing but censure for not having appreciated the value of the agent." But we must not let this manifest unfairness affect our judicial decision.

The issue, then, is a simple one: do we regard as the discoverer of anæsthesia the man who first used it or the man who first succeeded in giving it to the world? Here is a decision which each individual must make for himself, and amusingly enough it is usually made on geographic lines. Northerners express indignation at the very mention of Long, while doctors south of the Mason and Dixon line regard Morton as a despicable interloper. Perhaps the decision has usually gone to the Boston dentist because the Northern medical profession is more vocal and more powerful.

Let us not forget, however, that the two contenders made the discovery independently and that each according to his opportunities gave it to the world. Might not the warring factions settle the ether controversy amicably at last by agreeing that anæsthesia had two almost simultaneous discoverers, William Thomas Green Morton and Crawford W. Long? Certainly there is enough credit for two to share it.

Indeed, anæsthesia was the first of the four great discoveries made during the nineteenth century that went far to create modern medicine. After Virchow had established the cell doctrine in pathology, after Pasteur and Koch had demonstrated that germs cause contagious diseases, after Lister had developed antiseptic surgery, the foundation was virtually complete for the miraculous structure of healing which is being built higher and higher every year. New techniques, based on a greater understanding, have changed the practice of medicine until, looking back on the days of Morgan and McDowell, it seems that we are looking back a thousand years. Yet these valiant explorers in a wilderness of doubt blazed with their primitive instruments many trails that are being widened into highways by modern scientists equipped with the apparatus of a mechanical age. Those early doctors, pioneers not only in medicine but in the conquest of a new continent, were mighty influences in their own times, strong men who challenged the impossible and won sometimes against greater odds than any which exist today.

SELECTED BIBLIOGRAPHIES

AND

INDEX

SELECTED BIBLIOGRAPHIES

JOHN MORGAN

Morgan, John. *The Journal of Dr. John Morgan of Philadelphia from the City of Rome to the City of London, 1764* (with a biographical sketch by Julia Morgan Harding). Philadelphia, J. B. Lippincott, 1907.
A Discourse upon the Institution of Medical Schools in America. Philadelphia, 1765. (Facsimile of original edition, Baltimore, Johns Hopkins Press, 1937.)
A Vindication of His Public Character in the Station of Director General of the Military Hospitals and Physician-in-Chief of the American Army. Boston, 1777.
Middleton, William Shainline. "John Morgan." In: *Annals of Medical History*, vol. IX, pp. 13–26, New York, 1927.
"William Shippen, Jr." In: *Annals of Medical History*, new series, vol. IV, pp. 440–452, 538–549, New York, 1932.
Norris, George W. *The Early History of Medicine in Philadelphia.* Philadelphia, 1886.

Manuscript Material

Letters and papers in the collections of the American Philosophical Society, the Historical Society of Pennsylvania, the Ridgway Branch of the Library Company of Philadelphia, and the University of Pennsylvania.

MEDICINE IN THE REVOLUTION

Brown, Harvey E. *The Medical Department of the United States Army from 1775 to 1873.* Washington, Surgeon General's Office, 1873.
Duncan, Louis C. "Medical Men in the American Revolution, 1775–1783." In: *Army Medical Bulletin*, no. 25, Carlisle Barracks, Pennsylvania, 1931.
Gibson, James E. *Dr. Bodo Otto and the Medical Background of the American Revolution.* Springfield, Illinois, and Baltimore, Charles C. Thomas, 1937.
Lee, Richard Henry. *The Letters of Richard Henry Lee,* collected and edited by James Curtis Ballagh. 2 vols. New York, Macmillan, 1912–1914.
Owen, William O. "The Legislative and Administrative History of the Medical Department of the United States Army during the Revolutionary Period." In *Annals of Medical History*, vol. I, pp. 198–216, 261–280, 342–367, New York, 1917.

Thatcher, James. *A Military Journal during the American Revolutionary War from 1775–1783.* Boston, 1823.
Tilton, James. *Economical Observations on Military Hospitals and the Prevention and Cure of Diseases Incident to an Army.* Wilmington, 1813.
Toner, J. M. *The Medical Men of the Revolution.* Philadelphia, 1876.
Washington, George. *The Writings of George Washington from the Original Manuscript Sources,* edited by John G. Fitzpatrick. Vols. III–XVI. Washington, United States Government Printing Office, 1931–1936.

Manuscript Material

Documents in the Library of Congress and as listed under John Morgan and Benjamin Rush.

BENJAMIN RUSH

Rush, Benjamin. *A Memorial Containing Travels through Life or Sundry Incidents in the Life of Dr. Benjamin Rush. Written by Himself. Also Extracts from His Commonplace Book as Well as a Short History of the Rush Family in Pennsylvania.* Edited by Louis Alexander Biddle. Lanoraie, 1905.
An Account of the Bilious Remitting Yellow Fever as It Appeared in the City of Philadelphia in the Year 1793. Philadelphia, 1794.
Old Family Letters Relating to the Yellow Fever. Series B. Edited by Alexander Biddle. Philadelphia, J. B. Lippincott, 1892.
Carey, Mathew. *A Short Account of the Malignant Fever Lately Prevalent in Philadelphia.* Third edition. Philadelphia, 1793.
Cobbett, William. *Porcupine's Gazette.* Philadelphia, files for 1797. *The Rush Light.* New York, 1800.
Eve, Sarah, "Extracts from the Journal of Miss Sarah Eve While Living near the City of Philadelphia in 1772–3." In: *Pennsylvania Magazine of History and Biography,* vol. V, pp. 19–36, 191–205, Philadelphia, 1881.
Ford, Paul Leicester. "Dr. Rush and General Washington." In: *Atlantic Monthly,* vol. LXXV, pp. 633–640, Boston, 1895.
Good, Harry C. *Benjamin Rush and His Services to American Education.* Berne, Indiana, Witness Press, 1918.
Goodman, Nathan G. *Benjamin Rush, Physician and Citizen.* Philadelphia, University of Pennsylvania Press, 1934.
Lettsom, John Coakley. *Recollections of Dr. Rush.* London, 1815.
Mitchell, Silas Weir. "Historical Notes of Dr. Benjamin Rush." In:

SELECTED BIBLIOGRAPHIES   [357]

Pennsylvania Magazine of History and Biography, vol. XXVII, pp. 129–150, Philadelphia, 1903.
Ramsay, David. *An Eulogium upon Benjamin Rush.* Philadelphia, 1813.
A Report of an Action for Libel Brought by Benjamin Rush against William Cobbett. Philadelphia, 1800.
Shippen, Nancy. *Nancy Shippen, Her Journal Book*, compiled and edited by Ethel Armes. Philadelphia, J. B. Lippincott, 1935.

Manuscript Material

The Rush papers in the Ridgway Branch of the Library Company of Philadelphia. The journal of Rush's trip to Paris in the Pierpont Morgan Library. Miscellaneous letters and papers in the collections of the Historical Society of Pennsylvania, the New York Historical Society, and the New York Public Library.

EPHRAIM McDOWELL

Atlee, Washington L. *A Retrospect of the Struggles and Triumph of Ovariotomy in Philadelphia.* Philadelphia, 1875.
Chesney, J. P. "Interesting Incidents in the Private Life of Dr. Ephraim McDowell." In: *Cincinnati Medical Repertory*, vol. III, pp. 133–136, 1870.
Gross, Samuel David. "Ephraim McDowell." In: *Lives of Eminent American Physicians and Surgeons of the Nineteenth Century.* Philadelphia, 1861.
Memorial Oration in Honor of Ephraim McDowell. Louisville, 1879.
Kerr, Charles, editor. *History of Kentucky.* Vols. I and II. Chicago and New York, the American Historical Society, 1922.
McCormack, Mrs. Arthur Thomas. "Our Pioneer Heroine of Surgery—Mrs. Jane Todd Crawford." In: *Filson Club History Quarterly*, vol. VI, pp. 109–123, Louisville, 1932.
McCormack, J. N., editor. "Some of the Medical Pioneers of Kentucky." In: *Kentucky Medical Journal*, supplement to vol. XV, Louisville, 1917.
Ridenbaugh, Mary Y. (later editions signed Mary Thompson Valentine). *The Biography of Ephraim McDowell.* New York, 1890.
Schachner, August. *Ephraim McDowell, "Father of Ovariotomy" and Founder of Abdominal Surgery*, with an appendix on Jane Todd Crawford. Philadelphia, J. B. Lippincott, 1921.
Smith, Emily A. *The Life and Letters of Nathan Smith.* New Haven, Yale University Press, 1914.

Speed, Thomas. *The Political Club, Danville, Kentucky, 1786–90.* Louisville, John P. Morton, 1894.

Manuscript Material

Several letters in the collection of Dr. Marshall McDowell of Cynthiana, Kentucky.

DANIEL DRAKE

Drake, Daniel. *Pioneer Life in Kentucky, a Series of Reminiscential Letters from Daniel Drake to His Children,* edited with notes and a biographical sketch by his son, Charles D. Drake. Cincinnati, 1870.
Discourses Delivered by Appointment before the Cincinnati Medical Library Association. Cincinnati, 1852.
A Narrative of the Rise and Fall of the Medical College of Ohio. Cincinnati, 1822.
Practical Essays on Medical Education and the Medical Profession in the United States. Cincinnati, 1832.
The Principal Diseases of the Interior Valley of North America. Cincinnati, 1850–1854.
Anonymous. "An Inquiry into the Causes That Have Retarded the Prosperity of the Medical College of Ohio." Supplement to *Cincinnati Whig and Commercial Intelligencer,* 1835.
Gross, Samuel David. *A Discourse on the Life, Character, and Services of Daniel Drake, M.D.* Louisville, 1853.
Juettner, Otto. *Daniel Drake and His Followers.* Cincinnati, Harvey Publishing Co., 1909.
Mansfield, Edward D. *Memoirs of the Life and Services of Daniel Drake, M.D.* Cincinnati, 1855.

WILLIAM BEAUMONT

Beaumont, William. *Experiments and Observations.* Plattsburg, 1833. (Facsimile of original edition, Boston, XIIIth International Physiological Congress, 1929.)
Cannon, Walter Bradford. "Some Modern Extensions of Beaumont's Studies on Alexis St. Martin." In: *Journal of the Michigan State Medical Society,* vol. XXXII, pp. 155–164, 215–224, Chicago, 1933.
Erlanger, Joseph. "William Beaumont's Experiments and Their Present Day Value." In: *Weekly Bulletin of the St. Louis Medical Society,* vol. XXVIII, pp. 180–192. 1933.

Myer, Jesse S. *Life and Letters of Dr. William Beaumont.* St. Louis, C. V. Mosby, 1912.

Outten, W. B. "Glimpses of Early St. Louis Medical History." (Joseph Nashe McDowell.) In: *The Medical Fortnightly,* pp. 143–146, St. Louis, 1908.

Steiner, Walter R. "Dr. William Beaumont." In: *New England Journal of Medicine,* vol. XXIII, pp. 1137–1139, Boston, 1935.

Wisconsin Historical Collections. Vols. I–XXIII. General index, vol. XXI. Madison, State Historical Society of Wisconsin, 1855–1916.

Wood, Edwin Orin. *Historic Mackinac; the Historical, Picturesque, and Legendary Features of Mackinac County.* 2 vols., New York, Macmillan, 1918.

Manuscript Material

The Beaumont papers at the library of the Washington University Medical School. Also letters in the collections of the Army Medical Library and the Beaumont Club at the Yale University Library.

The Death of Pain

Bigelow, Henry J. "A History of the Discovery of Modern Anæsthesia." In: *A Century of American Medicine,* Philadelphia, 1876.

Erving, Henry Wood. "The Discoverer of Anæsthesia: Dr. Horace Wells of Hartford." In: *The Yale Journal of Biology and Medicine,* vol. V, pp. 421–430, New Haven, 1933.

Jacobs, Joseph. *Some Personal Recollections and Private Correspondence of Dr. Crawford Williamson Long.* Atlanta, 1919.

Morton, Elizabeth Whitman (Mrs. William T. G. Morton). "The Discovery of Anæsthesia." In: *McClure's Magazine,* vol. VII, pp. 311–318, New York, 1896.

Packard, Francis R. *History of Medicine in the United States,* vol. II. New York, P. B. Hoeber, 1931.

Poore, B. P. *Historical Materials for the Biography of W. T. G. Morton.* Washington, 1856.

Rice, Nathan P. *Trials of a Public Benefactor* (Morton). New York, 1859.

Statements supported by evidence of Wm. T. G. Morton, M.D., on his claim to the discovery of the anæsthetic properties of ether, submitted to the honorable select committee appointed by the Senate of the United States, 32nd Congress, 2nd session, January 21st, 1853. Washington, 1853.

Taylor, Frances Long. *Crawford W. Long and the Discovery of Ether Anæsthesia.* New York, P. B. Hoeber, 1928.

INDEX

Académie Royale de Chirurgie, Paris, 14

Academy of Medicine, Paris, 160

Academy of Sciences, Paris, 337, 339

Adams, John, 71, 79, 81–3, 107, 115

Adams, John Quincy, 258–9

Adams, Samuel, 29–30, 43–4, 71, 81

Allen, William, 295

American flag designed, 13

American Fur Company, 238, 250, 259–60

American Medical Association, 231–232, 280, 334

American Medical Recorder, 151

American Philosophical Society, 23, 51–2, 97, 191

American Physiological Society, 276, 284

American Revolution, bibliography, 353–4; mortality, 3

American Society of Dental Surgeons, 316

Anæsthesia, 293–352; bibliography, 357; importance, 294–5; religious objections to, 334; term coined, 333

Apothecary, first in America, 21; separate profession, 21, 219

Appendicitis, 130, 161–2, 221

Apprentice system, 9–10, 20, 192, 217–8

Army Medical Museum, 288

Ashe, Thomas (d'Arville), 185–6

Atlee, Washington, 159

Audubon, John James, 198

Bad Axe River, Battle of, 264

Baker, Mrs., 125

Baltimore College of Dental Surgery, 316

Beaumont, Buddy, 280, 282–3, 287–288

Beaumont, Mrs. William, 237, 247–249, 266

Beaumont, Samuel, 247, 271, 282–3, 285

Beaumont, Sarah, 280

Beaumont, William, bibliography, 356–7; discoveries about digestion, 261, 266–71; on theoretical medicine, 267–8; quarrels, 246, 249, 258, 277–80; religion, 241, 286–7; youth, 241–3; at Champlain, 243–4; studies medicine, 244–5; War of 1812, 245–7; practice in Plattsburg, 247–8; marries, 247–9; at Mackinac, 237–41, 248–55; treats St. Martin's wound, 250–2; begins experiments, 252–7; personal relation to St. Martin, 255, 257, 260–1, 265, 274, 283, 285; St. Martin runs away, 257; at Green Bay, 259; fights Indians, 259, 262–4; at Prairie du Chien, 260–4; second series of experiments, 260–2; in Washington, 265–6, 273; third and fourth series of experiments, 264–6; publishes book, 271, 281; exhibits St. Martin, 271–2; St. Martin fails to return, 274–5; negotiates with St. Martin, 281–6; in St. Louis, 275–87; resigns from army, 276–7; death, 286–7

Bell, John, 124, 144–5, 149, 151, 155, 157

Bernard, Claude, 284

Berzelius, Jöns Jakob, 266

Bethlehem, hospital at, 3, 75–7

Bigelow, Henry J., 308–9, 328–9, 333–5, 350–1

Binney, Dr., 30

Black Hawk War, 263–4

361

ery, 341, 344; during Civil War, 345, 347; death, 347–9
Mosby, Count. *See* Otto, Louis-Guillaume

Nashville Journal of Medicine and Surgery, 200
National Intelligence, 185
Navy Department, 273, 335, 345
Nélaton, Auguste, 157
Newark Hospital, 36, 38
New York Assembly, 37
New York Convention, 35
New York Independent Reflector, 9
Niagara, Battle of, 246
Nitrous oxide. *See* Laughing gas
Northern campaign (1776), 4, 33–4
Northfield Academy, 315
Nottingham School, 8, 59

Occupational diseases, 230
Occupational therapy, 116
Operation before anæsthesia, 294
Osler, William, 57, 113, 288, 310
Otto, Louis-Guillaume, 86–7
Ovariotomy, 121–31, 144–5, 148–150, 153–60
Overton, John, 153–4
Oxford Academy, 315

Paine, Thomas, 72
Parker, Willard, 221
Pasteur, Louis, 352
Pathological anatomy, first chair of, 221
Pavlov, Ivan Petrovich, 262, 270
Penn, Thomas, 17, 19
Pennington, Dr., 100
Pennock, 231
Pennsylvania Hospital, 10, 16, 20, 51, 116
Pennsylvania Packet, 69, 85
Pepsin, 266
Philadelphia, yellow fever epidemics, 93–101, 105–7

Philadelphia College of Physicians, 98
Philadelphia dispensary, 92, 149
Philadelphia Gazette, 106
Philadelphia Medical Society, 23
Physick, Philip Syng, 117, 149
Plattsburg, siege of, 246
Point Pleasant, Battle of, 147
Polk, James K., 145
Porcupine's Gazette, 106–7
Potts, Dr. Jonathan, 33, 60, 78
Powel, Samuel, 7, 14–5, 17
Prairie du Chien, 260–4, 266–7
Premedical requirements, 20, 53, 218
Princeton, Battle of, 73–4
Princeton University. *See* College of New Jersey
Pringle, Henry, 13
Prout, William, 269
Psychoanalysis, 116
Pus, nature of, 14
Putnam, Israel, 4, 35

Quarrels among doctors, 210–2, 277–80
Quincy's *Dispensatory*, 181

Ramsay, David, 63, 83
Réaumur, René, 61, 268
Redman, John, 9–10, 60, 63, 89
Reese, Dr., 302
Regimental surgeons, 25–6, 28–31, 39, 74
Reid, Andrew, 142–4
Reynolds, Joshua, 62
Rice, Nathan P., 320, 329
Richardson, William H., 196–7
Richmond, John Lambert, 205–9, 219, 264
Riddell, John Leonard, 221
Rogers, Coleman, 194, 198, 201–3, 212
Rush, Benjamin, autobiography, 58, 70, 113–4; bibliography, 353–5; career in general, 57–8; influence,